THE FABRIC SELECTOR

The essential guide to working with fabrics, trimmings & notions

Dana Willard

SEARCH PRESS

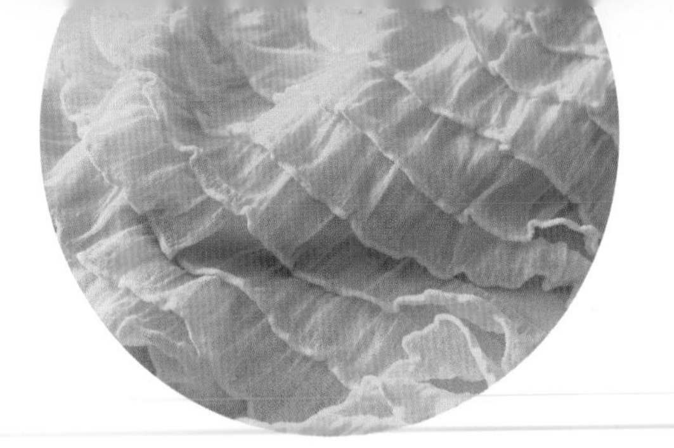

A RotoVision book

Published in 2011 by Search Press Ltd.
Wellwood, North Farm Road,
Tunbridge Wells, Kent TN2 3DR

This book is produced by
RotoVision SA
Sheridan House
114 Western Road
Hove
BN3 1DD

ISBN: 978-1-84448-742-4

Commissioning Editor: Isheeta Mustafi
Art Director: Emily Portnoi
Design: Emily Portnoi
Layout: Rebecca Stephenson

Printed in China by 1010 Printing International Ltd.

CONTENTS

INTRODUCTION

Why do we love fabrics so dearly? Well, what's not to like? They're beautiful, soft, rough, colourful, appealing to the eye and they spark creativity. Fabrics themselves are works of art. And just when you think you've found your most favourite textile ever, you click to another fabric site and fall in love with two others just as easily. Hey, we're equal opportunity employers when it comes to 'pretty things'. Nothing wrong with that.

Until we actually do something with these fabrics, however, they're nothing more than a pretty collection. Manipulating fabrics and sewing them into new creations is thrilling and exciting. It takes the art form to a new level. Whether sewing for yourself, your children, your business, or for friends, sewing is an adventure; there's nothing to fear.

You might be surprised at how often I hear someone say: 'I'm afraid to sew with knits', or 'I'm so scared to try elastic thread in my machine, so I just won't do it' or 'You can sew with that fabric? Really? I'm scared to try!'.

My two-year-old son is often afraid to try new things. He went through a period where taking a bath freaked him out. To me it seemed silly, but to him, he didn't want water poured on his head because it dripped in his eyes. I explained that he should close his eyes and tip his head back, and followed up the process by reassuring him 'That wasn't so bad!'. The phrase quickly caught on and soon the whole family was shouting it right and left, 'That wasn't so bad!'. Owen now loves taking baths.

Sometimes we need a little reassurance and explanation of facts to help us get past our fears. And sewing is no different. This book is designed to help you put your feet in the bath and experience the unknown. Sewing is fun and experimental, but typically when people think of fabrics, beautiful printed cotton comes to mind. While there's clearly a market for it, don't get stuck in a cotton rut. The world of textiles goes far beyond simple cotton and is just waiting for your discovery.

Use this book to help you think outside of the box. Have you sewn with shantung? Velvet? Nylon? Lycra? How about double cloth or jersey knit? All of these fabrics and many more are described in this book, along with quick pointers, references to needles and presser feet, and sewing tips. See! You don't need to be afraid anymore! Sewing with new fabrics might sound scary at first, but now you have the resources to guide you. And when you're done sewing, you too can exclaim, 'That wasn't so bad!'.

So with your book in hand, head to the fabric shop, grab a textile you've never sewn with and see where it takes you. The more you branch out, the more your sewing confidence will grow.

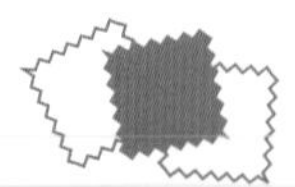

SECTION ONE: SELECTING FABRICS

The hardest part about writing this book was deciding how to organise the fabrics. Many fabrics overlap into more than one category. For instance, cotton may be blended with elastane; satin, once made from silk, is now often created from synthetic fibres; and so on. To overcome this problem, I decided to base the categories on how the fabrics are created. There are two main ways to create fabrics: by weaving or by knitting fibred yarns. Beyond this, almost all fabrics are man-made from plastics and vinyl. We also find textiles made from animal skins and furs, and often, many of our favourite fabrics are a blend of multiple fibres. Because of this, the fabrics in this book are divided into five sections: Woven Fabrics, Knit Fabrics, Specialty Fabrics, Blended Fabrics and Patterned Fabrics.

HOW TO USE THIS BOOK

There are a few things to remember when using this book and when planning a project:

- Fabric categories will overlap. For example, some cottons can be both woven and knit.
- Look for fabrics in their family of origin. Most natural fabrics have a synthetic counterpart, but these fabrics have been kept in the category of their origination. For example, chiffon was originally made of silk, but is now generally made from synthetic nylon. Instead of categorizing it as synthetic, you'll find it in the silk section of this book.
- This book provides basic information about washing, drying and pressing each type of fabric, but many fabrics are a mix of various fibres, so always double-check the manufacturer's instructions.
- Lining and interfacing information has been included, where appropriate, for each fabric. If nothing is listed, then the fabric isn't typically paired with interfacing or lining. However this is only a recommendation – my philosophy is to do what works best for you! Always refer to your pattern for additional information.

BEST USES FOR FABRICS

The best applications for each fabric are discussed in the text, but there are also icons at the top of each page that provide a quick reference to the best uses for each fabric. The icons represent three categories of applications.

FASHION: Garments and garment linings for women, men and children; bags, purses and other fashion accessories.

HOME FURNISHING: Curtains, cushion covers, bed linen, table linen, upholstery.

CRAFT/MISC.: Quilts, craft projects, testing fashion garments.

IDENTIFYING FIBRE CONTENT

Have you ever inherited a box of old fabrics and not known what they are? The detailed information in this book will help you to identify them, but for further investigation, a burn test will reveal a fabric's fibre content. To conduct a test, cut a small sample of fabric, hold it with a pair of tweezers and place it over a small flame. Take all necessary precautions and keep a bowl of water nearby to extinguish the flame when the test is complete. Observe the sample for the results listed here to determine the fibre content.

NATURAL FIBRES

COTTON: Burns quickly and steadily with a yellow flame. Continues to burn if flame is removed. Smells like burning leaves or paper. Leaves soft, grey ash.

SILK: Burns slowly and will self-extinguish if flame is removed. Smells like burning hair. Leaves crushable black beads of ash.

WOOL: Burns slowly and will self-extinguish if flame is removed. Smells like burning hair or feathers. Leaves brittle, black ash.

LINEN: Burns quickly and steadily with a yellow flame, but takes longer to ignite than cotton. Continues to burn if flame is removed. Smells like burning paper or rope. Leaves soft, grey ash.

MANUFACTURED FIBRES

ACETATE: Burns slowly and melts. Continues to burn if flame is removed. Smells like vinegar. Leaves hard, black beads.

ACRYLIC: Burns, melts and sputters. Continues to burn if flame is removed. Smells acidic. Leaves hard, black crust.

NYLON: Burns slowly and melts. Will self-extinguish if flame is removed. Smells like celery. Leaves hard, grey beads.

POLYESTER: Burns slowly and melts, with black smoke. Will self-extinguish if flame is removed. Smells sweet or fruity. Leaves hard black and brown beads.

RAYON: Burns quickly and steadily with a yellow flame. Continues to burn if flame is removed. Smells like burning wood. Leaves very little, fluffy ash.

PART ONE:
WOVEN FABRICS

NATURAL FABRICS

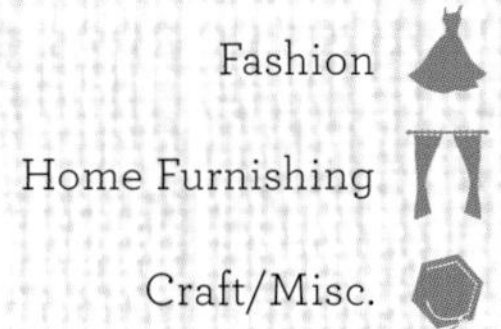

SUSTAINABLE FABRICS

MANUFACTURED FABRICS

WOVEN FABRICS

A woven cloth is just as simple as it sounds. Think back to your childhood – did you ever create a potholder with a plastic loom and some nylon strands, using your hands to weave them over and under? It's a simple process, and when you're done you have a colourfully woven cloth. With modern machinery, this process is far more advanced and there are numerous variations, but the basics are still the same:

- Weaving is typically done using two sets of yarn or thread.
- One set of threads is called the warp. These threads run vertically.
- The other set is the filling or weft, and these threads weave side to side through the warp.
- A loom is a huge device that holds the threads in place as they are woven.
- The way in which the threads are interlaced is called the weave.

Most woven fabrics are a plain weave, with threads going up and down and from side to side, but centuries of textile-making have inspired new methods. Here is a list of weave types, arranged from the most to the least commonly used.

PLAIN: Simple criss-cross pattern.
TWILL: Diagonal pattern of parallel ribs.
RIBBED: Variation of plain, with visible ribs.
SATIN: Fabric is glossy/smooth on the right side, with a dull matt finish on the wrong side. This is achieved by weaving the weft yarns less frequently so that long warp threads seem to float on the surface, giving sheen to the fabric.
PILE: Fabrics have a short 'pile' of threads – or nap – on the right side. This is achieved by adding looped yarns into the weave that stand perpendicular to the fabric. When the looped yarns are cut, the pile is exposed.
DOUBLE-WEAVE: Two layers of cloth interconnect, forming a double-sided, reversible fabric.
PIQUE: Diamond-shaped waffled weave.
DAMASK: Decorative weave using monochromatic or multicoloured threads. The image on the wrong side of the fabric is an inverse of what you see on the right side.
DOBBY: Decorative weave, creating small geometric shapes.
BROCADE: Decorative weave; gives the appearance that the weave is actually embroidered on to the fabric.
JACQUARD: Complex patterned weave, similar in look to damask. Jacquard looms use a punch-card technique that controls the warp yarn individually to create detailed designs.
IKAT: Resist-dyeing method used on only the warp or only the weft threads before weaving to create a graphic image or pattern.

Fashion 

Home Furnishing 

Craft/Misc.

BASKET: Multiple yarns are clumped together as one unit and woven into a plain weave, which looks like a woven basket.
LENO: A twisted-looking weave in which warp yarns are twisted together before being woven with the weft. The fabric can be sheer, yet very durable.

Woven cloths can be simple and plain, or complex and decorative. They make up the majority of the fabrics around us and can be further categorised according to the types of fibres they are made from. Textile fibres come in all forms, including cotton plants, sheep's wool and silkworm cocoons. They have been used since the dawn of time and refined through the ages, but let's start at the very beginning with one of humankind's most beloved fibres - cotton.

COTTON: An Overview

Cotton is grown in more than 80 countries and accounts for 40 per cent of the total fibre production in the world. The US, China and India produce more than half of that output. Cotton is, undoubtedly, the most important textile in the world. It is worn by every class of people, in almost every nation. Not to mention it is comfortable, durable, breathes well and has a wide range of uses.

Cotton is also one of the oldest fibres known to humankind. Archaeology traces cotton back to ancient Egypt, as early as 12,000 BC. By 3,000 BC cotton was also well established in India and parts of Peru. Today cotton is often blended with rayon, polyester and wool to produce even stronger textiles. You'll find it woven and knitted, unbleached and dyed, in varying weights and colours, and featuring a variety of patterns and prints. Cotton is, literally, all over the map.

PRODUCTION & PROCESSES

Cotton plants grow best in warmer climates, with most cotton being grown in regions of the US, China, India and Eastern Europe. In fact, a large area of southern states in the US known for their cotton production is referred to as the 'Cotton Belt'.

The planting of cotton seeds typically begins in the springtime, with large machine planters poking small holes in the earth, dropping in the seeds and then covering the holes back up with soil. Three months after being planted, the cotton plant produces a delicate yellow/white flower. As time goes by, the flower changes colour and falls off, exposing the boll, or rounded seed, of the plant. When the boll matures, the seed bursts open and we're left with beautiful white cotton, ready to be picked. Though once done by hand, large machinery is now used, working at a rate 50 times faster than human hands.

After harvesting, the cotton is combed to remove any seeds. Once a tedious process, the invention of the cotton gin by Eli Whitney in 1793 industrialised cotton production with its ability to separate seeds from fibres and prepare them for spinning. Cotton fibres alone are not very robust, but they are twisted and spun together to form strong threads that can be

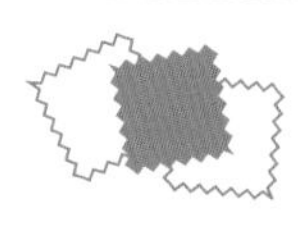

knitted or woven to create cotton fabric. The woven fabric then passes through several processing stages, including singeing (burning off unwanted fibres), desizing (a chemical process that removes excess size materials from finished cotton), scouring (washing the fabric to remove impurities and pectin), bleaching, dyeing and finishing, and eventually makes it way to the fabric shop shelf. The quality of cotton fabric depends on the fineness of the fibre, the thread count (number of threads per inch/2.5cm) used and the amount of foreign matter it contains.

ORGANIC & FAIR TRADE

The commercial cotton industry relies heavily on chemicals such as fertilisers and insecticides, which can have damaging effects on the environment and the health of cotton workers. Additionally, many cotton farmers and garment workers in the developing world suffer poor working conditions and are paid very low wages. In response to this, some farmers and garment manufacturers have switched to organic and fair trade methods. For more on this, see pages 114–115 and 119.

USES

Because it is readily available and easy to work with, cotton can be used for almost any sewing project. It is typically used for all types of clothing and a variety of home furnishings, quilting and craft projects. You can rarely go wrong with cotton.

CHARACTERISTICS

- Comfortable and soft.
- Durable.
- Can be chemically treated to reduce its flammability.
- Good colour retention; prints well.
- Absorbs and releases perspiration easily.
- Drapes well.
- Stronger wet than dry.
- Frequently shrinks.
- Machine-washable or can be dry-cleaned.
- Easy to handle and sew.

BATISTE

Batiste is a lightweight, semi-soft, plain-weave fabric that has a variety of uses. In fact, you've probably sewn with batiste without even being aware of it. Similar to lawn cotton, it is modest yet elegant. You can use it to make an everyday summer shirt for the office, or dress it up as a chic evening blouse. Due to its lightweight quality, batiste also works well as an underlining for dresses, nightgowns and other lightweight sleepwear – just be careful not to snag the fabric when pinning it. When in doubt, use a scrap piece first.

PROPERTIES

- CHARACTER: Lightweight, semi-soft and delicate.
- WEAVE: Plain weave.
- WEIGHT: Lightweight.
- SPECIAL CONSIDERATIONS: Shrinks and wrinkles easily. Due to shrinkage, consider washing/drying more than once before sewing.

WORKING WITH

- TO CUT: Use sharp scissors or a rotary cutter and mat.
- HANDLING FOR SEWING: Easy to sew; great for beginners.
- NEEDLES: Universal H, size 60/8 to 80/12.
- THREAD: All-purpose polyester or cotton.
- STITCH LENGTH: 2–2.5mm.
- SEWING MACHINE FEET: Standard.
- INTERFACING/LINING: Lightweight sew-in or fusible interfacing. Lining is optional, but when preferred, something lightweight should be used.

CARE

- WASHING: Machine wash.
- DRYING: Air-dry or normal tumble dry.
- IRONING: Medium heat and steam.
- SHRINKAGE: High.

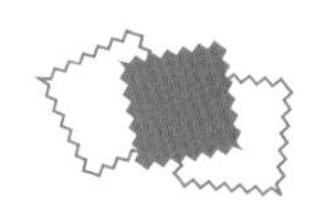

BEDFORD CORD

Bedford cord is a heavyweight fabric known for its lengthwise ribbed weave. Though similar in look to corduroy, the twill-woven ribs of Bedford cord are created in the weave itself (while corduroy is created with cut piles or nap in a plain weave).

Embraced by England's Duke of Bedford in the fifteenth century, it was originally used for military uniforms, but today has a wide range of uses, from home furnishings and upholstery to shorts, jackets and trousers. In fact, trousers manufactured from this fabric are often referred to as Bedford cords. It is also commonly used to make durable, heavy bedspreads. Bedford cord washes well, is easy to spot clean and, when used in upholstery, can last for years.

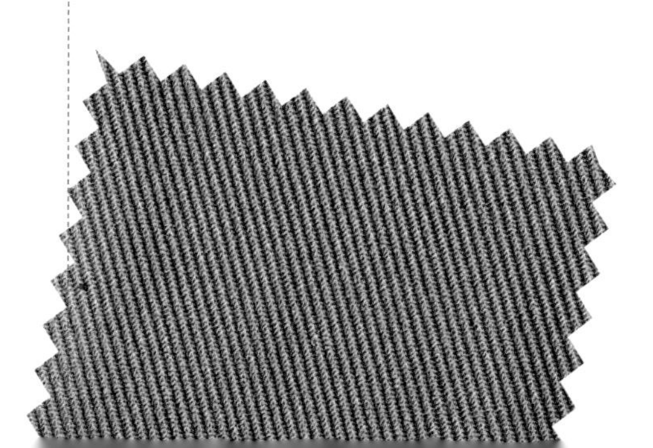

PROPERTIES

- CHARACTER: Lengthwise ribs, similar to corduroy.
- WEAVE: Twill with ribs.
- WEIGHT: Heavy.
- SPECIAL CONSIDERATIONS: Very durable, washes well and lasts for many years.

WORKING WITH

- TO CUT: Use sharp scissors or a rotary cutter and mat. With-nap layout is recommended when cutting out patterns.
- HANDLING FOR SEWING: Can feel bulky but sews easily.
- NEEDLES: Jeans/Denim HJ, sizes 100/16 or 110/18.
- THREAD: All-purpose polyester or cotton.
- STITCH LENGTH: 2–2.5mm.
- SEWING MACHINE FEET: Roller or standard.
- INTERFACING/LINING: Sew-in or fusible interfacing. Use acetate or other lightweight fabric linings for outerwear.

CARE

- WASHING: Machine wash.
- DRYING: Air-dry or normal tumble dry.
- IRONING: Medium to high steam heat. Press on the wrong side to protect the fabric cords.
- SHRINKAGE: Minimal to moderate.

BROADCLOTH

Broadcloth is a semi-soft, densely woven cotton that is readily available in most fabric shops, and is usually seen in solid colours rather than printed designs. Similar to poplin, broadcloth has a dense weave and is very easy to use. It works well for casualwear, shirts, skirts, pyjamas, childrenswear and sheets. It is also widely used in the quilting world.

PROPERTIES

- CHARACTER: Dense weave, similar to poplin.
- WEAVE: Plain weave.
- WEIGHT: Medium.
- SPECIAL CONSIDERATIONS: To avoid excessive fraying, overlock the edges or stitch the ends together before washing and drying.

WORKING WITH

- TO CUT: Use sharp scissors or a rotary cutter and mat.
- HANDLING FOR SEWING: Easy to sew; great for beginners.
- NEEDLES: Universal H, size 80/12.
- THREAD: All-purpose polyester or cotton.
- STITCH LENGTH: 2–2.5mm.
- SEWING MACHINE FEET: Standard.
- INTERFACING/LINING: Lightweight sew-in or fusible interfacing. Lining is optional, but when preferred, something lightweight should be used.

CARE

- WASHING: Machine wash.
- DRYING: Air-dry or normal tumble dry.
- IRONING: Medium steam heat.
- SHRINKAGE: Moderate.

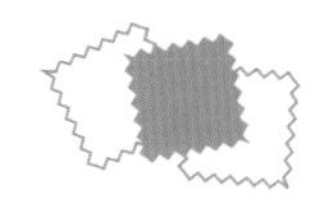

BUCKRAM

Buckram, sometimes referred to as book crinoline, is a stiff, heavy, open-weave cotton commonly used to cover and protect books. It is also used as a stabiliser in items such as bags, purses, hats and caps to help them stand upright and hold their shape. When used for hat-making it is called millinery buckram and comes in three weights: baby buckram (used for children's and doll's hats), single-ply buckram and double buckram (also known as theatrical crown).

DID YOU KNOW?

To make a hat, millinery buckram is infused with starch and left to dry into a hard shape.

PROPERTIES

- CHARACTER: Very stiff; stands upright on its own.
- WEAVE: Open.
- WEIGHT: Heavy.
- SPECIAL CONSIDERATIONS: Very economical; often found in the curtains section of a fabric shop, sold on a roll that measures approximately 50cm wide.

WORKING WITH

- TO CUT: Use sharp scissors or a rotary cutter and mat.
- HANDLING FOR SEWING: To avoid pinning, use a temporary spray-adhesive to hold the fabric in place while sewing.
- NEEDLES: Universal H or Sharp HG, sizes 70/10–110/18.
- THREAD: All-purpose polyester or cotton.
- STITCH LENGTH: 2–3mm.
- SEWING MACHINE FEET: Standard or roller.
- INTERFACING/LINING: No interfacing or lining. Buckram is stiff enough on its own.

CARE

- WASHING: Dry-clean only.
- DRYING: Dry-clean only.
- IRONING: Medium dry heat.
- SHRINKAGE: Will shrink and lose its stiffness if washed/dried, so should be dry-cleaned.

CANVAS and DUCK

Canvas is a heavy-duty, plain-weave fabric. Also referred to as duck cloth (from the Dutch word *doek*, meaning 'linen canvas'), canvas was once primarily used to make sailor's trousers, but today can be found in all sorts of objects, such as tote bags, art canvases, tents, backpacks, umbrellas, awnings, upholstery and shoes. Canvas is durable, strong and available in many solid colours.

HANDY HINT

While canvas fabric makes a great tote bag or pair of shoes, it's a shame to see it tarnished by dirt and spills. To protect your fabric from soils and help it repel water, spray a fabric protector over the fabric surface. Wait approximately 24 hours for the protector to dry. It's always best to perform a test on a sample piece first to ensure that it works.

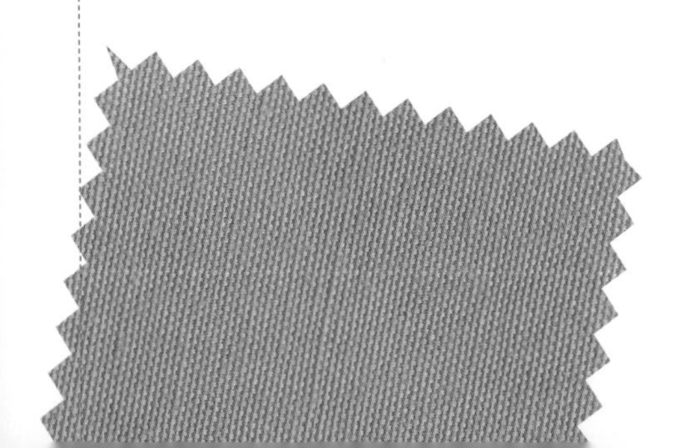

PROPERTIES

- CHARACTER: Heavy-duty, durable, strong.
- WEAVE: Plain.
- WEIGHT: Heavy.
- SPECIAL CONSIDERATIONS: Because canvas is very heavy, it isn't ideal for most types of clothing. It can be softened by pre-shrinking and you can use a fabric protector spray to help repel water and block stains.

WORKING WITH

- TO CUT: Use sharp scissors or a rotary cutter and mat.
- HANDLING FOR SEWING: Can feel bulky, so give yourself plenty of space to sew and spread out.
- NEEDLES: Jeans/Denim HJ, sizes 100/16 or 110/18.
- THREAD: All-purpose polyester or cotton.
- STITCH LENGTH: 2–3mm.
- SEWING MACHINE FEET: Standard.
- INTERFACING/LINING: No interfacing or lining. The fabric is sturdy enough on its own.

CARE

- WASHING: Can be washed or dry-cleaned.
- DRYING: Air-dry or normal tumble dry.
- IRONING: Medium to high steam.
- SHRINKAGE: Will shrink and soften if washed/dried.

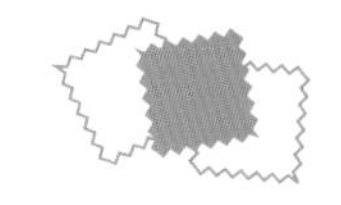

CHAMBRAY

Chambray is a soft, plain-weave cotton, once referred to as cambric. It is made by weaving coloured threads through a white weft (similar to denim), which results in a pleasing 'watered down' shade of the original thread colour. Think of it as adding white paint to a bright pigment. If you look at the cut end of chambray, you'll see white weft threads running in one direction and vibrant coloured thread in the other. Available in a spectrum of shades, the most common is blue chambray. It is a wonderful choice for clothing, shirts, dresses, childrenswear and even pyjamas.

PROPERTIES

- CHARACTER: Coloured thread woven through a white weft, resulting in a 'watered down' shade of the original thread colour.
- WEAVE: Plain weave.
- WEIGHT: Light to medium.
- SPECIAL CONSIDERATIONS: To avoid excessive fraying, overlock the edges or stitch the ends together before washing and drying.

WORKING WITH

- TO CUT: Use sharp scissors or a rotary cutter and mat.
- HANDLING FOR SEWING: Easy to sew; great for beginners.
- NEEDLES: Universal H, size 80/12.
- THREAD: All-purpose polyester or cotton.
- STITCH LENGTH: 2–2.5mm.
- SEWING MACHINE FEET: Standard.
- INTERFACING/LINING: Lightweight sew-in or fusible interfacing. Lining is optional, but when prefered, something lightweight should be used.

CARE

- WASHING: Machine wash.
- DRYING: Air-dry or normal tumble dry.
- IRONING: Medium steam.
- SHRINKAGE: Moderate.

CHENILLE

Chenille, the French word for 'caterpillar', is just what you would imagine: soft, fuzzy fabric that you can wrap cosily around your body. This makes the fabric an excellent choice for blankets, soft tunic tops and home furnishing projects.

Chenille is made by placing short pieces of yarn between two longer strands of yarns and twisting them together. The yarns are then woven to create an extremely soft, elegant fabric that denotes luxury without being too expensive. Some chenilles are a simple plain weave, while others are woven with a tufted pile design on top. Similar in appearance to velvet, all chenilles catch light from different angles, making the fabric iridescent at times. Chenille can be used for loose clothing, jumpers and jackets, and is an ideal choice for throws, home furnishings, bedspreads, baby toys and bathrobes.

PROPERTIES

- CHARACTER: Extremely soft and fuzzy. Sometimes seen with tufted piles.
- WEAVE: Plain weave or tufted piles.
- SPECIAL CONSIDERATIONS: Chenille can grow and stretch as it is worn. If creating a garment, use a knit or tricot interfacing to give it more structure. After washing, lay your clothing out flat to dry rather than hanging.

WORKING WITH

- TO CUT: Use sharp scissors or a rotary cutter and mat. Use with-nap layout when cutting out patterns.
- HANDLING FOR SEWING: It is easier to sew than other tufted fabrics.
- NEEDLES: Universal H, size 80/12.
- THREAD: All-purpose polyester or cotton.
- STITCH LENGTH: 2–2.5mm.
- SEWING MACHINE FEET: Standard, roller or walking.
- INTERFACING/LINING: Fusible knit or tricot interfacing.

CARE

- WASHING: Hand wash or machine wash on a low/gentle cycle.
- DRYING: Air-dry by laying out flat (don't hang).
- IRONING: Low to medium steam heat. To minimise crushing piles while you iron, first lay a towel on your ironing surface then place your fabric on top. Don't press directly on the pile as it will flatten; iron on the wrong side of the fabric.
- SHRINKAGE: Minimal to moderate.

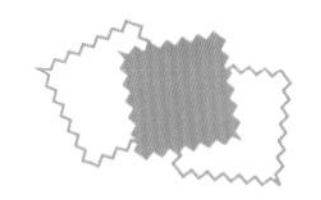

CHINO

Chino (the Spanish term for 'Chinese') is a kind of twill woven fabric. Ever heard of chinos? You guessed it; these trousers are made from chino fabric. As the name denotes, it was originally developed in China and was often worn by peasants. It was later used by Europeans and Americans to make military uniforms, and from there was introduced into everyday fashion.

Though sometimes labelled as khaki trousers (since they are often khaki colour), chino fabric covers a wide colour spectrum and is used for a variety of garments such as trousers, shorts, casual skirts and bags.

PROPERTIES

- CHARACTER: A form of twill that is often khaki in colour.
- WEAVE: Twill.
- WEIGHT: Medium.
- SPECIAL CONSIDERATIONS: Though often seen in a khaki colour, chino fabric can be found in a spectrum of colours.

WORKING WITH

- TO CUT: Use sharp scissors or a rotary cutter and mat.
- HANDLING FOR SEWING: Easy to sew.
- NEEDLES: Universal H, size 80/12.
- THREAD: All-purpose polyester or cotton.
- STITCH LENGTH: 2–2.5mm.
- SEWING MACHINE FEET: Standard.
- INTERFACING/LINING: No interfacing or lining. The fabric is sturdy on its own.

CARE

- WASHING: Machine wash or dry-clean.
- DRYING: Air-dry or normal tumble dry.
- IRONING: Medium steam.
- SHRINKAGE: Moderate.

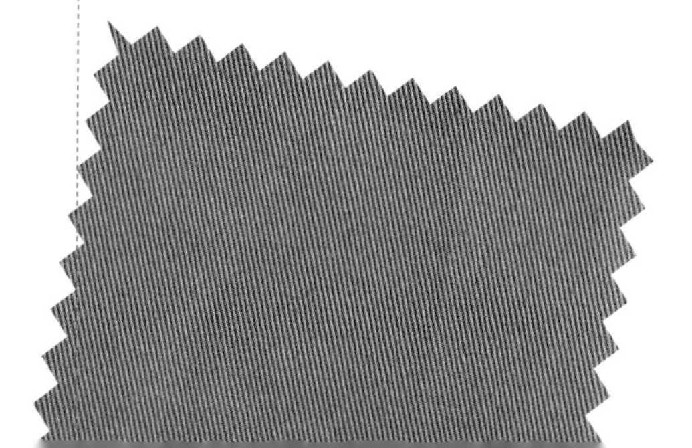

CHINTZ

Chintz is a plain-weave cotton that is characterised by a light background colour with bright, bold, often floral patterns on top. It can be used for curtains, bedding, tablecloths and upholstery. Some chintz fabrics have a glazed finish, which may be permanent or may wash out.

Chintz was originally produced in India (the name 'chintz' derives from the Hindi wozrd *chit*, meaning spotted or variegated), where patterns of birds, plants and flowers were painted on by hand. The fabric became wildly popular in Europe in the seventeenth and eighteenth centuries, and in order to meet demand, European textile manufacturers began developing their own methods for mass producing chintz using synthetic dyes. In contemporary interiors, chintz is best used in small amounts as an accent so as not to overpower a room.

PROPERTIES

- CHARACTER: Light background colour with bright, bold, often floral printed patterns.
- WEAVE: Plain weave.
- WEIGHT: Medium.
- SPECIAL CONSIDERATIONS: Some chintz fabrics have a glazed finish. Some glazes wash out and some are permanent.

WORKING WITH

- TO CUT: Use sharp scissors or a rotary cutter and mat.
- HANDLING FOR SEWING: Easy to sew.
- NEEDLES: Universal H, sizes 70/10 or 80/12.
- THREAD: All-purpose polyester or cotton.
- STITCH LENGTH: 2–3mm.
- SEWING MACHINE FEET: Standard.
- INTERFACING/LINING: Lightweight sew-in or fusible interfacing. Lining is optional, but when preferred, something lightweight should be used.

CARE

- WASHING: Machine wash or dry-clean.
- DRYING: Air-dry or normal tumble dry.
- IRONING: Medium steam.
- SHRINKAGE: Moderate.

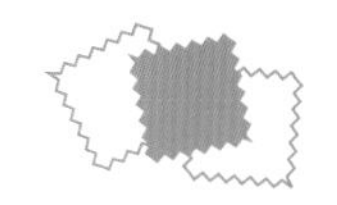

CORDUROY

Corduroy is a durable ribbed fabric, characterised by its parallel, lengthwise cords. These cords are created by adding looped yarns in the weave that stand upright on the fabric. When the looped yarns are cut, the pile - or napped - cords are exposed. The lengthwise cords are called wales and the narrow spaces that run between them are called channels. Corduroy is sold in different wale widths (usually marked on the fabric bolt), and the more narrow and slim the wale, the softer and less durable the fabric. Smaller wales are perfect for shirts, caps, jackets and childrenswear, and because of its durability, wider wale corduroy works well for upholstery and trousers.

DID YOU KNOW?

People often mistake the word corduroy to mean 'cord of kings', from the French *corde du roi*. But in fact, there's no such phrase in the French language! It's more likely to come from the British words 'cord' and 'duroy', which is a rough wool fabric.

PROPERTIES

- CHARACTER: Lengthwise ribs known as wales.
- WEAVE: Ribbed.
- WEIGHT: Medium to heavy (depending on the wale width).
- SPECIAL CONSIDERATIONS: Darker colours are more flattering on adults. If you are heavier-set, avoid wearing wider-waled cords as they add extra bulk.

WORKING WITH

- TO CUT: Use sharp scissors or a rotary cutter and mat. Use with-nap layout when cutting out patterns.
- HANDLING FOR SEWING: Rub fabrics against each other to restore the nap.
- NEEDLES: Universal H or HJ, size 80/12.
- THREAD: All-purpose polyester or cotton.
- STITCH LENGTH: 2–3mm.
- SEWING MACHINE FEET: Roller, walking or standard.
- INTERFACING/LINING: Sew-in or fusible interfacing. Lining is recommended for outerwear.

CARE

- WASHING: Machine wash.
- DRYING: Air-dry or normal tumble dry. Restore flattened wales by throwing the fabric in the dryer along with a damp cloth and tumble drying inside out for a few minutes.
- IRONING: Medium to high steam heat. Press on the wrong side of the fabric with a towel as your underlying surface to protect the wales on the right side.
- SHRINKAGE: Minimal to moderate.

DENIM

Denim is a dense, twill-woven fabric, famously known for its use in blue jeans. It is slightly similar to chambray, as it has coloured threads in the warp and white threads in the filling. Once used solely for workwear, denim can now be found virtually everywhere, and is even used in high-end fashion.

Similar to the twill fabric serge, denim is thought to have originated in Nîmes, France. Denim was traditionally dyed blue using natural dyes from the indigo plant. The colour struck a chord and today blue denim is worn by billions of people worldwide, thanks in part to Levi Strauss who developed the timeless blue jeans.

Though blue is king, time and innovation have developed denim even further, and the fabric is now available in many different weights, colours, washes and fibre blends.

Here are some of the different types of denim available on the market:

RAW DENIM: The purest form of denim. It is unwashed, stiff, very dark blue in colour and fades with wash and wear. Some prefer a natural method of washing/ageing raw denim compared to factory-created distressed looks.

WASHED DENIM: Refers to a variety of washes such as 'classic wash' (washed raw denim that is substantially faded), 'stone wash' (denim washed with stones to create a worn look) and 'acid wash' (achieved using chemicals to strip the denim of its colour).

STRETCH DENIM: Denim that is blended with small amounts of elastane for added comfort and stretch.

LIGHTWEIGHT DENIM: Used for shirts, dresses and crafts.

HEAVYWEIGHT DENIM: Used for trousers, shorts, skirts and jackets.

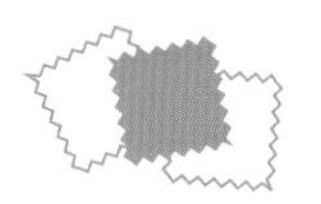

PROPERTIES

- CHARACTER: Durable; white thread woven with coloured thread.
- WEAVE: Twill.
- WEIGHT: Heavy or lightweight.
- SPECIAL CONSIDERATIONS: Denim fabrics are usually dyed in a 'wash' to create varying colours and looks. Darker denim washes will bleed when thrown in a washing machine, so wash them with similar colours. You can create your own 'faded wash' look by bleaching and washing denim multiple times.

WORKING WITH

- TO CUT: Use sharp scissors or a rotary cutter and mat.
- HANDLING FOR SEWING: Hold fabric taut while sewing through multiple layers. Keep everything straight to avoid skipped stitches.
- NEEDLES: Jeans/Denim HJ, sizes 90/14 (lightweight) and 100/16 (heavyweight).
- THREAD: All-purpose polyester or cotton.
- STITCH LENGTH: 2–3mm.
- SEWING MACHINE FEET: Standard, straight-stitch, roller or jeans.
- INTERFACING/LINING: Washable, sew-in, or fusible interfacing, depending on fabric weight. Heavier denim does not need interfacing – it's sturdy enough on its own. Some denim (such as a jacket) is lined with fleece to make the garment warmer.

CARE

- WASHING: Machine wash with similar colours. Darker denims will bleed with each wash.
- DRYING: Tumble dry on a low setting or hang to dry (to avoid shrinking).
- IRONING: Medium to high steam heat.
- SHRINKAGE: Moderate.

HANDY HINT

There is a trend towards re-purposing clothing in the sewing world, and an old pair of denim jeans is the perfect specimen for upcycling. Turn a pair of trousers into a skirt, make a small tote bag or zipped pouch from a denim pocket, or cut up old pairs of jeans and transform then into a denim quilt with a soft fleece backing. 'Fabric' doesn't always mean 'fresh off the bolt'; you can find it in a variety of places.

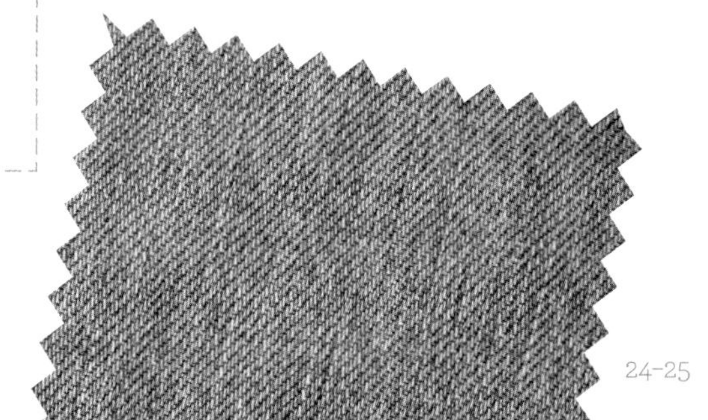

DIMITY

Dimity comes from the Greek word *Dirnitos* meaning 'double thread'. It is a thin fabric with two or three additional warp yarns added to the weave to create a slightly raised, patterned effect. Dimity is sheer yet strong, with a crisp texture. The raised warp is usually woven into checked or striped patterns.

Dimity was once manufactured in all white, but because it holds colour well, it is now seen in a variety of shades and patterns. It is easy to sew with and washes very well, making it ideal for hardwearing curtains, sleepwear and aprons.

PROPERTIES

- CHARACTER: Unique texture with a raised pattern on one side; lightweight yet strong.
- WEAVE: Plain with dimity woven pattern.
- WEIGHT: Sheer to lightweight.
- SPECIAL CONSIDERATIONS: Typically made from pre-shrunk cotton so there is little concern for the fabric shrinking or losing its shape.

WORKING WITH

- TO CUT: Use sharp scissors or a rotary cutter and mat.
- HANDLING FOR SEWING: Rub fabrics against each other to restore the nap.
- NEEDLES: Sharp HM or HJ or Universal H, size 70/10.
- THREAD: All-purpose polyester or cotton.
- STITCH LENGTH: 2–2.5mm.
- SEWING MACHINE FEET: Standard.
- INTERFACING/LINING: Lightweight sew-in or fusible interfacing. Lining is optional, but when preferred, something lightweight should be used.

CARE

- WASHING: Machine wash.
- DRYING: Air-dry or normal tumble dry.
- IRONING: Low, medium or high heat.
- SHRINKAGE: Minimal.

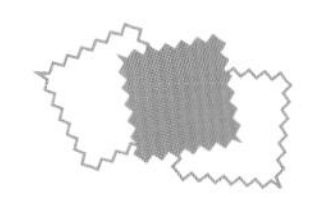

DOTTED SWISS

Dotted Swiss is a cute fabric, so it's no surprise that it is often used to create baby clothes, blouses and summer dresses. It was originally produced on handlooms in Switzerland in the 1700s, and became especially popular in the 1950s. Dotted Swiss is a sheer batiste fabric with small raised dots decorating its surface. It comes in a variety of colours and dot sizes, and is a beautiful choice for clothing, sheer curtains, bedding and aprons. Its youthful charm gives off a feeling of happiness.

DID YOU KNOW?

Aside from fabric, the term 'dotted Swiss' has been applied to cake decorating and pottery, and simply refers to the decorated arrangement of small raised dots.

PROPERTIES

- CHARACTER: Small raised dots arranged in a pattern over sheer cotton fabric.
- WEAVE: Plain weave with woven or embroidered plush dots (this differs from standard 'polka dot' fabric, which is typically printed).
- WEIGHT: Sheer.
- SPECIAL CONSIDERATIONS: Often found in pastel colours. If you can't find a shade you like, grab some fabric dye and create your own colour.

WORKING WITH

- TO CUT: Use sharp scissors or a rotary cutter and mat.
- HANDLING FOR SEWING: Easy to sew; great for beginners.
- NEEDLES: Universal H, size 80/12.
- THREAD: All-purpose polyester or cotton.
- STITCH LENGTH: 2–2.5mm.
- SEWING MACHINE FEET: Standard.
- INTERFACING/LINING: Lightweight sew-in or fusible interfacing. Lining is optional, but when preferred, something lightweight should be used.

CARE

- WASHING: Machine wash.
- DRYING: Air-dry or normal tumble dry.
- IRONING: Medium steam heat.
- SHRINKAGE: Moderate.

DRILL

Similar to canvas and duck, drill is a highly durable fabric known for its twill (or diagonal) weave. Drill is often grey in colour, but can be bleached or dyed, and is commonly used to make khaki trousers. A versatile fabric, drill comes in two weights – lightweight, which is used for shirts, blouses, sportswear and light jackets; and heavy, which is used for workwear and a variety of uniforms, including martial-arts clothing.

DID YOU KNOW?

Drill is widely used in the manufacture of chefs' uniforms. While cool to the skin, the fabric doesn't melt at high temperatures and therefore protects the wearer.

PROPERTIES

- CHARACTER: Sturdy and durable.
- WEAVE: Twill, bias/diagonal.
- WEIGHT: Lightweight to heavy.
- SPECIAL CONSIDERATIONS: Drill can withstand high temperatures without melting.

WORKING WITH

- TO CUT: Use sharp scissors or a rotary cutter and mat.
- HANDLING FOR SEWING: Easy to work with.
- NEEDLES: Universal H, size 80/12 or Jeans/Denim HJ, sizes 100/16 or 110/18.
- THREAD: All-purpose polyester or cotton.
- STITCH LENGTH: 2–3mm.
- SEWING MACHINE FEET: Standard.
- INTERFACING/LINING: Washable, sew-in, or fusible interfacing, depending on fabric weight. Heavier drill does not need interfacing – it's sturdy enough on its own.

CARE

- WASHING: Can be washed or dry-cleaned.
- DRYING: Air-dry or normal tumble dry.
- IRONING: Medium to high steam heat.
- SHRINKAGE: Will shrink and soften if washed/dried.

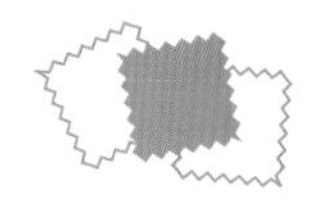

EYELET and BRODERIE ANGLAISE

Eyelet and Broderie Anglaise are both lightweight cotton fabrics featuring cut-out pieces outlined with embroidered thread. Although both fabrics have a similar appearance, the production of Broderie Anglaise is done by hand. To create Broderie, a small hole is pierced in the fabric, the hole is outlined by hand with embroidered stitches to create a larger circle around the hole, and the fabric inside the circle is then cut out to create an outlined eyelet look. This time-consuming technique is known as 'whitework' because white thread is sewn on to white fabric.

Eyelet is a modernised version of Broderie. Lightweight and dainty, it is often used for summer dresses and baby clothing, and comes in a variety of colours. The cut-out designs appear in recurring patterns, and often the fabric requires a garment lining. Eyelet is inexpensive and gives a shabby chic feel when used for home furnishings.

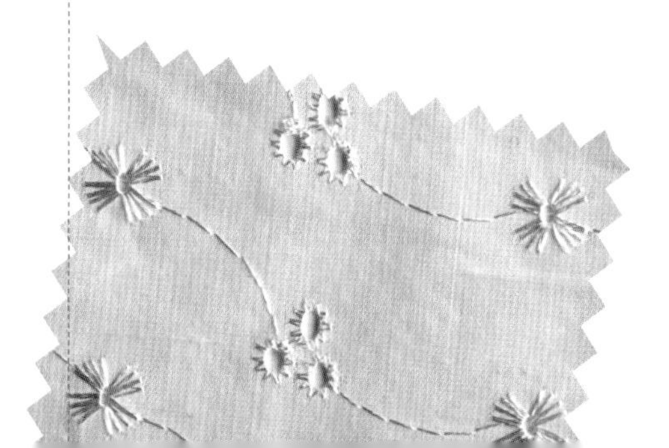

PROPERTIES

- CHARACTER: Embroidered cut-out patterns; dainty and feminine.
- WEAVE: Plain weave with embroidery.
- WEIGHT: Lightweight.
- SPECIAL CONSIDERATIONS: When choosing a fabric lining, consider your desired look. A lining in a contrasting colour will make the eyelets pop and stand out, while a matching lining gives a subtle look.

WORKING WITH

- TO CUT: Use sharp scissors or a rotary cutter and mat.
- HANDLING FOR SEWING: Easy to sew.
- NEEDLES: Universal H, size 80/12.
- THREAD: All-purpose polyester or cotton.
- STITCH LENGTH: 2–2.5mm.
- SEWING MACHINE FEET: Standard.
- INTERFACING/LINING: Lightweight sew-in or fusible interfacing. Use lightweight cotton for lining.

CARE

- WASHING: Machine wash.
- DRYING: Air-dry or normal tumble dry.
- IRONING: Medium steam heat.
- SHRINKAGE: Moderate.

FLANNEL (Flannelette)

Cotton flannel is a favourite among sewers and crafters. It has a soft-brushed nap and a tight weave, making it both comfortable and durable.

The terms flannelette and flannel have different meanings depending on where you are in the world. In North America, 'flannel' is used to refer to cotton flannel; however, in some countries, such as the UK, the term 'flannelette' is used. If that wasn't confusing enough, the term flannel is also used to refer to clothing made from flannelette, such as the tartan-printed shirts popular among outdoor adventurers. The fabric is also used to create sleepwear, bed sheets, baby receiving blankets, crafts, jacket linings and even quilt wadding. It is lightweight yet warm, and is great for winter projects.

PROPERTIES

- CHARACTER: Soft-brushed nap.
- WEAVE: Plain weave.
- WEIGHT: Medium.
- SPECIAL CONSIDERATIONS: To avoid excessive fraying, overlock the edges or stitch the ends together before washing and drying; wrinkles easily.

WORKING WITH

- TO CUT: Use sharp scissors or a rotary cutter and mat.
- HANDLING FOR SEWING: Easy to sew; frays easily. Trim cut edges of pattern pieces with pinking shears. Finish off seams with an overlocker or a zigzag stitch.
- NEEDLES: Universal H, size 80/12.
- THREAD: All-purpose polyester or cotton.
- STITCH LENGTH: 2–2.5mm.
- SEWING MACHINE FEET: Standard.
- INTERFACING/LINING: Lightweight sew-in or fusible interfacing. Flannel is itself often used as a lining for jackets or as an alternative to quilt wadding.

CARE

- WASHING: Machine wash.
- DRYING: Air-dry or normal tumble dry.
- IRONING: Medium heat and steam.
- SHRINKAGE: Shrinks more than typical cottons.

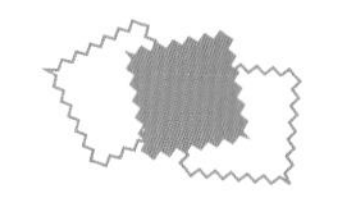

GAUZE

Gauze is a very lightweight, open-weave fabric that is often used to dress wounds, however variations of gauze (both cotton and blended) have made their way into the fashion world. With a billowy drape and breathable weave, gauze is a wonderful choice for summer dresses and comfortable skirts, and is available in a wide variety of colours.

DID YOU KNOW?

Due to its lightweight and breathable characteristics, gauze and muslin have become popular fabrics for making baby receiving blankets, and both are especially good choices if you live in a warm climate.

PROPERTIES

- CHARACTER: Lightweight open weave; billows in the wind; wrinkles easily (although this can enhance the fabric's appearance).
- WEAVE: Plain or leno (where warp yarns are twisted around each other).
- WEIGHT: Lightweight.
- SPECIAL CONSIDERATIONS: Due to a unique leno weave, some gauze fabrics can feel like they have a slight stretch to them. If this concerns you, consider lining your garment with a lightweight woven fabric of similar colour to help stabilise the stretch.

WORKING WITH

- TO CUT: Use sharp scissors or a rotary cutter and mat.
- HANDLING FOR SEWING: Easy to sew.
- NEEDLES: Universal H, size 80/12.
- THREAD: All-purpose polyester or cotton.
- STITCH LENGTH: 2–2.5mm.
- SEWING MACHINE FEET: Standard.
- INTERFACING: Lightweight sew-in or fusible interfacing. Lining is optional, but when preferred, something lightweight should be used.

CARE

- WASHING: Machine wash.
- DRYING: Air-dry or normal tumble dry.
- IRONING: Medium steam heat
- SHRINKAGE: Moderate.

LAMINATED COTTON

Have you ever wished your favourite cotton print was water resistant? If so, you'll love the movement towards laminated fabrics. Laminated cotton is just what you would imagine – cotton fabric that is laminated on one side with a lightweight clear polyurethane coating. Compared to oilcloth and vinyl, laminated cotton gives you the designer printed look found in normal cotton varieties, but with an added benefit: You can use it to make raincoats, summer tote bags, lunch bags, tablecloths, baby bibs and purses. Many top-name fabric designers carry a few laminates in their collection, although they can be pricey.

HANDY HINT

Oilcloth vs. laminated cotton – which should you choose? Your decision really depends on the nature of the project. Oilcloth is stiff yet bendable, works well for upholstery, tablecloths and beach bags, but is made of polyvinyl chloride, which makes it unsuitable for items that may go in a child's mouth. Laminated cotton, on the other hand, is a more well-rounded fabric. It's pliable, drapes better than oilcloth and doesn't contain PVC. Laminated cotton can be used for aprons, bags, wallets, tablecloths, clothing and even umbrellas. It's easier to sew than oilcloth and can be ironed (on the wrong side using a pressing cloth). The main disadvantage is that laminated cotton costs twice as much as oilcloth.

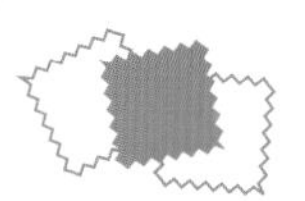

PROPERTIES

- CHARACTER: Printed cotton, laminated on one side with clear polyurethane coating; water resistant.
- WEAVE: Plain weave.
- WEIGHT: Medium.
- SPECIAL CONSIDERATIONS: Although the Consumer Product Safety Improvement Act of 2008 (CPSIA) in the US prohibits the use of oilcloth in baby bibs and toys for children under the age of 12, most laminated cottons are deemed 'child-safe' by manufacturers.

WORKING WITH

- TO CUT: Use sharp scissors or a rotary cutter and mat.
- HANDLING FOR SEWING: Pins will leave holes, so only pin in the seam allowance. Change your needle when starting a new project. Consider using a walking or Teflon foot. When using a standard foot, the laminated side of the fabric has a tendency to stick under the presser foot. Here are three ideas to combat sticking:

1. Sandwich the fabric with a piece of tissue paper on the top and bottom. When you've finished sewing, carefully tear the tissue paper off.
2. Apply masking or painter's tape to the bottom of your presser foot and to the top of your machine plate, which will help the fabric slide through more smoothly.
3. Use a non-stick, Teflon or roller foot.

- NEEDLES: Universal H, size 80/12 or Jeans/Denim HJ, size 70/10.
- THREAD: All-purpose polyester or cotton.
- STITCH LENGTH: 2–3mm.
- SEWING MACHINE FEET: Standard, walking or Teflon.
- INTERFACING/LINING: Since the fabric is only laminated on one side, consider using another water-resistant fabric, such as nylon, to line a bag.

CARE

- WASHING: Hand wash, spot clean or machine wash on a very delicate cycle. The polyurethane coating wipes clean with a damp cloth.
- DRYING: Some laminates can be tumble dried on low heat. Refer to the manufacturer's care instructions or experiment with a sample piece. When in doubt, lay flat to dry.
- IRONING: To remove wrinkles, lay the fabric face down on your ironing surface, cover with a pressing cloth and iron on the wrong side of the fabric on high steam heat (the standard cotton setting). Never iron on the laminated side.
- SHRINKAGE: None.

LAWN

Lawn is a plain-weave cotton with a high thread count, which can make it very soft and almost silky. It is often found in dainty floral prints (such as those produced by Liberty of London), but is also available in solid colours. Lawn cotton is a wonderful choice for blouses, dresses, shirts, curtains, nightgowns, baby clothing and quilting.

PROPERTIES

- CHARACTER: A high thread count makes it very soft.
- WEAVE: Plain weave.
- WEIGHT: Lightweight to medium; can be sheer.
- SPECIAL CONSIDERATIONS: Shrinks and wrinkles easily. Due to shrinkage, consider washing and drying more than once before sewing.

WORKING WITH

- TO CUT: Use sharp scissors or a rotary cutter and mat.
- HANDLING FOR SEWING: Easy to sew; great for beginners.
- NEEDLES: Universal H, size 80/12.
- THREAD: All-purpose polyester or cotton.
- STITCH LENGTH: 2–2.5mm.
- SEWING MACHINE FEET: Standard.
- INTERFACING: Lightweight sew-in or fusible interfacing. Lining is optional, but when preferred, something lightweight should be used.

CARE

- WASHING: Machine wash.
- DRYING: Air-dry or normal tumble dry.
- IRONING: Medium steam heat.
- SHRINKAGE: Shrinks easily.

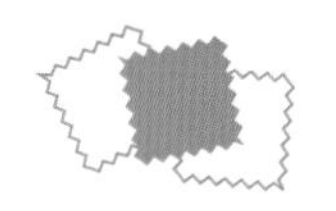

MATELASSÉ

Matelassé, the French word for 'quilted' or 'padded', is a heavy quilted cotton that appears to be padded, though it isn't. It looks elegant and feels comfortable, and the fabric softens with every wash. Meant to echo hand-stitched quilts made in France, the fabric was originally quilted by hand but today it is machine woven on a Jacquard loom. The fabric is typically found in solid colours, and the quilted designs range from simple graphics to ornate florals.

Matelassé is best used for home furnishing projects such as pillow shams, bedspreads, duvet covers, throw cushions and slip covers, and is often used for shabby chic furnishing looks. Matelassé is also ideal for apparel, jackets and handbags.

PROPERTIES

- CHARACTER: Quilted look with a padded feel.
- WEAVE: Plain, Jacquard loom or dobby.
- WEIGHT: Heavy.
- SPECIAL CONSIDERATIONS: The fabric softens with each wash.

WORKING WITH

- TO CUT: Use sharp scissors or a rotary cutter and mat.
- HANDLING FOR SEWING: Matelassé can tear easily when removing stitches - sew carefully to avoid mistakes. On the reverse side, its uneven surface actually hides irregular and messy stitches.
- NEEDLES: Sharp HM or Universal H, sizes 70/10 or 80/12.
- THREAD: All-purpose polyester or cotton.
- STITCH LENGTH: 2–3mm.
- SEWING MACHINE FEET: Standard, roller or zigzag.
- INTERFACING/LINING: Sew-in interfacing. When used in clothing, you may want to add an organza, voile or crisp cotton lining.

CARE

- WASHING: Machine wash or dry-clean.
- DRYING: Air-dry or normal tumble dry.
- IRONING: To avoid flattening, place a towel under your fabric. Use a cloth on top of your fabric when pressing the right side.
- SHRINKAGE: Moderate.

MERCERISED COTTON

Mercerised cotton is cotton that has been treated with sodium hydroxide to give it a shiny, smooth appearance. The process was discovered in 1844 by chemist and fabric printer John Mercer and was patented in 1851. Mercer found that immersing cotton strands in a soda bath made them stronger and better able to retain coloured dye.

Today, mercerised cotton is seen in fabrics, threads and manufactured clothing. It is sometimes referred to as pearl (or perle) cotton due to its shiny appearance, and because the cotton is pre-shrunk, mercerised cotton tends not to shrink as much as regular cotton.

PROPERTIES

- CHARACTER: Shiny, smooth look; stronger than regular cotton.
- WEAVE: Plain weave.
- WEIGHT: Lightweight to medium.
- SPECIAL CONSIDERATIONS: Mercerised cotton strands are pre-shrunk so the fabric tends to shrink less than regular cotton.

WORKING WITH

- TO CUT: Use sharp scissors or a rotary cutter and mat.
- HANDLING FOR SEWING: Easy to sew; great for beginners.
- NEEDLES: Universal H, size 80/12.
- THREAD: All-purpose polyester or cotton.
- STITCH LENGTH: 2–2.5mm.
- SEWING MACHINE FEET: Standard.
- INTERFACING: Lightweight sew-in or fusible interfacing. Lining is optional, but when preferred, something lightweight should be used.

CARE

- WASHING: Machine wash.
- DRYING: Air-dry or normal tumble dry.
- IRONING: Medium steam heat.
- SHRINKAGE: Shrinks less than regular cotton.

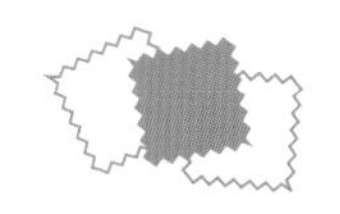

MOLESKIN

Moleskin is a densely woven twill that doesn't wrinkle or stretch out of shape. Designed to mimic the fur of a mole, it is extremely soft, with a short raised nap on one side that feels similar to suede. Moleskin is a great choice for apparel and is typically used for men's shirts and trousers. It is comfortable, cosy, easy to clean and very durable. Lighter-weight moleskin is often used in military clothing, while heavier grades are used as linings for winter coats.

DID YOU KNOW?

Moleskin is popular among film-makers, but not for its wardrobe uses. The flesh-coloured fabric works well as a cover-up for private parts in scenes where nudity is suggested but not actually shown.

PROPERTIES

- CHARACTER: Durable, extremely soft and feels similar to suede.
- WEAVE: Twill.
- WEIGHT: Lightweight to medium.
- SPECIAL CONSIDERATIONS: Tends not to wrinkle or lose shape from stretching.

WORKING WITH

- TO CUT: Use sharp scissors or a rotary cutter and mat.
- HANDLING FOR SEWING: Easy to sew.
- NEEDLES: Sharp Microtex HM, size 70/10.
- THREAD: All-purpose polyester or cotton.
- STITCH LENGTH: 2–2.5mm.
- SEWING MACHINE FEET: Standard.
- INTERFACING: Fusible tricot interfacing.

CARE

- WASHING: Machine wash on a gentle cycle (turn inside out before washing). Washing helps to maintain the tightness of the twill weave. Can also be dry-cleaned.
- DRYING: Air-dry or normal tumble dry.
- IRONING: Press on the wrong side of the fabric using the steam and 'synthetic' setting.
- SHRINKAGE: Shrinks less than regular cotton.

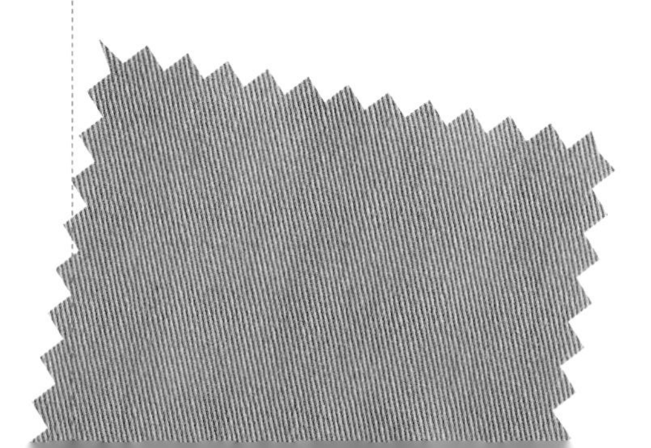

MUSLIN (Calico)

Calico is a loosely woven, inexpensive fabric that is most often an unbleached white or natural tan colour (although it also holds dye well). You'll find bolts of calico in your local fabric shop in varying grades and thread counts. In the fashion world, calico is often used to make a test garment (known as a *toile*) to avoid making mistakes when cutting and sewing expensive fabric.

DID YOU KNOW?

The firm cloth with everyday uses, known as calico in the UK, is called muslin in the US; calico describes a fabric featuring a small repeated pattern. In the UK, muslin usually refers to a sheer, gauzy fabric.

PROPERTIES

- CHARACTER: Lightweight with an open weave; often white.
- WEAVE: Plain weave.
- WEIGHT: Lightweight.
- SPECIAL CONSIDERATIONS: Shrinks and wrinkles easily. Typically inexpensive but prices vary with thread count.

WORKING WITH

- TO CUT: Use sharp scissors or a rotary cutter and mat.
- HANDLING FOR SEWING: Easy to sew.
- NEEDLES: Universal H, size 80/12.
- THREAD: All-purpose polyester or cotton.
- STITCH LENGTH: 2–2.5mm.
- SEWING MACHINE FEET: Standard.
- INTERFACING/LINING: Interfacing and lining are not necessary since muslin is often used as a test garment or as a lining itself.

CARE

- WASHING: Machine wash.
- DRYING: Air-dry or normal tumble dry.
- IRONING: Medium steam heat.
- SHRINKAGE: Moderate.

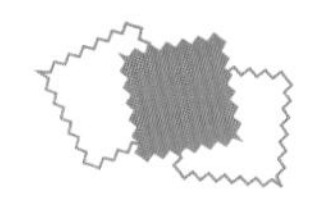

ORGANDY

Organdy (or organdie) is the sheerest cotton fabric available. Similar to silk organza, it is very lightweight with a plain, open weave. Organdy is typically stiff due to a calendering finishing process (which washes out), and it tends to wrinkle easily. Calendering involves folding the fabric and then passing it under rollers at a high temperature and at high pressure.

Stiff organdy can create a puffy, bouffant fullness that is ideal for evening dresses, while soft organdy is best used for garment linings, summer dresses, skirts and curtains.

PROPERTIES

- CHARACTER: Lightweight and very sheer.
- WEAVE: Plain weave.
- WEIGHT: Lightweight.
- SPECIAL CONSIDERATIONS: Wrinkles easily but can be smoothed with an iron.

WORKING WITH

- TO CUT: Use sharp scissors or a rotary cutter and mat.
- HANDLING FOR SEWING: Sew tautly to avoid puckering in seams. If fabric frays, sew a basting stitch first to keep fibres in place.
- NEEDLES: Sharp HM and Universal H, sizes 60/8 or 70/10.
- THREAD: Lightweight and all-purpose cotton.
- STITCH LENGTH: 2–2.5mm.
- SEWING MACHINE FEET: Standard, wide straight stitch, roller or a single-hole plate.
- INTERFACING/LINING: Lightweight sew-in or fusible interfacing. Lining is optional, but when preferred, something lightweight should be used.

CARE

- WASHING: Machine wash (note: washing will soften fabric and reduce calendering).
- DRYING: Air-dry or normal tumble dry.
- IRONING: Medium steam heat.
- SHRINKAGE: Minimal.

PIQUÉ

Piqué cotton is characterised by its own unique weave, which has a raised diamond and waffle-like effect on top. The name is derived from the French word *piquer*, meaning 'to quilt'. The fabric holds more starch than standard cotton, making it a stiffer, medium-weight fabric. Piqué is a wonderful choice for fitted tops and jackets.

PROPERTIES

- CHARACTER: Diamond, waffled look; stiffer than normal cotton.
- WEAVE: Piqué weave.
- WEIGHT: Medium.
- SPECIAL CONSIDERATIONS: Holds more starch than standard cotton and is stiff.

WORKING WITH

- TO CUT: Use sharp scissors or a rotary cutter and mat.
- HANDLING FOR SEWING: Easy to sew.
- NEEDLES: Universal H, sizes 70/10 or 80/12.
- THREAD: All-purpose cotton or polyester.
- STITCH LENGTH: 2–2.5mm.
- SEWING MACHINE FEET: Standard.
- INTERFACING/LINING: Fusible tricot or sew-in interfacing.

CARE

- WASHING: Machine wash.
- DRYING: Air-dry or normal tumble dry.
- IRONING: Steam iron, medium heat.
- SHRINKAGE: Minimal to moderate.

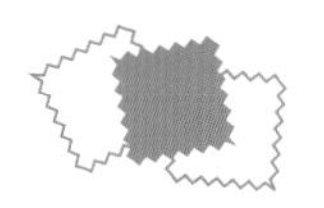

POPLIN

Poplin is similar to broadcloth, but has a slight cross-ribbed weave with noticeable ridges, which makes it dense, sturdy and heavy. Sometimes poplin is woven with a silk warp and a worsted yarn weft. When made from cotton, however, it is often a mix of softer and heavier grade yarns. It has a soft feel and sometimes a slight shine. Originally produced in France to make church vestments, poplin is an excellent choice for shirts, trousers, dresses and fine upholstery.

DID YOU KNOW?

Today poplin is associated with 100 per cent high-quality cotton men's shirts, and can be quite expensive, but in *Little Women*, the March sisters thought their poplin dresses were plain and not up to par. This just goes to show that fashion trends are a revolving cycle.

PROPERTIES

- CHARACTER: Dense weave with noticeable ridges; heavier than broadcloth.
- WEAVE: Plain weave with cross ribs.
- WEIGHT: Medium to heavy.
- SPECIAL CONSIDERATIONS: Tends not to wrinkle.

WORKING WITH

- TO CUT: Use sharp scissors or a rotary cutter and mat.
- HANDLING FOR SEWING: Easy to sew.
- NEEDLES: Sharp HJ or Universal H, sizes 70/10 and 80/12.
- THREAD: All-purpose polyester or cotton.
- STITCH LENGTH: 2.5mm.
- SEWING MACHINE FEET: Standard.
- INTERFACING/LINING: Rarely needed.

CARE

- WASHING: Machine wash.
- DRYING: Air-dry or normal tumble dry.
- IRONING: Medium steam heat.
- SHRINKAGE: Minimal to none.

QUILTING COTTONS

Quilting cottons encompasses a wide range of light- to medium-weight fabrics that are slightly stiffer than standard batiste, voile or lawn. The fabric washes well, holds up over time, creases nicely when ironed, comes in a large variety of printed designs and batiks, and is used for one main purpose - to make quilts! Of course quilting cotton can also be used for clothing and accessories - and works very well for totes and handbags - but the fabric isn't as soft and doesn't drape as well as other cottons.

HANDY HINT

Designers release new lines of quilting fabrics once or twice a year, with approximately six to 10 design variations in each line. This makes it easy for a quilter to pick up a stack of coordinating fat quarters (approximately 45 x 55cm) from the same, or similar, lines and start quilting!

PROPERTIES

- CHARACTER: Slightly stiffer than other standard cottons. Typically with a printed or batik-dyed design on top.
- WEAVE: Plain weave.
- WEIGHT: Light to medium.
- SPECIAL CONSIDERATIONS: Washes well and creases well when ironed. It has a stiffer drape than other cottons and is not ideal for some clothing. Pre-shrink the fabric before sewing.

WORKING WITH

- TO CUT: Use sharp scissors or a rotary cutter and mat.
- HANDLING FOR SEWING: Easy to sew; excellent choice for beginners.
- NEEDLES: Universal H sizes 70/10–80/12.
- THREAD: All-purpose polyester or cotton.
- STITCH LENGTH: 2–2.5mm.
- SEWING MACHINE FEET: Standard.
- INTERFACING/LINING: Lightweight sew-in or fusible interfacing.

CARE

- WASHING: Machine wash.
- DRYING: Air-dry or tumble dry.
- IRONING: Medium to high heat with steam.
- SHRINKAGE: Moderate. Machine wash and dry more than once before sewing to shrink the fabric.

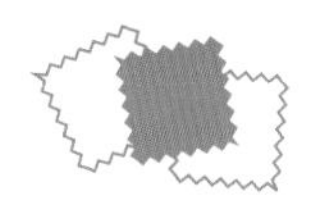

SATEEN

Not to be confused with satin, which is made from silk, sateen is a mercerised cotton that has a lustre and sheen that resembles satin. The sheen is mostly due to its unique weaving process. While plain weaves are one over, one under, sateen is four over, one under. This places most of the threads on top of the fabric, creating softness but also less durability. Satin is woven in the same manner, but with silk or polyester threads.

Sateen can be made of cotton, wool, nylon or polyester. The fabric is soft, drapes well and has a very high thread count, which explains its popularity as bed sheets. Sateen is also used for clothing, as a lining for jackets and for garments with a vintage look. It is cheaper than satin and is also machine washable.

PROPERTIES

- CHARACTER: High lustre and sheen that is similar to satin.
- WEAVE: Plain weave of four over, one under.
- WEIGHT: Medium.
- SPECIAL CONSIDERATIONS: Looks similar to satin but is machine washable; frays easily.

WORKING WITH

- TO CUT: Use sharp scissors or a rotary cutter and mat.
- HANDLING FOR SEWING: Easier to sew than satin; not as slippery.
- NEEDLES: Sharp HM, HJ or Universal H, sizes 60/8 and 70/10.
- THREAD: Lightweight, all-purpose polyester or cotton.
- STITCH LENGTH: 2.5mm.
- SEWING MACHINE FEET: Wide straight stitch, roller, single-hole plate.
- INTERFACING/LINING: Lightweight sew-in or fusible interfacing. Organza, polyester, rayon or chiffon as lining.

CARE

- WASHING: Machine wash.
- DRYING: Air-dry or normal tumble dry.
- IRONING: Low to medium steam heat; you may want to use a pressing cloth on the right side of the fabric.
- SHRINKAGE: Minimal to moderate.

SEERSUCKER

Seersucker screams summertime with its unique lightweight, slack-tension weave. To achieve this look, groups of yarn are bunched together in certain parts of the fabric to form a puckered effect. These puckers create air pockets between the body and the fabric, keeping the wearer cool in hot temperatures. It is often found in striped, checked or tartan patterns and has a trademark wrinkled look. This makes it a great choice for summer holiday clothing, as it travels well and doesn't need ironing.

Seersucker was once a fabric of the working classes in the US, but over time was adopted by upper-class men. If you were a gentleman in the South, a seersucker suit was the only way to survive hot summers while still being fashionable. This puckered fabric isn't just limited to men's suits, however. It is a popular fabric for skirts, summer dresses, blouses, shirts, trousers and shorts, and is very easy to sew with.

DID YOU KNOW?

Every June, US senators pay homage to the southern seersucker style by donning suits made from this lightweight summer fabric. Known as Seersucker Thursday, the tradition started in 1996 when Senator Trent Lott from Mississippi wanted to bring some southern charm to the Senate.

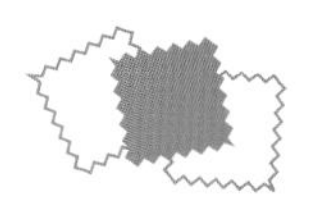

PROPERTIES

- CHARACTER: Small patterned puckers throughout with a wrinkled look.
- WEAVE: Slack-tension.
- WEIGHT: Light to medium.
- SPECIAL CONSIDERATIONS: Ironing is unnecessary since the fabric is supposed to look slightly wrinkled.

WORKING WITH

- TO CUT: Use sharp scissors or a rotary cutter and mat.
- HANDLING FOR SEWING: Easy to sew; great for beginners.
- NEEDLES: Universal H, sizes 70/10 or 80/12.
- THREAD: All-purpose polyester or cotton.
- STITCH LENGTH: 2–2.5mm.
- SEWING MACHINE FEET: Standard.
- INTERFACING/LINING: Lightweight sew-in or fusible interfacing. Lining is optional, but when preferred, something lightweight should be used.

CARE

- WASHING: Machine wash.
- DRYING: Air-dry or normal tumble dry.
- IRONING: Medium dry heat. Use a light touch and the tip of your iron when pressing seams to avoid crushing the wrinkled texture. If texture is ironed out, it will bounce back again once washed/dried.
- SHRINKAGE: Moderate.

SHIRTING

Shirting is probably better described as a category rather than a specific type of cotton fabric. Whether voile, batiste, lawn or broadcoth, it refers to a crisp cotton that is used for making shirts and blouses. It is typically seen in striped and checked patterns, or anything similar to the fabric you'd find on a men's shop-bought shirt.

PROPERTIES

- CHARACTER: Crisp, quality cotton used for shirts.
- WEAVE: Plain weave.
- WEIGHT: Medium.
- SPECIAL CONSIDERATIONS: Available in a variety of fabrics (voile, batiste, lawn, broadcloth).

WORKING WITH

- TO CUT: Use sharp scissors or a rotary cutter and mat.
- HANDLING FOR SEWING: Easy to sew.
- NEEDLES: Universal H, size 70/10.
- THREAD: Quality cotton.
- STITCH LENGTH: 2–2.5mm.
- SEWING MACHINE FEET: Standard.
- INTERFACING/LINING: Fusible or sew-in interfacing for collars and cuffs.

CARE

- WASHING: Machine wash.
- DRYING: Air-dry or normal tumble dry. Remove from dryer when slightly damp and iron dry.
- IRONING: Medium steam heat.
- SHRINKAGE: Moderate.

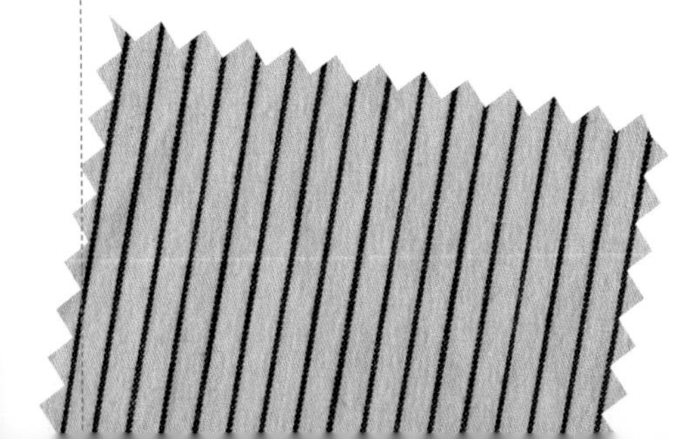

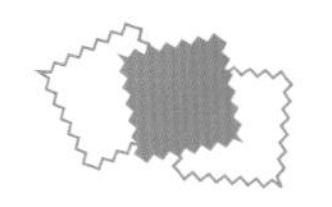

STRETCH WOVEN (Cotton)

Woven fabrics don't have much give, but when blended with a small amount of elastance, or Lycra, the result is a stretch woven fabric. The fabric has the same rigid structure as other woven fabrics, but the added stretch allows you to make form-fitting clothes that are comfortable to wear.

Stretch wovens are found in a variety of textiles such as corduroy, cotton, denim, lace, linen, satin, seersucker, twill and velour, and they all typically contain less than 5 per cent elastane. Stretch wovens are used for trousers, jeans, skirts, fitted jackets and other casualwear, and should be sewn in the same way as their non-stretch counterparts. Care should be given not to pull or stretch the fabric when sewing; let the machine naturally feed the fabric for you.

PROPERTIES

- CHARACTER: Woven fabric with a bit of stretch.
- WEAVE: Plain weave.
- WEIGHT: Light to medium.
- SPECIAL CONSIDERATIONS: Fabrics should be sewn and cared for in a similar way to their non-stretch counterparts.

WORKING WITH

- TO CUT: Use sharp scissors or a rotary cutter and mat.
- HANDLING FOR SEWING: Let the machine naturally feed the fabric for you. Do not pull or stretch it as you sew.
- NEEDLES: Universal H or Sharp HM and HJ, sizes 70/10–90/14.
- THREAD: All-purpose polyester or cotton.
- STITCH LENGTH: 2–2.5mm.
- SEWING MACHINE FEET: Standard.
- INTERFACING/LINING: Lining recommended for tailored garments.

CARE

- WASHING: Most stretch wovens are machine washable, but consult the manufacturer's care instructions for details.
- DRYING: Air-dry or tumble dry. Consult the manufacturer's care instructions for details.
- IRONING: Medium heat, steam and a pressing cloth are recommended.
- SHRINKAGE: Moderate; should be similar to the fabric's non-stretch counterpart.

TERRY CLOTH

Terry cloth (also known as terry towelling) is famous for its high absorbency, making it the go-to fabric for towels and bathrobes. It is woven on a dobby loom and characterised by uncut loops of thread that create a soft pile on each side of the fabric. Be careful not to snag one of the loops, however, or the entire thread row will pull out along with the snag, creating a run in your fabric.

Terry cloth is perfect for any project requiring an absorbent textile. Although it is soft and cosy, there are some downsides to sewing with it. The edges will fray or piece-off very easily and, depending on the thickness of the pile, can create a mess in your workspace when cutting out a pattern. Edges and seams should be finished off with an overlocker (or serger) or edged with bias tape and fabric. Terry cloth also shrinks easily, so it's a good idea to wash and dry it twice before starting your project.

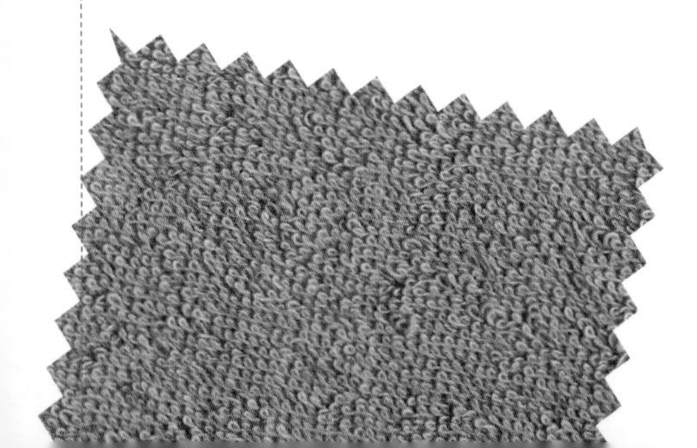

PROPERTIES

- CHARACTER: Soft looped piles on each side of the fabric; very absorbent.
- WEAVE: Dobby loom.
- WEIGHT: Medium to heavy.
- SPECIAL CONSIDERATIONS: Terry cloth can snag and shrink easily. It also frays badly and raw edges must be finished off.

WORKING WITH

- TO CUT: Use sharp scissors or a rotary cutter and mat.
- HANDLING FOR SEWING: All edges and seams should be bound with bias tape or finished off with an overlocker.
- NEEDLES: Universal H 80/12 or 90/14.
- THREAD: All-purpose polyester or cotton.
- STITCH LENGTH: 3mm.
- SEWING MACHINE FEET: Roller, wide straight stitch or Teflon.
- INTERFACING/LINING: Rarely used.

CARE

- WASHING: Machine wash on normal cycle.
- DRYING: Air-dry or tumble dry.
- IRONING: Medium to high steam heat.
- SHRINKAGE: Shrinks easily. Wash and dry fabric twice before cutting.

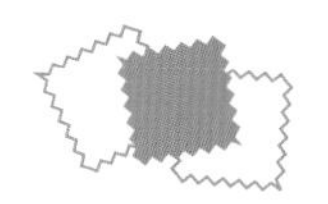

TWILL

The term twill describes any fabric created with a twill weave. Examples include chino, drill, denim, gabardine, tweed and serge. The twill weave is recognizable due to the parallel diagonal ribs in the fabric. This diagonal weave produces a fabric that is durable, sturdy and drapes well. The right side of the fabric has the most pronounced wale - it is more durable and attractive than the wrong side, and is usually on the outside of a garment.

Twill can be made from a variety of fibres (wool, cotton, polyester and rayon), but cotton and wool are favoured in the fashion world. Cotton twill works well for trousers such as chinos, as well as upholstery, skirts, purses and bags.

PROPERTIES

- CHARACTER: A diagonal weave.
- WEAVE: Twill.
- WEIGHT: Medium.
- SPECIAL CONSIDERATIONS: It's important to identify the right and wrong side of the fabric and to cut your pattern accordingly. Trim cut edges of pattern pieces with pinking shears to avoid excess fraying. Finish off seams with an overlocker or a zigzag stitch.

WORKING WITH

- TO CUT: Use sharp scissors or a rotary cutter and mat.
- HANDLING FOR SEWING: Easy to sew.
- NEEDLES: Universal H, size 80/12.
- THREAD: All-purpose polyester or cotton.
- STITCH LENGTH: 2–2.5mm.
- SEWING MACHINE FEET: Standard.
- INTERFACING/LINING: No interfacing or linings. The fabric is sturdy on its own.

CARE

- WASHING: Machine wash or dry-clean.
- DRYING: Air-dry or normal tumble dry.
- IRONING: Medium heat.
- SHRINKAGE: Moderate.

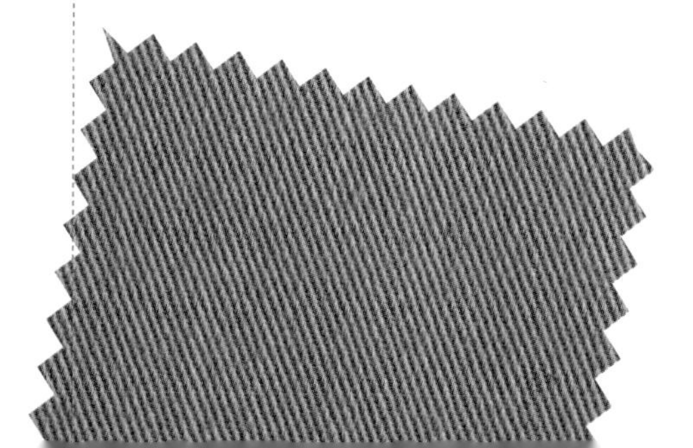

VELVETEEN

Velveteen is a modern adaptation of velvet – it has more give than real velvet, is easier to care for and costs considerably less. It is woven and then sheared to create a short pile on top. Made from cotton rather than silk, it is soft to the touch and luxurious in appearance. Velveteen is a good choice for dresses, trousers, skirts, jackets, childrenswear, home furnishings and craft projects.

PROPERTIES

- CHARACTER: Soft, luxurious appearance that is similar to velvet.
- WEAVE: Woven with a short pile.
- WEIGHT: Medium to heavy.
- SPECIAL CONSIDERATIONS: Easy to care for and is considerably cheaper than velvet.

WORKING WITH

- TO CUT: Use sharp scissors or a rotary cutter and mat. Use with-nap layout when cutting patterns.
- HANDLING FOR SEWING: Shrinks and frays more than real velvet. Work carefully to avoid mistakes and remove stitches gently. Only use pins in the seam allowance.
- NEEDLES: Universal H or Sharp HM/HJ, sizes 70/10 to 90/14, depending on fabric weight.
- THREAD: All-purpose polyester or cotton.
- STITCH LENGTH: 2.5–3mm.
- SEWING MACHINE FEET: Roller, wide straight stitch.
- INTERFACING/LINING: Optional; sew-in interfacing.

CARE

- WASHING: Machine wash or dry-clean. For best results, finished garments should be dry-cleaned.
- DRYING: Air or tumble dry; dry-clean.
- IRONING: Medium to high heat with steam.
- SHRINKAGE: Moderate.

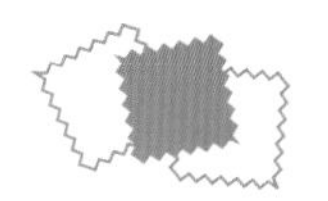

VOILE

Voile, the French word for 'veil', is a lightweight, sheer, crisp fabric similar to batiste. Cotton voile is breathable, breezy and makes a beautiful set of sheer curtains. It is also used for childrenswear, lingerie, summer dresses and blouses.

PROPERTIES

- CHARACTER: Lightweight, sheer, crisp.
- WEAVE: Plain weave.
- WEIGHT: Lightweight.
- SPECIAL CONSIDERATIONS: Shrinks and wrinkles easily. Due to shrinkage, consider washing/drying more than once.

WORKING WITH

- TO CUT: Use sharp scissors or a rotary cutter and mat.
- HANDLING FOR SEWING: Easy to sew; great for beginners.
- NEEDLES: Universal H, size 80/12.
- THREAD: All-purpose polyester or cotton.
- STITCH LENGTH: 2–2.5mm.
- SEWING MACHINE FEET: Standard.
- INTERFACING: Lightweight sew-in or fusible interfacing. Lining is optional, but when preferred, something lightweight should be used.

CARE

- WASHING: Machine wash.
- DRYING: Air-dry or normal tumble dry.
- IRONING: Medium steam heat.
- SHRINKAGE: Moderate.

SILK: An Overview

We often associate the word silk with something of luxury and beauty, and for justifiable reasons. For centuries, silk production was a well-kept secret in China and was guarded with great pride until 300 AD, when Korea and Japan began cultivating silk as well. Today, the secret of silk is public knowledge and silk is produced all around the world, although it is still an expensive fabric to produce. Silk is exquisite in every shape and form; it can be smooth and glossy like charmeuse and satin, or rough and nubby like dupioni and tussah. It is warm but lightweight, comfortable and feminine.

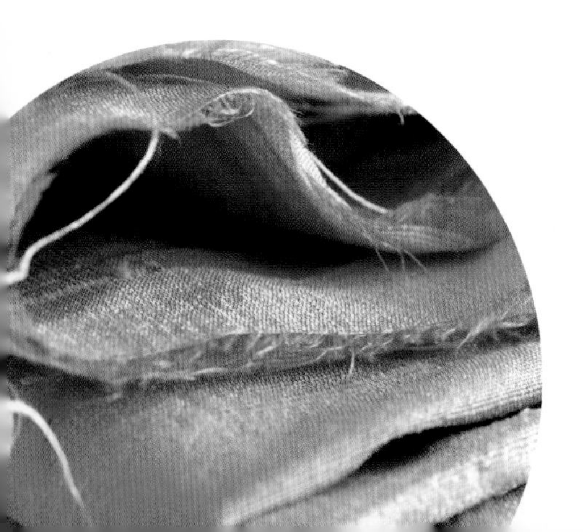

PRODUCTION & PROCESSES

Silk fibres are cultivated from the cocoons of silk worms, requiring a great deal of effort for very little output. Thousands of silk worms together produce only a small piece of fabric. For this reason alone silk is costly and continues to carry an elite status in the textile world.

The process starts with silkworm eggs that are incubated and hatch, growing into worms that then form cocoons. The worms are then killed before they can break out of the cocoons (which would damage the continuous fibres). The cocoons are sorted for size, colour and texture and then softened in hot water, which causes the cocoon to unwind, releasing the fibres. Since the fibres are too fine to be used alone, they are grouped together to form thick strands, which are wound with additional strands and finally spun into yarn. The yarn is then dyed and woven into colourful fabrics.

While China once had a monopoly on the production and trade of silk, India is now the second largest producer, and is also the number one consumer of this fabric. Thailand is also a big player, with the trade being passed down from generation to generation. Often woven on handlooms, it can take 40 hours to produce 1.5kg of Thai silk.

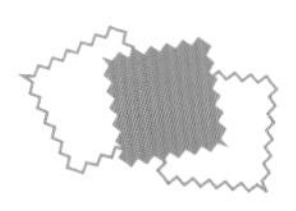

It is unclear how silk was originally discovered. Chinese tradition claims that thousands of years ago, Empress Si Ling-Chi was drinking tea when a silkworm cocoon accidently fell into her cup. While fishing it out, she discovered that the hot liquid had softened the cocoon and it was easily unwound into one long, continuous fibre. Whether or not this is true, history does show that in the second century BC the Chinese figured out how to cultivate silkworms and turn their cocoons into glorious fabrics.

NATURAL vs SYNTHETIC

With all of its beauty and shine, it's no wonder manufacturers have found ways to mimic silk by using synthetic fibres. In fact, almost every type of silk fabric has a synthetic version. The real draw to synthetic silks (typically made of nylon, polyester, rayon or acetate) is that they are a fraction of the cost - some are even non-fray and machine washable, but even with all of its benefits, synthetic silk just doesn't have that same feel as real silk.

SELECTING FABRICS

When deciding between silk or synthetic, weigh up your sewing needs versus cost and availability. Read the labels on fabric bolts and cross-reference them with the fabrics outlined in this section. Some manufacturers create their own names for blended and synthetic silks, but the origins of the fabrics are the same and should be identifiable with those described here.

USES

Silk fabric is favoured for high-end garments, home furnishings and for some everyday clothing.

CHARACTERISTICS

- Elegant and dressy.
- Warm yet lightweight.
- Dyes well and comes in a variety of colours.
- Resists wrinkles.
- Holds shape well and drapes beautifully (depending on the type and weave).
- Very absorbent and dries quickly.
- Some silks are washable; most finished garments require dry-cleaning.
- The strongest of all natural fibres.
- Weaker when wet.
- Can yellow with age and sunlight.
- Is easily damaged by improper ironing and seam-ripping.

CHARMEUSE

Charmeuse is a quintessential luxury fabric. This shiny, floating fabric drapes beautifully, slips under your fingers and feels expensive. Due to its lustrous finish it is easily mistaken for satin, but the fabric is more lightweight and, at times, paper thin. Though originally made from silk fibres, today you'll find polyester and rayon versions at your fabric shop for a fraction of the price. Charmeuse is an excellent choice for blouses, dresses, dressy garments, eveningwear, hair accessories, bags, lingerie, baby blankets and linings.

Charmeuse is a satin weave, which means the weft yarns are woven less frequently so that long warp threads seem to float on the surface. This creates a very glossy sheen to the right side of the fabric and a matt, almost rough, appearance on the wrong side. Because of its slinky nature, the fabric can be hard to work with. Pins should only be used in the seam allowances of your garment and pinned parallel to the selvedge to avoid snags or runs in the fabric. When cutting patterns, use weights instead of pins to hold the pattern in place. Make sure you always have a fresh, sharp needle in place when starting a new project. This all might sound like a lot of work, but with a little sewing practice you'll fall in love with the beauty of charmeuse.

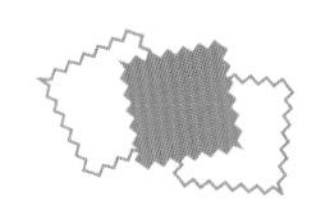

PROPERTIES

- CHARACTER: Shiny, slinky, glossy on top and matt on the back.
- WEAVE: Satin weave.
- WEIGHT: Lightweight.
- SPECIAL CONSIDERATIONS: Frays very easily. Due to its slippery nature, can be hard to work with. Fabric should not be cut until you are ready to sew. Trim cut edges of pattern pieces with pinking shears. Finish off seams with an overlocker or a French seam.

WORKING WITH

- TO CUT: To keep fabric from misshaping and slinking away from you while cutting, a rotary cutter and mat work best. A handy method is to sandwich the fabric between two pieces of tissue paper on a cutting mat (one tissue on top, one underneath the fabric), pin the three layers together in the seam allowance and carefully cut with scissors or rotary cutter.
- HANDLING FOR SEWING: When starting a new seam, do not backstitch. Use your left hand to hold both machine threads to avoid the fabric being sucked down into the machine plate. As you sew, hold the fabric taut using both hands. Pins should only be used in the seam allowances of your garment and pinned parallel to the selvedge to avoid snags and runs in the fabric. To prevent charmeuse from fraying all the way down to the seam and creating a hole, it's important to use a wider seam allowance in your garments, especially seams that will have the most stress placed on them. Fabric is easily snagged with a seam ripper, so work carefully to avoid errors.
- NEEDLES: Sharp HM and HJ or Universal H, sizes 60/8 or 70/10.
- THREAD: Lightweight all-purpose cotton or silk.
- STITCH LENGTH: 2mm.
- SEWING MACHINE FEET: Standard, straight stitch or roller with a single-hole needle plate.
- INTERFACING/LINING: Lightweight sew-in or fusible interfacing. Use chiffon lining for a draped look or organza for a crisp look.

CARE

- WASHING: Machine wash (for synthetics) or dry-clean (for silk).
- DRYING: Air-dry or tumble dry (for synthetics) or dry-clean (for silk).
- IRONING: Low dry heat. Fabric may show discoloration when ironing but the faded look is only temporary. Water and steam may cause water spots unless fabric is pre-washed.
- SHRINKAGE: Minimal shrinking.

CHIFFON

Chiffon is a lightweight, often transparent, slippery fabric. It gathers and ruffles beautifully and is an excellent choice for dresses, skirts, petticoats, lightweight blouses, eveningwear, lingerie, wraps, scarves and linings.

Chiffon is often layered over the top of another fabric to give a floating or draped look. While real silk chiffon drapes wonderfully, nylon and polyester versions are a great way to replicate this look as they have the same appearance but are easier to care for and cost much less.

HANDY HINT

Standard silk chiffon will fray with time, however non-fray nylon chiffon doesn't fray at all, allowing you to create interesting ruffles and petticoats with raw edges, and opening up a whole range of project ideas. While not often available in small fabric shops, many online stockists carry non-fray chiffons in a range of colours.

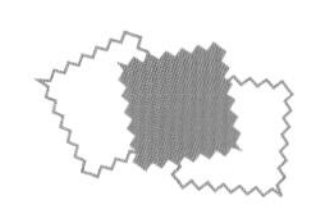

PROPERTIES

- CHARACTER: Is slippery and can be transparent.
- WEAVE: Plain weave.
- WEIGHT: Lightweight.
- SPECIAL CONSIDERATIONS: Will fray unless specified as non-fray. Fabric is slippery and can be hard to work with.

WORKING WITH

- TO CUT: To keep fabric from misshaping and slinking away from you while cutting, a rotary cutter and mat work best. A handy method is to sandwich the fabric between two pieces of tissue paper on a cutting mat (one tissue on top, one underneath the fabric), pin the three layers together in the seam allowance and carefully cut with scissors or rotary cutter.
- HANDLING FOR SEWING: When starting a new seam, do not backstitch. Use your left hand to hold both machine threads to avoid the fabric being sucked down into the machine plate. As you sew, hold the fabric taut using both hands. Pins should only be used in the seam allowances of your garment and pinned parallel to the selvedge to avoid snags and runs in the fabric. Machine or hand-rolled hems, such as the hem around a finished silk scarf, work beautifully on chiffon.
- NEEDLES: Sharp HM and HJ or Universal H, sizes 60/8 or 70/10.
- THREAD: Lightweight cotton or silk.
- STITCH LENGTH: 2mm.
- SEWING MACHINE FEET: Standard, straight stitch or roller with a single-hole needle plate.
- INTERFACING/LINING: Lightweight sew-in interfacing. Lining is recommended if chiffon is transparent. Coordinate or contrast your lining colour with your chiffon overlay to create an interesting look.

CARE

- WASHING: Machine wash (for synthetics) or dry-clean (for silk).
- DRYING: Air-dry or tumble dry (for synthetics) or dry-clean (for silk).
- IRONING: Low dry heat. Chiffon is easily damaged with too much heat. Read the manufacturer's recommendation for more information.
- SHRINKAGE: Minimal.

CHINA SILK

China silk (also known as Habotai) is a plain-weave fabric that can range from very lightweight to medium. Heavier China silk is used for shirts, dresses and other garments, while lightweight fabric is ideal for billowy scarves and sheer clothing. With a smooth, semi-soft finish, China silk also works well as a lining for many types of fabrics.

PROPERTIES

- CHARACTER: Semi-soft, often looks the same on both sides.
- WEAVE: Plain weave.
- WEIGHT: Lightweight to medium.
- SPECIAL CONSIDERATIONS: To avoid excessive fraying, overlock all edges or stitch the ends together before washing/drying.

WORKING WITH

- TO CUT: Use a rotary cutter and mat to keep fabric from misshaping and slinking away from you while cutting. A handy method is to sandwich the fabric between two pieces of tissue paper on a cutting mat (one tissue on top, one underneath the fabric), pin the three layers together in the seam allowance and carefully cut with scissors or rotary cutter.
- HANDLING FOR SEWING: When starting a new seam, do not backstitch. Use your left hand to hold both machine threads to avoid the fabric being sucked down into the machine plate. As you sew, hold the fabric taut using both hands. Pins should only be used in the seam of your garment and pinned parallel to the selvedge to avoid snags and runs in the fabric.
- NEEDLES: Sharp HM and HJ or Universal H, sizes 60/8 or 70/10.
- THREAD: Lightweight all-purpose cotton, polyester or silk.
- STITCH LENGTH: 2mm.
- SEWING MACHINE FEET: Standard, straight stitch or roller with a single-hole needle plate.
- INTERFACING/LINING: It is often used as a lining itself.

CARE

- WASHING: Hand wash.
- DRYING: Air- or drip-dry.
- IRONING: Low dry heat.
- SHRINKAGE: Minimal.

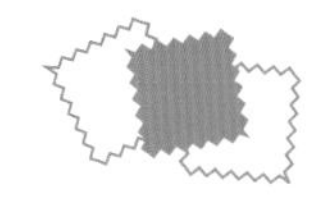

CRÊPE DE CHINE

Not to be confused with China silk, crêpe de Chine is woven with twisted yarns, giving it a slightly crinkled look. It has a dull lustre, drapes beautifully and is available in real silk (which tends not to pucker) or polyester. Crêpe de Chine also comes in three weights: two-ply is the most common, three-ply has a finer feel and four-ply is used for high-end garments. Crêpe de Chine is often used for blouses, shirts, dresses, skirts, trousers, lingerie and jackets.

PROPERTIES

- CHARACTER: Crinkled with a dull lustre.
- WEAVE: Plain weave.
- WEIGHT: Lightweight to medium.
- SPECIAL CONSIDERATIONS: Comes in three different weights – two-ply is the most common.

WORKING WITH

- TO CUT: Use a rotary cutter and mat and cut through multiple layers at once. Sharp scissors will also work.
- HANDLING FOR SEWING: As you sew, hold the fabric taut using two hands. Pins should only be used in the seam allowances of your garment and pinned parallel to the selvedge to avoid snags and runs in the fabric.
- NEEDLES: Sharp HM and HJ or Universal H, sizes 60/8 or 70/10.
- THREAD: Lightweight all-purpose cotton, polyester or silk.
- STITCH LENGTH: 2mm.
- SEWING MACHINE FEET: Standard, straight stitch or roller with a single-hole needle plate.
- INTERFACING/LINING: Featherweight sew-in interfacing. Silk organza or China silk linings may help prevent wrinkling on fitted garments.

CARE

- WASHING: Dry-clean or hand wash.
- DRYING: Dry-clean or air-dry.
- IRONING: Low dry heat.
- SHRINKAGE: Minimal.

DEVORÉ (Burnout)

Devoré, or burnout, is a type of fabric that has been treated with chemicals to 'burn' through part of the existing surface. The process leaves sheer, exposed areas behind, creating interesting designs. Burnout can only be achieved on fabrics that are a blend of cellulose plant fibres (such as cotton and linen) mixed with protein animal fibres (such as wool and silk) or with man-made fibres (such as nylon and polyester). This fibre blend is important since the acidic chemicals will eat through cotton, leaving the protein or synthetic fibre behind.

Devoré typically requires a lining for modesty. Velvet devoré is used for fancy dresses, skirts, jackets, gowns and some home furnishings, while casual cotton-blended devoré makes an interesting T-shirt or pair of leggings.

HANDY HINT

Feeling ambitious? Burnout can actually be created in your own home using a simple fibre-etching solution. After washing and drying your fabric, place a piece of cling film under it to avoid bleed-through, and draw your design on to the fabric. Then apply the etching solution and watch as the acid eats away part of the fabric.

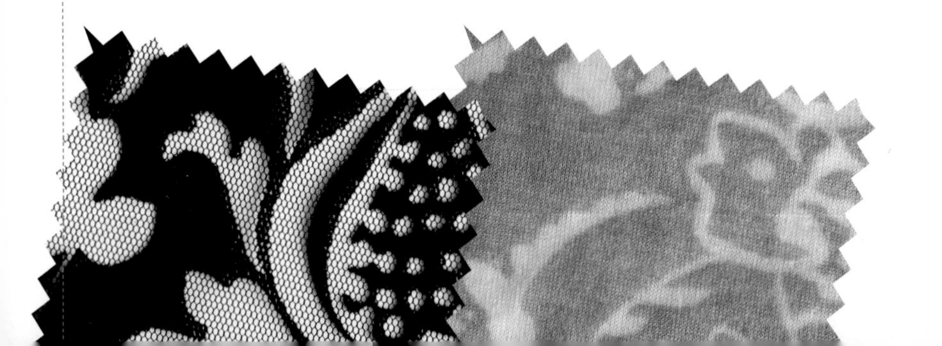

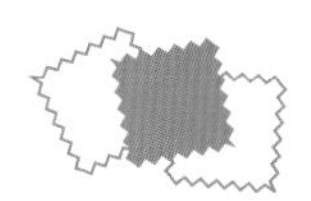

PROPERTIES

- CHARACTER: Burned-out sheer areas create interesting designs on the right side.
- WEAVE: Knit or plain weave with burned-out areas on the surface.
- WEIGHT: Lightweight to medium.
- SPECIAL CONSIDERATIONS: Devoré can be made from a variety of fibres, though it's often seen in velvet. Sew the fabric according to the fibre content.

WORKING WITH

- TO CUT: Use sharp scissors or a rotary cutter and mat. Use with-nap layout when cutting pattern pieces.
- HANDLING FOR SEWING: Where possible, sew in the direction of the pile. Periodically lift your presser foot to allow the fabric to bounce back.
- NEEDLES: Sharp HM and HJ or Universal H, sizes 70/10 or 80/12.
- THREAD: All-purpose polyester or cotton.
- STITCH LENGTH: 2.5–3mm.
- SEWING MACHINE FEET: Standard, walking foot or roller.
- INTERFACING/LINING: Lining is recommended for modesty. Use a contrasting lining colour to create additional interest.

CARE

- WASHING: Dry-clean or machine wash. Washing may change the nap but can also give your fabric a vintage look. When in doubt, read the manufacturer's care instructions or stick with dry-cleaning.
- DRYING: Dry-clean or air-dry.
- IRONING: Cotton-based fabrics can be ironed with medium heat and steam. It's best to avoid ironing velvet devoré unless you have a specialised needle board, although you can iron it if you place a towel or another piece of velvet on your pressing surface, then lay the fabric on top with the pile facing down. The pile of your fabric and the pile of the ironing surface will mesh into each other and prevent the fabric from crushing. Hold a steam iron about 1cm above the fabric for best results. If you damage silk velvet with an iron, your fabric will look crushed or have a shine and usually the damage is permanent. You can try to revive the pile with steam, but it will never look as luxurious as it once did. Always test-iron a sample of your fabric before pressing on your finished project.
- SHRINKAGE: Minimal.

DUPIONI and SHANTUNG

Dupioni silk is easily characterised by its rough, nubby, uneven threads and subtle sheen. Far different from the glossy look of satin, this bumpy texture gives dupioni a unique personality. The fabric is created from double silk cocoons, which are spun side by side and interlocked together. These rough fibres are uneven and irregular and when woven together, create small slubs with a bumpy effect. Dupioni is beautiful to look at and resistant to wrinkles. It's a wonderful choice for home furnishings, cushions, fitted dresses, straight skirts, tailored trousers and fine suits.

Shantung is a type of dupioni that comes from the Shantung province of China. It is often more refined, lighter weight and contains slubs in a more regular pattern, compared to the random slubs and roughness of dupioni. It works well for garments and home furnishings.

DID YOU KNOW?

A synthetic version of dupioni made from fibres such as polyester and acetate is sometimes referred to as dupionini. Though a wonderful alternative to the real silk version (and significantly cheaper), it doesn't carry the same beauty. The slubs are not authentic and look pre-planned (rather than appearing randomly); they are also less bumpy.

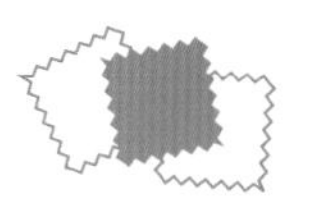

PROPERTIES

- CHARACTER: Rough, nubby, with bumpy slubs; resists wrinkles.
- WEAVE: Plain weave.
- WEIGHT: Lightweight.
- SPECIAL CONSIDERATIONS: To avoid excessive fraying, overlock all edges or stitch the ends together before washing/drying. Trim cut edges of pattern pieces with pinking shears. Finish off seams with an overlocker, zigzag stitch or French seams.

WORKING WITH

- TO CUT: Use sharp scissors or a rotary cutter and mat.
- HANDLING FOR SEWING: When starting a new seam, do not backstitch. Use your left hand to hold both machine threads to avoid the fabric being sucked down into the machine plate. As you sew, hold the fabric taut using both hands. Pins should only be used in the seam allowances of your garment and pinned parallel to the selvedge to avoid snags and runs in the fabric.
- NEEDLES: Sharp HM and HJ or Universal H, sizes 60/8 or 70/10.
- THREAD: Lightweight all-purpose cotton, polyester or silk.
- STITCH LENGTH: 2–2.5mm.
- SEWING MACHINE FEET: Standard.
- INTERFACING/LINING: Lightweight fusible or sew-in interfacing. Silk organza, rayon or polyester chiffon lining.

CARE

- WASHING: Dry-cleaning versus washing depends on the look you desire. To maintain crispness and shine, dry-cleaning is recommended; for a softer, more informal look, machine wash and air-dry your fabric.
- DRYING: Dry-clean or air-dry.
- IRONING: Low to medium dry heat.
- SHRINKAGE: Minimal.

FAILLE

Faille (pronounced 'file') is woven with a subtle ribbed pattern, creating a texture similar to grosgrain ribbon. It is somewhat stiff with a slight shine, making it ideal for clothing. Faille tends not to deform or wrinkle and looks great after hours of wear. Faille is often used for jackets, waistcoats, formal dresses and gowns as well as home furnishings, including curtains.

PROPERTIES

- CHARACTER: Subtle ribbed pattern; somewhat stiff with a slight shine.
- WEAVE: Ribbed.
- WEIGHT: Medium.
- SPECIAL CONSIDERATIONS: Tends not to deform or wrinkle, but frays easily. To avoid excessive fraying, overlock all edges or stitch the ends together before washing/drying. Trim cut edges of pattern pieces with pinking shears. Finish off seams with an overlocker, zigzag stitch or French seams.

WORKING WITH

- TO CUT: Use sharp scissors or a rotary cutter and mat.
- HANDLING FOR SEWING: When starting a new stitch, do not backstitch. Use your left hand to hold both machine threads to avoid the fabric being sucked down into the machine plate. As you sew, hold the fabric taut using both hands. Pins should only be used in the seam allowances of your garment and pinned parallel to the selvedge to avoid snags and runs in the fabric.
- NEEDLES: Sharp HM and HJ or Universal H, sizes 60/8 or 70/10.
- THREAD: Lightweight all-purpose cotton, polyester or silk.
- STITCH LENGTH: 2–2.5mm.
- SEWING MACHINE FEET: Standard.
- INTERFACING/LINING: Fusible or sew-in interfacing. Silk organza, rayon or polyester chiffon lining.

CARE

- WASHING: Can be washed but dry-cleaning is recommended. Fabric softens and loses some of its sheen when washed/dried.
- DRYING: Dry-clean or air-dry.
- IRONING: Low to medium dry heat.
- SHRINKAGE: Minimal.

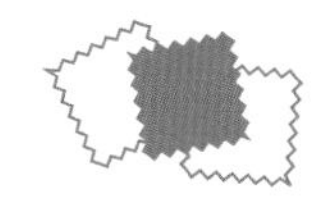

GAUZE

It can be difficult to distinguish silk gauze from organza. Both fabrics are sheer and lightweight, but gauze has more strength due to an interlocking leno weave, which reduces tearing and fraying. Gauze comes in varying weights, colours and Holes Per Inch (HPI). It is often used as a lining, but can also be used for clothing such as dresses, scarves, eveningwear and blouses.

PROPERTIES

- CHARACTER: Sheer and thin.
- WEAVE: Plain or leno (warp yarns are twisted around each other).
- WEIGHT: Lightweight.
- SPECIAL CONSIDERATIONS: Minimal fraying; washing softens the fibres.

WORKING WITH

- TO CUT: To keep fabric from misshaping and slinking away from you while cutting, a rotary cutter and mat work best. A handy method is to sandwich the fabric between two pieces of tissue paper on a cutting mat (one tissue on top, one underneath the fabric), pin the three layers together in the seam allowance and carefully cut with scissors or a rotary cutter.
- HANDLING FOR SEWING: When starting a new seam, do not backstitch. Use your left hand to hold both machine threads to avoid the fabric being sucked down into the machine plate. As you sew, hold the fabric taut using both hands. Pins should only be used in the seam allowances of your garment and pinned parallel to the selvedge to avoid snags and runs in the fabric.
- NEEDLES: Sharp HM and HJ or Universal H, sizes 60/8 or 65/9.
- THREAD: Lightweight all-purpose cotton, polyester or silk.
- STITCH LENGTH: 2mm.
- SEWING MACHINE FEET: Standard or straight stitch with a single-hole needle plate.
- INTERFACING/LINING: Lightweight sew-in or fusible interfacing. No lining; it is often used as a lining itself.

CARE

- WASHING: Dry-clean or hand wash.
- DRYING: Dry-clean or air-dry.
- IRONING: Low to medium dry heat.
- SHRINKAGE: Minimal.

GAZAR

Gazar is a lightweight silk made of twisted yarns. The fabric has a tight weave, is somewhat crisp and is an excellent choice for clothing and linings. Use gazar for skirts, blouses, jackets, suits, linings and home furnishings.

PROPERTIES

- CHARACTER: Lightweight with crispness and little drape.
- WEAVE: Plain weave with twisted yarns.
- WEIGHT: Lightweight to medium.
- SPECIAL CONSIDERATIONS: To avoid excessive fraying, overlock all edges or stitch the ends together before washing/drying. Washing will considerably soften the fibres. Trim cut edges of pattern pieces with pinking shears. Finish off seams with an overlocker, zigzag stitch or French seams.

WORKING WITH

- TO CUT: To keep fabric from misshaping and slinking away from you while cutting, a rotary cutter and mat work best. A handy method is to sandwich the fabric between two pieces of tissue paper on a cutting mat (one tissue on top, one underneath the fabric), pin the three layers together in the seam allowance and carefully cut with scissors or a rotary cutter.
- HANDLING FOR SEWING: When starting a new seam, do not backstitch. Use your left hand to hold both machine threads to avoid the fabric being sucked down into the machine plate. As you sew, hold the fabric taut using both hands. Pins should only be used in the seam of your garment and pinned parallel to the selvedge to avoid snags and runs in the fabric.
- NEEDLES: Sharp HM and HJ or Universal H, sizes 60/8 or 65/9.
- THREAD: Lightweight all-purpose cotton, polyester or silk.
- STITCH LENGTH: 2mm.
- SEWING MACHINE FEET: Standard or straight stitch with a single-hole needle plate.
- INTERFACING/LINING: Lightweight sew-in or fusible interfacing.

CARE

- WASHING: Dry-clean or hand wash.
- DRYING: Dry-clean or air-dry.
- IRONING: Low to medium dry heat.
- SHRINKAGE: Minimal.

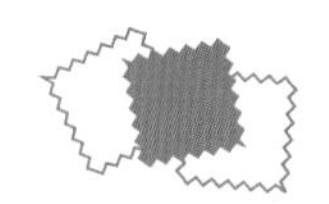

GEORGETTE

Georgette is a sheer crêpe silk that is similar in appearance to chiffon, but is slightly heavier and more durable. It is typically made of silk, although synthetic versions are available in rayon and polyester. Georgette wrinkles and frays easily and can be damaged by seam ripping and improper pressing. It is used for dresses, blouses, shirts, special occasion gowns and linings.

PROPERTIES

- CHARACTER: Often sheer, similar to chiffon.
- WEAVE: Plain.
- WEIGHT: Lightweight.
- SPECIAL CONSIDERATIONS: Frays very easily. Easier to sew than chiffon, but is still slippery and requires patience. Trim cut edges of pattern pieces with pinking shears. Finish off seams with an overlocker, zigzag stitch or French seams.

WORKING WITH

- TO CUT: Cut fabrics in layers using a rotary cutter and mat. Sharp scissors will also work.
- HANDLING FOR SEWING: When starting a new seam, do not backstitch. Use your left hand to hold both machine threads to avoid the fabric being sucked down into the machine plate. As you sew, hold the fabric taut using both hands. Pins should only be used in the seam of your garment and pinned parallel to the selvedge to avoid snags and runs in the fabric. Georgette can fray easily. To prevent the fabric from fraying all the way down to the seam and creating a hole, use a wide seam allowance in your garments or use French seams. Fabric is easily snagged with a seam ripper, so work carefully to avoid errors.
- NEEDLES: Sharp HM and HJ or Universal H, sizes 60/8 or 70/10.
- THREAD: Lightweight all-purpose cotton, polyester or silk.
- STITCH LENGTH: 2–2.5mm.
- SEWING MACHINE FEET: Standard, straight stitch or roller with a single-hole needle plate.
- INTERFACING/LINING: Lightweight sew-in interfacing.

CARE

- WASHING: Machine wash (for synthetics) or dry-clean (for silk).
- DRYING: Air-dry or tumble dry (for synthetics) or dry-clean (for silk).
- IRONING: Cool to medium dry heat. A pressing cloth is recommended. Georgette is easily ruined with improper pressing and too much heat.
- SHRINKAGE: Minimal shrinking but frays easily.

MATKA

Matka is a plain-woven silk fabric that resembles the look of linen fabric. Just like linen, it is very comfortable to wear, but the main difference is that matka doesn't wrinkle. Matka is cool, breathable, comes in a variety of colours, and is quite versatile; however some matka can stretch and unravel badly, so it requires a bit of patience when cutting and sewing. Matka is used for skirts, trousers, suits, dresses, jackets, home furnishings and even bags.

PROPERTIES

- CHARACTER: Looks like linen.
- WEAVE: Plain.
- WEIGHT: Lightweight to medium.
- SPECIAL CONSIDERATIONS: Frays very easily and can stretch. Trim cut edges of pattern pieces with pinking shears. Finish off seams with an overlocker, zigzag stitch or French seams.

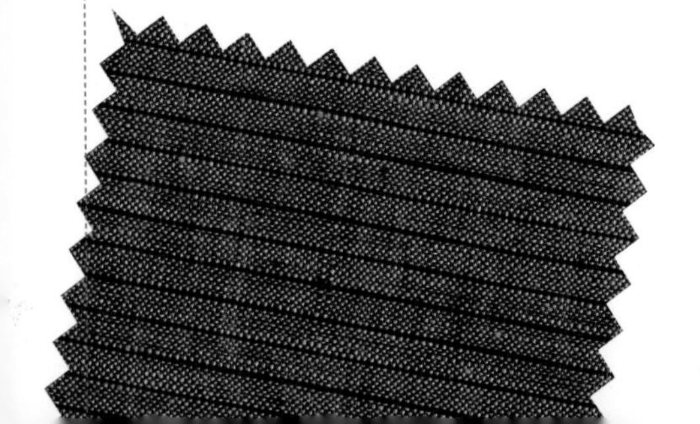

WORKING WITH

- TO CUT: Cut fabric in layers using a rotary cutter and mat. Sharp scissors will also work.
- HANDLING FOR SEWING: Let the fabric feed itself through the machine so you don't stretch the fabric. When starting a new seam, do not backstitch. Use your left hand to hold both machine threads to avoid the fabric being sucked down into the machine plate.
- NEEDLES: Sharp HM and HJ or Universal H, sizes 70/10 or 90/14.
- THREAD: All-purpose cotton or polyester.
- STITCH LENGTH: 2–3mm.
- SEWING MACHINE FEET: Straight stitch or roller.
- INTERFACING/LINING: Lightweight sew-in or fusible interfacing. Silk organza, rayon or polyester chiffon lining for suiting and high-quality looks.

CARE

- WASHING: Dry-clean or hand wash.
- DRYING: Dry-clean or air-dry.
- IRONING: Low to medium dry heat, no steam. A pressing cloth is recommended.
- SHRINKAGE: Minimal shrinking but will fray.

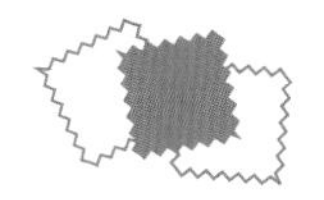

ORGANZA

Organza is a sheer, lightweight and sometimes stiff fabric that can be made of pure silk or synthetic nylon and polyester. It's often used to make wedding gowns and evening dresses, skirts, blouses, costumes and home furnishings. It also works beautifully as a simple window treatment or room-dividing screen.

Organza's sheer beauty can be left plain, ruffled or gathered for a feminine look, or even painted with a design. Organza can also be draped over bedposts to create a romantic setting and hung over lampshades for diffused lighting (with low-heat light bulbs). The uses for organza are far-reaching.

PROPERTIES

- CHARACTER: Sheer, lightweight, sometimes stiff.
- WEAVE: Plain weave.
- WEIGHT: Lightweight.
- SPECIAL CONSIDERATIONS: Though commonly made from nylon or polyester, high quality organza made from silk is easier to sew with. Silk organza tends not to pucker at the seams the way synthetic fabrics can. Of course, holding the fabric taut while sewing will help.

WORKING WITH

- TO CUT: To keep fabric from misshaping and slinking away from you while cutting, a rotary cutter and mat work best.
- HANDLING FOR SEWING: When starting a new stitch, do not backstitch. Use your left hand to hold both machine threads to avoid the fabric being sucked down into the machine plate. As you sew, hold the fabric taut using both hands. Pins should only be used in the seam of your garment and pinned parallel to the selvedge to avoid snags and runs in the fabric. ▶

ORGANZA continued

- NEEDLES: Sharp HM and HJ or Universal H, sizes 60/8 or 70/10.
- THREAD: Lightweight all-purpose cotton, polyester or silk.
- STITCH LENGTH: 2–2.5mm.
- SEWING MACHINE FEET: Standard, straight stitch or roller with a single-hole needle plate.
- INTERFACING/LINING: Lightweight sew-in or fusible interfacing. Lightweight lining is typically needed for modesty.

HANDY HINT

One of the beauties of silk organza is that it can withstand high temperatures, so although it may be the most expensive rag you own, it makes a wonderful pressing cloth. Lay it over the top of other fabrics when ironing, and then throw it in the washing machine when needed.

CARE

- WASHING: Dry-cleaning versus washing depends on the look you desire. To maintain crispness and shine, dry-cleaning is recommended; for a softer more informal look, machine wash and air-dry your fabric.
- DRYING: Dry-clean or air-dry.
- IRONING: Low dry heat. A pressing cloth is recommended, as synthetic organza is easily damaged with improper pressing.
- SHRINKAGE: None.

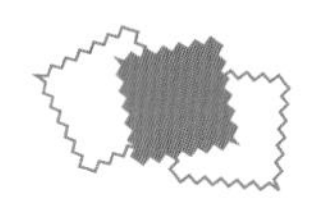

PEAU DE SOIE

Peau de soie, meaning 'skin of silk' in French, is medium-weight delustred satin, sometimes referred to as duchess satin. It has the rich, luxurious look of charmeuse but with slightly less shine and a stiffer drape.

Quality peau de soie (pronounced 'poe duh swah') looks the same on both sides, making it reversible. It is commonly used for wedding gowns, bridesmaid and mother of the bride dresses, as well as other elegant attire. It is easy to sew with but pins will leave marks, so only pin in the seam allowances of your garment.

PROPERTIES

- CHARACTER: Delustred satin; looks the same on both sides.
- WEAVE: Satin weave.
- WEIGHT: Medium.
- SPECIAL CONSIDERATIONS: Because it looks the same on both sides you can use either side of the fabric.

WORKING WITH

- TO CUT: To keep fabric from misshaping and slinking away from you while cutting, a rotary cutter and mat work best. A handy method is to sandwich the fabric between two pieces of tissue paper on a cutting mat (one tissue on top, one underneath the fabric), pin the three layers together in the seam allowance and carefully cut with scissors or a rotary cutter. Use with-nap layout when cutting pattern pieces. ▶

PEAU DE SOIE continued

- HANDLING FOR SEWING: When starting a new seam, do not backstitch. Use your left hand to hold both machine threads to avoid the fabric being sucked down into the machine plate. As you sew, hold the fabric taut using both hands. Pins should only be used in the seam allowances of your garment and pinned parallel to the selvedge to avoid snags and runs in the fabric.
- NEEDLES: Sharp HM and HJ or Universal H, sizes 60/8 or 70/10.
- THREAD: Lightweight all-purpose cotton or silk.
- STITCH LENGTH: 2–2.5mm.
- SEWING MACHINE FEET: Standard, straight stitch or roller with a single-hole needle plate.
- INTERFACING/LINING: Lightweight sew-in interfacing. Organza or other lightweight silk lining is recommended and makes it possible to hand sew an invisible hem by attaching the fabric to the lining.

CARE

- WASHING: Machine wash or dry-clean.
- DRYING: Air-dry, tumble dry or dry-clean.
- IRONING: Cool to medium dry heat. Fabric may show discoloration when ironing but the faded look is only temporary. Water and steam may cause water spots unless fabric is pre-washed. A pressing cloth is recommended.
- SHRINKAGE: Minimal.

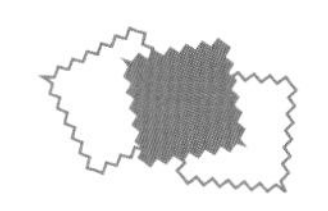

RAW SILK (Noil, Tussah and Pongee)

Raw silk, also known as noil, is a nubby fabric with a similar feel to dupioni. Pongee and tussah are also forms of raw silk and are cultivated from wild silk worms. They are all made from the shortest, discarded fibres in a silk cocoon, which are spun into noil yarns and then woven into fabric. Subtle flecks in the silk are actually natural particles from the cocoon and add to the fabric's charm. The finish is dull and uneven, and the look is more 'raw' and casual than other silks in the family. Noil is an excellent choice for full skirts, blouses, jackets, waistcoats and loose dresses. It is wrinkle resistant and great for travelling.

PROPERTIES

- CHARACTER: Rough and nubby with subtle flecks.
- WEAVE: Plain weave.
- WEIGHT: Lightweight.
- SPECIAL CONSIDERATIONS: Wrinkle-resistant. Some wild silks can shrink when washed.

WORKING WITH

- TO CUT: Use sharp scissors or a rotary cutter and mat.
- HANDLING FOR SEWING: When starting a new seam, do not backstitch. Use your left hand to hold both machine threads to avoid the fabric being sucked down into the machine plate. As you sew, hold the fabric taut using both hands. Pins should only be used in the seam of your garment and pinned parallel to the selvedge to avoid snags and runs in the fabric.
- NEEDLES: Sharp HM and HJ or Universal H, size 80/12.
- THREAD: Lightweight all-purpose cotton, polyester or silk.
- STITCH LENGTH: 2–2.5mm.
- SEWING MACHINE FEET: Standard.
- INTERFACING/LINING: Lightweight fusible or sew-in interfacing. Silk organza, rayon or polyester chiffon lining.

CARE

- WASHING: Dry-cleaning versus washing depends on the look you desire. To maintain crispness, dry-cleaning is recommended; for a softer more informal look, machine-wash and air-dry.
- DRYING: Dry-clean or air-dry.
- IRONING: Low to medium dry heat. A pressing cloth is recommended.
- SHRINKAGE: Moderate to extreme.

SATIN

Satin is probably the 'it' fabric when it comes to silks, and is well-known for its glossy, elegant appearance. In fact, satin is so widely known that the word is used to describe things other than textiles - lotions and paint are often referred to as having a 'satin' finish.

Satin fabric originated in China and was once only made of silk fibres, but today you'll find synthetic versions made from acetate, polyester and rayon. Satin is its own weave, with weft yarns woven less frequently so that long warp threads seem to float on the surface. This creates a very glossy sheen on the right side of the fabric and a matt, almost rough appearance on the wrong side.

Satin is primarily used for garments such as wedding gowns and formal dresses. Peau de soie or duchess satin is delustred satin that has slightly less shine and is finished on both sides.

DID YOU KNOW?

When it came to US prom fashion in the 1980s it was all about matching your shoes with your dress. Because white satin holds colour well, shoe retailers would sell cheap white satin heels and dye them to match the colour of any gown.

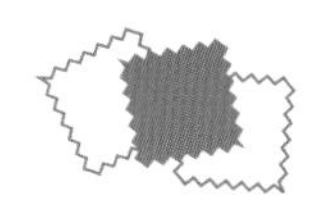

PROPERTIES

- CHARACTER: Shiny, slinky, glossy on the right side and matt, dull finish on the wrong side; usually thicker than charmeuse.
- WEAVE: Satin weave.
- WEIGHT: Medium.
- SPECIAL CONSIDERATIONS: Polyester and rayon satin will water spot.

WORKING WITH

- TO CUT: To keep fabric from misshaping and slinking away from you while cutting, a rotary cutter and mat work best. A handy method is to sandwich the fabric between two pieces of tissue paper on a cutting mat (one tissue on top, one underneath the fabric), pin the three layers together in the seam allowance and carefully cut. Use with-nap layout when cutting pattern pieces.
- HANDLING FOR SEWING: Always use a new sharp needle to prevent snags in the fabric. When starting a new seam, do not backstitch. Use your left hand to hold both machine threads to avoid the fabric being sucked down into the machine plate. As you sew, hold the fabric taut using both hands. Pins should only be used in the seam allowances of your garment and pinned parallel to the selvedge to avoid snags and runs in the fabric.
- NEEDLES: Sharp HM and HJ or Universal H, sizes 60/8 or 70/10.
- THREAD: Lightweight all-purpose cotton or silk.
- STITCH LENGTH: 2–2.5mm.
- SEWING MACHINE FEET: Standard, straight stitch or roller with a single-hole needle plate.
- INTERFACING/LINING: Lining recommended for quality garments. Use China silk or silk or polyester organza and chiffon.

CARE

- WASHING: Dry-clean or machine wash. Finished garments should be dry-cleaned.
- DRYING: Dry-clean or air-dry.
- IRONING: Cool to medium dry heat. Fabric may show discoloration when ironing, but the faded look is only temporary. Water and steam may cause water spots unless fabric is pre-washed. A pressing cloth is recommended.
- SHRINKAGE: Minimal.

SILK BROCADE

Brocade is a decorative fabric with a slightly embossed design against a contrasting background. Woven on a Jacquard loom, the patterns can be subtle or ornate, and range from floral designs to animals and geometric shapes. Brocade can also be fancy in colour with rich golds and reds, or simpler with pale pinks and blues. Regardless of the design, brocade looks luxurious and has been used for centuries for the finest of projects. It was once the fabric of choice for home furnishings, and is still favoured today for curtains, furniture upholstery and throw cushions. Silk brocade is also used for wedding gowns, costumes, slim-fitted trousers, waistcoats and theatrical costumes.

Though the finest brocades are made of silk, it's easy to find polyester and other synthetic versions in fabric shops. These variations are slightly easier to work with compared to real silk and won't break your budget.

HANDY HINT

If you need a splash of colour in a room, silk brocade makes a beautiful throw pillow for a couch or bed. The detailed fabric livens up the room without overpowering other decor.

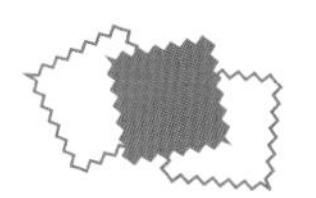

PROPERTIES

- CHARACTER: Decorative with an embossed, contrasting design.
- WEAVE: Jacquard.
- WEIGHT: Medium to heavy.
- SPECIAL CONSIDERATIONS: Ravels and snags easily. Can be bulky and difficult to work with, but its decorative pattern is forgiving and helps disguise uneven stitching and mistakes.

WORKING WITH

- TO CUT: Use sharp scissors or a rotary cutter and mat. Use with-nap layout when cutting pattern pieces.
- HANDLING FOR SEWING: Brocade can fray easily. To prevent the fabric from fraying all the way down to the seam and creating a hole, use wider seams in your garments and finish off all seams with an overlocker or pinking shears.
- NEEDLES: Sharp HM and HJ or Universal H, sizes 70/10–90/14.
- THREAD: All-purpose polyester or cotton.
- STITCH LENGTH: 2.5mm.
- SEWING MACHINE FEET: Standard.
- INTERFACING/LINING: Sew-in interfacing. Charmeuse or China silk lining is recommended for high-quality garments.

CARE

- WASHING: Dry-clean or machine wash. Dry-cleaning will keep your fabric just as it was the day you bought it, but washing may make fabric shrink.
- DRYING: Dry-clean or air-dry.
- IRONING: Medium dry heat. It's a good idea to press on the wrong side of the fabric where possible and to use a pressing cloth when ironing on the right side in order to avoid flattening the fabric.
- SHRINKAGE: Minimal shrinking.

TAFFETA

Taffeta is a tightly woven, stiff fabric made of silk, nylon or rayon. While it is sometimes used as an underlining, taffeta is ideal for party dresses and skirts. It's considered a 'noisy' fabric since it rustles with your every move, and it is famous for its iridescent lustre and shine. Taffeta requires a bit of patience when sewing as it can pucker at the seams and the fabric creases badly. Lining your garment with organza or tulle will reduce creasing and add personality to your party-going attire.

PROPERTIES

- CHARACTER: Stiff and noisy; rustles as you walk.
- WEAVE: Very tight plain weave.
- WEIGHT: Medium to heavy.
- SPECIAL CONSIDERATIONS: Taffeta puckers easily at the seams, so extra patience is required when sewing.

WORKING WITH

- TO CUT: Rotary cutter and mat work best, though sharp scissors will also work.
- HANDLING FOR SEWING: Pins should only be used in the seam of your garment and pinned parallel to the selvedge to avoid snags and runs in the fabric. As you sew, hold the fabric taut using both hands.
- NEEDLES: Sharp HM and HJ or Universal H, sizes 60/8 or 70/10.
- THREAD: All-purpose cotton, polyester or silk.
- STITCH LENGTH: 2.5mm.
- SEWING MACHINE FEET: Standard, straight stitch with a single-hole needle plate.
- INTERFACING/LINING: Lining recommended for quality garments. Use silk or polyester organza and chiffon or China silk.

CARE

- WASHING: Dry-clean (silk) or machine wash (synthetic), but check the manufacturer's instructions. Dry-cleaning will maintain crispness. For a softer, more informal look, machine wash and air-dry your fabric.
- DRYING: Dry-clean or air-dry.
- IRONING: Low to medium dry heat. Steam will cause water spots. Use an organza pressing cloth.
- SHRINKAGE: Minimal.

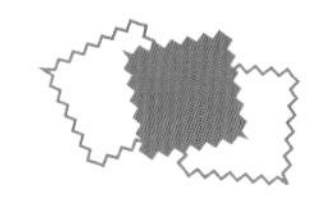

TULLE

Tulle is an open-mesh net fabric that was once solely made of silk, but is now often found in nylon, rayon and cotton. The fabric is often used for wedding decorations, veils and gowns; for adding puffy layers to skirts and dresses; and is famous for its use on ballet tutus. Tulle is often woven in a 15 denier weight (though you can sometimes find wider mesh holes and weights). Most fabric shops carry a variety of colours, but online shops tend to have a wider selection.

PROPERTIES

- CHARACTER: Open-mesh netting.
- WEAVE: Plain weave.
- WEIGHT: Lightweight.
- SPECIAL CONSIDERATIONS: Tulle can be difficult to cut and sew. Because the fabric is sheer and lightweight, layers tend to stick together and are hard to distinguish from each other.

WORKING WITH

- TO CUT: To keep fabric from misshaping while cutting, a rotary cutter and mat work best. A handy method is to sandwich the fabric between two pieces of tissue paper on a cutting mat (one tissue on top, one underneath the fabric), pin the three layers together in the seam allowance and carefully cut with scissors or a rotary cutter.
- HANDLING FOR SEWING: When starting a new seam, do not backstitch. Use your left hand to hold both machine threads to avoid the fabric being sucked down into the machine plate. As you sew, hold the fabric taut using both hands. Pins should only be used in the seam of your garment and pinned parallel to the selvedge to avoid snags and runs in the fabric.
- NEEDLES: Sharp HM and HJ or Universal H, sizes 60/8 or 70/10.
- THREAD: All-purpose cotton or polyester.
- STITCH LENGTH: 2mm.
- SEWING MACHINE FEET: Standard or straight stitch.
- INTERFACING/LINING: It is often used as a lining itself.

CARE

- WASHING: Dry-clean or machine wash.
- DRYING: Dry-clean or air-dry.
- IRONING: Very low dry heat. Tulle is easily damaged by an iron. See manufacturer recommendations for more info.
- SHRINKAGE: Minimal.

VELVET

Velvet is a soft pile fabric that connotes luxury. Traditionally made of silk, velvet is now created from almost any fibre: rayon, polyester, acetate, cotton, elastane, microfibre and other blends. It is used for dresses, skirts, jackets, waistcoats, furniture upholstery, throw cushions and other home furnishings.

Velvet is created by weaving the warp threads between two cloths (instead of one). The cloths are then cut right down the middle and each finished cloth is wound on a separate roll. The resulting fabric has soft, tiny threads that stick up, similar to freshly cut grass. This is known as pile.

Since velvet comes in a range of fibres, check the manufacturer's notes for specific care and washing instructions. Real silk velvet is easily damaged; creasing and folding the fabric can flatten the pile. When storing, hang by the selvedge rather than folding. Blended velvets tend to drape the best, while stretch and microfibre velvets can be machine washed.

HANDY HINT

A walking foot is recommended when sewing with velvet because it can cause shifting. It works in a similar way to the feed dogs on the bottom of your machine plate, but it feeds the fabric from the top as well as from the bottom. A walking foot is also used for quilting.

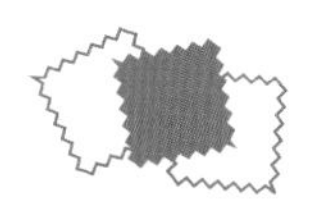

PROPERTIES

- CHARACTER: Soft pile, luxurious.
- WEAVE: Plain with pile.
- WEIGHT: Medium to heavy.
- SPECIAL CONSIDERATIONS: Since velvet is easily damaged by seam-ripping, try using a pattern you've sewn with before or make a test garment to work out the problem areas before cutting into the velvet. Polyester and other synthetic velvets are easier to sew with than real silk. Cotton velvet is the easiest of all the fibres, making it a good option for beginners.

WORKING WITH

- TO CUT: Use sharp scissors or a rotary cutter and mat. Use with-nap layout when cutting pattern pieces.
- HANDLING FOR SEWING: Where possible, sew in the direction of the pile. Periodically lift your presser foot to allow the fabric to bounce back. Baste stitch all seams to avoid ripping. Do not use pins, as they will leave marks in the fabric. Instead, use double-sided tape in your seams to keep them from shifting. Do not sew through the tape but just next to it.
- NEEDLES: Sharp HM and HJ or Universal H, sizes 70/10 or 80/12.
- THREAD: All-purpose polyester or cotton.
- STITCH LENGTH: 2.5–3mm.
- SEWING MACHINE FEET: Walking foot, velvet 'V' foot, roller or straight stitch.
- INTERFACING/LINING: Sew-in interfacing and linings only (no fusibles). Use silk or polyester organza and chiffon or China silk.

CARE

- WASHING: Dry-clean or machine wash. Washing may change the nap but can also give your fabric a vintage look. When in doubt, read the manufacturer's care instructions or stick with dry-cleaning.
- DRYING: Dry-clean or air-dry. Never fold velvet; hang it from the selvedge.
- IRONING: It is best to avoid ironing velvet unless you have a specialised needle board, although you can get a similar result by using another piece of velvet or a towel as an underlying cloth. Place the towel or extra velvet on your pressing surface, then lay the fabric on top with the pile facing down. The pile of your fabric and the pile of the ironing surface will mesh into each other and prevent the fabric from crushing. Hold a steam iron about 1cm above the fabric for best results. If you damage silk velvet with an iron, your fabric will look crushed or have a shine. Usually the damage is permanent. You can try to revive the pile with steam but it will never look as luxurious as it once did. Always test-iron a sample of fabric before pressing on a finished project.
- SHRINKAGE: Minimal.

WOOL: An Overview

Just the mention of wool fabric has me dreaming of autumn clothing, pleated skirts and beautifully tailored coats. But wool offers much more than warmth; in fact, it's one of the most versatile fabrics. With amazing wicking abilities, it pulls moisture away from the skin, which means a lightweight wool shirt can actually keep you cool in the summer. It can be fuzzy, smooth, twill woven or plain. We use it for crafts, to decorate our homes and even to cover billiard tables. But most importantly, we love to use wool for garments of utility and style.

PRODUCTION & PROCESSES

A natural animal protein, wool primarily comes from the fleece of sheep and lambs. Varying types of wool are also found in other animals, such as alpacas, Angora rabbits and goats.

Since the beginning of time humans have been using wool for some sort of protection or clothing. Over time, our production skills have evolved, and today approximately 1.3 million tonnes of wool is produced every year, with 60 per cent of it being used for apparel. Australia is the number one producer, with China, New Zealand and Russia close behind.

The production of wool starts with the annual shearing of sheep. The process requires specialist skills in order to avoid nicking or injuring the sheep. After shearing, the fleece is sorted by colour, length and quality, and given a soapy bath to remove dirt, burrs and other debris. Then the fibres will go in one of two processing directions: they will become either woollen or worsted wool.

WOOLLEN: Once the fleece is washed, any fibres that are less than 8cm/3in long are carded or pulled straight out from the wool. The fibres are spun and woven into yarn, which is further woven into fabric. These short fibres create a unique hairy surface on the fabric. Woollens are soft, with a rough texture, and compared to worsted wools, are easier to sew with and cost less, but can easily pill and snag.

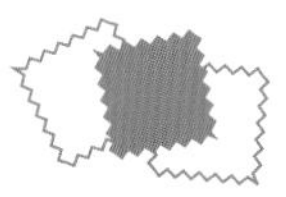

WORSTED: After the short woollen fibres are carded out, the longer fibres are combed and spun. The smooth and lustrous resulting yarn is then tightly woven into worsted fabric. Although worsteds cost slightly more than woollens, they are more durable, look wonderful on tailored garments, rarely snag and press well. They have a slight shine and are a lighter weight fabric compared to woollens.

ORGANIC & FAIR TRADE

When wool is produced, livestock may be subject to synthetic pesticides, hormones, genetic engineering and non-organic food, thus the methods for producing organic wool have become an increasing concern for consumers. In the UK, the Soil Association has a long list of requirements for a fabric to be certified as organic. In addition to being void of the traditional pesticides and hormones listed above, livestock used for organic wool must graze on land that is large enough to accommodate the number of animals.

USES

Woollens are used for trousers, skirts, jackets, coats, bow ties, luggage and shoes. Worsteds are used for tailored garments, trousers, skirts, dresses, waistcoats, jackets and coats.

CHARACTERISTICS

- Extremely versatile.
- Light in summer, warm in winter.
- Insulates and retains body heat.
- Wonderful wicking abilities, pulling moisture away from the skin.
- Water resistant. Wool can absorb 30 per cent of its weight without feeling wet.
- Resists wrinkling.
- Blends well with other natural and synthetic fibres.
- Works well for tailored garments.
- Wool can felt and shrink when washed and dried.
- Some wools are washable, but most finished garments require dry-cleaning.
- Is easily damaged by improper ironing, seam-ripping, moths and carpet beetles.

ALPACA

Alpaca wool is known as a hair fibre textile, which is characterised by small visible hairs scattered throughout the fabric (similar to mohair, cashmere, camel's hair and angora). While standard 'wool' comes from a sheep, alpaca fibres are from the alpaca. Alpacas are similar to llamas but are much smaller and bred specifically for their wool. Alpaca yarn can be knit or woven. When woven, it is used for jackets, coats, capes, wraps and trousers. The beauty of alpaca is that it is very warm without being bulky; it can feel itchy to the skin, so it's best to line your garments with a thin cotton voile or China silk.

DID YOU KNOW?

Alpaca wool comes in a wide range of natural colours, depending on the country of origin. Peru classifies 52 natural colours, Australia classifies 12 and the US classifies 16.

PROPERTIES

- CHARACTER: Small hair fibres covering the surface.
- WEAVE: Plain.
- WEIGHT: Medium to heavy.
- SPECIAL CONSIDERATIONS: Very warm without feeling bulky. Can be costly.

WORKING WITH

- TO CUT: Use sharp scissors or a rotary cutter and mat.
- HANDLING FOR SEWING: Lift your presser foot periodically to help the fabric relax and to keep it from bunching up.
- NEEDLES: Universal H, size 80/12.
- THREAD: All-purpose polyester or cotton.
- STITCH LENGTH: 2.5mm.
- SEWING MACHINE FEET: Standard.
- INTERFACING/LINING: Sew-in interfacings only. Line jackets and coats with cotton batiste, voile, organza, chiffon or China silk.

CARE

- WASHING: Dry-clean or hand wash.
- DRYING: Dry-clean or lay flat to dry.
- IRONING: Always test-press first. For best results, use another piece of wool as your underlying surface, place your fabric on top of that with the right side of the fabric facing down, then sandwich it with another wool pressing cloth on top. Use medium heat and steam.
- SHRINKAGE: Moderate.

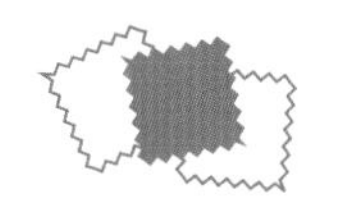

ANGORA

Angora wool is an extremely soft hair fibre textile made from the fur of Angora rabbits – not to be confused with Angora goat hair, which is known as mohair. Rabbit fur on its own is silky, extraordinarily soft and, because the fibres are hollow, almost seems to float. As rabbit leather and fur for clothing is deemed inhumane by some, angora fabric is made of fibres from sheared rabbits – a process that does not hurt the animals.

Throughout the year, angora rabbits in varying shades of white and black are shorn. The long and short hairs are spun with other fibres, such as cashmere, to create structured yarn. Typically, the yarn is knitted into jumpers and scarves, but when woven with wool fibres, the result is an extremely soft fabric with visible hair fibres on the surface. It is durable, warm and may be a good alternative for people with wool allergies. Angora wool fabric is used for coats, outerwear and trims. Due to its laborious production processes, however, the textile is costly.

PROPERTIES

- CHARACTER: Extremely soft with small hair fibres covering the surface.
- WEAVE: Plain.
- WEIGHT: Medium to heavy.
- SPECIAL CONSIDERATIONS: Warmer than wool and a possible alternative for people with wool allergies. Can be expensive.

WORKING WITH

- TO CUT: Use sharp scissors.
- HANDLING FOR SEWING: Lift your presser foot periodically to help the fabric relax and to keep it from bunching up.
- NEEDLES: Universal H, size 80/12.
- THREAD: All-purpose polyester or cotton.
- STITCH LENGTH: 2.5mm.
- SEWING MACHINE FEET: Standard.
- INTERFACING/LINING: Sew-in interfacings only. Line jackets and coats with cotton batiste, voile, organza, chiffon or China silk.

CARE

- WASHING: Dry-clean or hand wash.
- DRYING: Dry-clean or lay flat to dry.
- IRONING: Always test-press first. For best results, use another piece of wool as your underlying surface, place your fabric on top of that with the right side face down, then sandwich it with another wool pressing cloth on top. Use medium heat and steam.
- SHRINKAGE: Moderate.

BAIZE

Baize is a wool fabric you may not have heard of, but it's likely you've touched it before. True professional billiard and gaming tables are often covered in felted wool, but for the average household or pool hall, baize is an inexpensive alternative. It's also a good choice for card tables because it keeps the cards from sliding excessively, and the bold colour contrast between the table and the cards can help prevent players from cheating.

Though traditionally green, online fabric shops carry baize in a variety of colours and even patterns. The fabric is not designed to be washed and can warp when exposed to water.

PROPERTIES

- CHARACTER: Thick, soft wool; similar to felted wool.
- WEAVE: Plain.
- WEIGHT: Medium to heavy.
- SPECIAL CONSIDERATIONS: Not designed for washing. Will warp when exposed to water.

WORKING WITH

- TO CUT: Use sharp scissors or a rotary cutter and mat.
- HANDLING FOR SEWING: Can be bulky under your machine. If re-covering a table, sewing may not be necessary. Try stretching the fabric and stapling or use a glue gun.
- NEEDLES: Universal H, sizes 80/12 or 90/14.
- THREAD: All-purpose polyester or cotton.
- STITCH LENGTH: 2.5–3mm.
- SEWING MACHINE FEET: Standard or Teflon.
- INTERFACING/LINING: None.

CARE

- WASHING: Dry-clean only.
- DRYING: Dry-clean only.
- IRONING: Always test-press first. Use medium heat and steam with a wool press-cloth over the top.
- SHRINKAGE: Extreme. Fabric will warp when exposed to water.

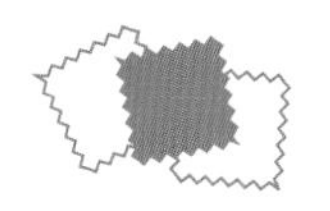

BOILED WOOL

Boiled wool is similar to felt. It is soft, warm, retains its shape well and doesn't wrinkle. Typically, boiled wool is made by boiling and shrinking knitted yards of merino wool using industrial machinery, but this process can be recreated on a small scale at home as well. Take a large woollen jumper or a knitted piece of fabric, wash it in hot water in the washing machine and then dry it in a hot dryer. The fibres will shrink up to 40–50 per cent, and you'll be left with a thicker, denser version of what you started with.

Boiled wool is an excellent choice for handbags, jackets, capes, coats, waistcoats, skirts, cardigans, fitted garments and toys.

PROPERTIES

- CHARACTER: Thick, compact, felted wool.
- WEAVE: Knit.
- WEIGHT: Medium to heavy.
- SPECIAL CONSIDERATIONS: Felting can easily be created at home using your washer and dryer.

WORKING WITH

- TO CUT: Use sharp scissors or a rotary cutter and mat.
- HANDLING FOR SEWING: Easy to sew; sewn like other woven fabrics.
- NEEDLES: Universal H, sizes 70/10-90/14.
- THREAD: All-purpose polyester or cotton.
- STITCH LENGTH: 2–3mm.
- SEWING MACHINE FEET: Standard.
- INTERFACING/LINING: Lining recommended for skirts, tailored jackets and coats.

CARE

- WASHING: Dry-clean.
- DRYING: Dry-clean.
- IRONING: Use medium heat and steam. A pressing cloth is recommended when pressing on the right side of the fabric.
- SHRINKAGE: None when dry-cleaned.

BOUCLÉ

Bouclé fabric is easily described by the name itself, which in French means 'curled'. Soft, looping curls cover the fabric's surface giving it a bumpy, nubby surface. It can be knit or woven and made of wool or wool blends. Bouclé resists wrinkles and the textured surface hides sewing irregularities and mistakes, although it can be bulky to sew and may pill or snag. If you catch one yarn loop on a piece of jewellery, the entire row can pull out and ruin your garment. Bouclé is used for jackets, coats, waistcoats, tunics, skirts and dresses.

PROPERTIES

- CHARACTER: Woven or knitted with looping yarn curls give the fabric a bumpy, nubby surface; wrinkle-free.
- WEAVE: Plain or knit.
- WEIGHT: Lightweight to heavy.
- SPECIAL CONSIDERATIONS: Easily pulls and snags. The textured surface hides sewing irregularities and mistakes.

WORKING WITH

- TO CUT: Use sharp scissors or a rotary cutter and mat.
- HANDLING FOR SEWING: Lift your presser foot periodically to help the fabric relax and to keep it from bunching up.
- NEEDLES: Universal H, sizes 70/10–90/14.
- THREAD: All-purpose polyester or cotton.
- STITCH LENGTH: 2–3mm.
- SEWING MACHINE FEET: Roller, straight stitch or walking.
- INTERFACING/LINING: Sew-in interfacings (fusible may flatten the texture). Line jackets and coats with cotton batiste, voile, organza, chiffon or China silk.

CARE

- WASHING: Dry-clean or hand wash.
- DRYING: Dry-clean or lay flat to dry.
- IRONING: Typically not needed since bouclé is wrinkle resistant, but if pressing is desired, first place a towel on your ironing board, place the fabric on top of that with the right side of the fabric facing down, then lightly touch the back side of the fabric. Do not press too hard or you will crush the nubby texture. Use medium heat and steam.
- SHRINKAGE: Moderate.

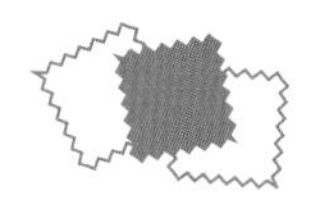

CAMEL HAIR

Camel hair fabric comes from the hair of the double-humped Bactrian camel. It is a hair fibre textile, and is similar to mohair, cashmere, alpaca and Angora. It has the same soft feel as cashmere and is just as costly. The fabric can be pure camel or blended with wool and other fibres.

Camel hair is frequently used to create coats for men and women, as well as fitted skirts and tailored trousers. It is often a sandy camel colour, but can range from red to brown and even black. These are not dyed fibres, but are the natural colours found on moulted camel hair.

PROPERTIES

- CHARACTER: Very soft, often a sandy camel colour (but can also come in red, brown or black).
- WEAVE: Plain.
- WEIGHT: Medium to heavy.
- SPECIAL CONSIDERATIONS: Very warm without feeling bulky. Similar softness as cashmere and can be costly.

WORKING WITH

- TO CUT: Use sharp scissors or a rotary cutter and mat.
- HANDLING FOR SEWING: Lift your presser foot periodically to help the fabric relax.
- NEEDLES: Universal H, size 80/12.
- THREAD: All-purpose polyester or cotton.
- STITCH LENGTH: 2.5mm.
- SEWING MACHINE FEET: Standard.
- INTERFACING/LINING: Sew-in interfacings only. Line jackets and coats with cotton batiste, voile, organza, chiffon or China silk.

CARE

- WASHING: Dry-clean or hand wash.
- DRYING: Dry-clean or lay flat to dry.
- IRONING: Always test-press. For best results, use another piece of wool as your underlying surface, place your fabric on top of that with the right side of the fabric facing down, then sandwich it with another wool pressing cloth on top. Use medium heat and steam.
- SHRINKAGE: Moderate.

CASHMERE

Cashmere is easily the most luxurious and desired fabric available, but is the obsession with cashmere warranted? Indeed. Due to the rarity of its wool, cashmere was once only worn by royalty, and owning anything made from the soft wool clearly marked your social status. As time passed, the fabric crept in to upper-class society, and by the 1940s movie stars brought the fabric to life with their high-fashion wardrobes. Today, cashmere is readily available, although it is still quite costly and continues to carry its elite status.

Like other hair fibre textiles, cashmere is characterised by small visible hairs scattered throughout the fabric, making it extremely soft. It is similar to mohair, camel hair, Angora and alpaca. While standard 'wool' comes from a sheep, these fibres are from goats. The wool is brushed annually, and sometimes spun with other fibres to create less expensive fabric. The finest cashmere comes from the underbelly and throat of the goats where the hair is extremely soft. Cashmere yarn can be knit or woven; knitted cashmere is used for jumpers, dresses, cardigans and even robes, and woven cashmere is used for skirts, trousers, scarves, jackets and coats.

DID YOU KNOW?

Sometimes cashmere is mixed with silk fibres for added strength, which results in pashmina. Manufactured in Tibet, pure pashmina can feel coarse and rough, so manufacturers put it through a softening process and the end result has a soft, silken quality very similar to pure cashmere.

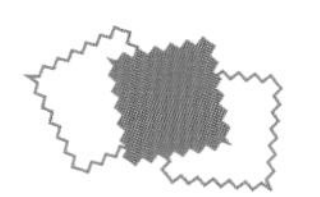

PROPERTIES

- CHARACTER: Extremely soft with small hairs scattered on the surface.
- WEAVE: Plain or knit.
- WEIGHT: Medium to heavy.
- SPECIAL CONSIDERATIONS: 50 per cent warmer than standard wool and available in a variety of blends.

WORKING WITH

- TO CUT: Use sharp scissors or a rotary cutter and mat.
- HANDLING FOR SEWING: Hold fabric taut and be careful not to stretch it. Lift your presser foot periodically to help the fabric relax.
- NEEDLES: Universal H, size 80/12 (wovens); Stretch HS, size 75/11 (knits).
- THREAD: All-purpose polyester or cotton.
- STITCH LENGTH: 2–2.5mm.
- SEWING MACHINE FEET: Standard (woven); Teflon (knits).
- INTERFACING/LINING: Interfacing is optional. Line jackets and coats with cotton batiste, voile, organza, chiffon or China silk.

CARE

- WASHING: Dry-clean or hand wash.
- DRYING: Dry-clean or lay flat to dry.
- IRONING: Always test-press first. For best results, use a piece of wool as your underlying surface, place your fabric on top of that with the right side of the fabric facing down, then sandwich it with another wool pressing cloth on top. Use a press-and-lift motion, and medium heat with steam.
- SHRINKAGE: Moderate.

CHALLIS

Challis (pronounced shall-ee) is one of those easy-to-love, go-to fabrics. Commonly made from wool, it can also be made from cotton or rayon. Challis is lightweight, breathable, drapes well, hardly wrinkles, is soft and silky, and is sometimes machine washable. In a nutshell, challis is easy to use and comprises many run-of-the-mill fabrics you may come across in a fabric shop. Challis is a wonderful fabric for shirts, dresses, A-line skirts, trousers and jackets.

PROPERTIES

- CHARACTER: Soft and drapeable.
- WEAVE: Plain.
- WEIGHT: Lightweight.
- SPECIAL CONSIDERATIONS: Easy to sew. Trim cut edges of pattern pieces with pinking shears to avoid fraying. Finish off seams with an overlocker, zigzag stitch or French seams.

WORKING WITH

- TO CUT: Use sharp scissors or a rotary cutter and mat.
- HANDLING FOR SEWING: Easy to sew.
- NEEDLES: Universal H, size 80/12.
- THREAD: All-purpose polyester or cotton.
- STITCH LENGTH: 2.5mm.
- SEWING MACHINE FEET: Standard.
- INTERFACING/LINING: Sew-in or fusible interfacings; lightweight linings.

CARE

- WASHING: Read manufacturer's label. Some challis can be machine washed. When in doubt, dry-clean or hand wash.
- DRYING: Read the manufacturer's label. Dry-clean or tumble dry.
- IRONING: Use medium heat and steam.
- SHRINKAGE: Will shrink moderately when machine washed.

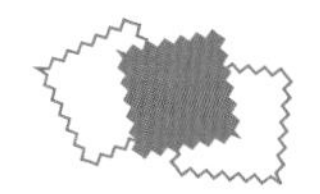

CRÊPE

Wool crêpe is woven with twisted yarns to give it a crinkled, pebbly surface. It comes in all weights, from light to heavy, and can make a garment look dressy or casual. The beauty of wool crêpe is that it resists wrinkles, making it perfect for winter travel. Wool crêpe is used for tailored clothing, trousers, dresses, skirts, jackets and coats.

PROPERTIES

- CHARACTER: Crinkled, pebbly surface.
- WEAVE: Plain and twisted.
- WEIGHT: Lightweight to heavy.
- SPECIAL CONSIDERATIONS: Very easy to sew. Made of wool, cotton or rayon.

WORKING WITH

- TO CUT: Use sharp scissors or a rotary cutter and mat.
- HANDLING FOR SEWING: Use stay tape in seams where the most stress will be placed (shoulders, crotch, etc.).
- NEEDLES: Universal H, size 80/12.
- THREAD: All-purpose polyester or cotton.
- STITCH LENGTH: 2–2.5mm.
- SEWING MACHINE FEET: Standard.
- INTERFACING/LINING: Sew-in or fusible interfacings; lightweight linings.

CARE

- WASHING: Fabric must be pre-shrunk by dry-cleaning before sewing or your finished garment will shrink significantly the first time it is dry-cleaned. You can mimic dry-cleaning by hanging it over a shower curtain rod in a steamy bathroom. Steam-shrinking with an iron will cause it to shrink unevenly.
- DRYING: Dry-clean.
- IRONING: Always test-press first. For best results, use another piece of wool as your underlying surface, place your fabric on top of that with the right side face down, then sandwich it with another wool pressing cloth on top. Use medium heat and steam.
- SHRINKAGE: Extreme.

FELT

A favoured fabric among crafters, felt is neither knitted or woven, but is instead made from fibres that are pounded, shrunk and compressed together to create a non-fray fabric without a visible grain. You can sew with it, glue it, shred it and it never frays, which makes it ideal for costumes and crafts. Felt comes in varying weights and fibres, including:

100 PER CENT WOOL: The finest felt available, it comes in a wide range of colours, is heavier and more compact than other felts, and can be expensive.

BLENDED WOOL: A wonderful alternative to pure wool, these felts are usually a mix of synthetic fibres and wool. They're less than half the price of 100 per cent wool, and are typically sold on bolts rather than pre-cut squares. You'll find beautiful jewel shades, soft pastel colours and everything in between.

ACRYLIC AND POLYESTER: The least expensive of all felts. They are sold on bolts or pre-cut into squares. The colour selection is quite limited (often in bold shades) and the felt is sometimes thin and of a poor quality.

PROPERTIES

- CHARACTER: Thick, compact, felted wool.
- WEIGHT: Medium.
- SPECIAL CONSIDERATIONS: Easy to sew.

WORKING WITH

- TO CUT: Use sharp scissors or a rotary cutter and mat.
- HANDLING FOR SEWING: Easy to sew.
- NEEDLES: Universal H, size 80/12.
- THREAD: All-purpose polyester or cotton.
- STITCH LENGTH: 2–2.5mm.
- SEWING MACHINE FEET: Standard.
- INTERFACING/LINING: Some felts are stiff on their own.

CARE

- WASHING: Machine-wash in cool water or hand wash. Do not wring water out or twist, as felt will bend out of shape. Felt tends to pill and ball when machine washed and dried. Do not dry-clean.
- DRYING: Form back into shape and lay flat to dry.
- IRONING: Test-press first. Use medium heat and steam.
- SHRINKAGE: Will shrink moderately when machine washed.

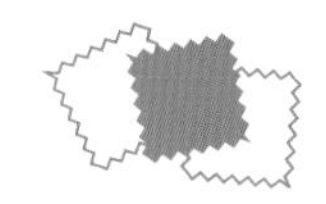

FLANNEL

Not to be confused with cotton flannel or flannelette, wool flannel comes in varying weights and quality. It sometimes has a slightly brushed napped finish and may be plain woven or twill. It's best used for dressy garments, trousers, shirts, coats, jackets, fitted dresses and skirts.

PROPERTIES

- CHARACTER: Soft-brushed look.
- WEAVE: Plain or twill.
- WEIGHT: Medium.
- SPECIAL CONSIDERATIONS: To avoid excessive fraying, overlock the edges or stitch the ends together before washing and drying.

WORKING WITH

- TO CUT: Use sharp scissors or a rotary cutter and mat. Use with-nap layout when cutting pattern pieces.
- HANDLING FOR SEWING: Easy to sew.
- NEEDLES: Universal H, size 80/12.
- THREAD: All-purpose polyester or cotton.
- STITCH LENGTH: 2–2.5mm.
- SEWING MACHINE FEET: Standard.
- INTERFACING/LINING: Sew-in or fusible interfacings. Lightweight linings.

CARE

- WASHING: Dry-clean or hand wash. Read the manufacturer's label.
- DRYING: Dry-clean or air-dry.
- IRONING: For best results, use another piece of wool as your underlying surface, place your fabric on top of that with the right side face down, then sandwich it with another wool pressing cloth on top. Use medium heat and steam.
- SHRINKAGE: Moderate.

GABARDINE

Gabardine dates back to the late nineteenth century when Thomas Burberry, of the iconic Burberry fashion brand, set out to design a fabric that was versatile and would hold up well to wear and tear. The result was a tightly twill-woven fabric, typically made from worsted wool yarn, but now commonly found in cotton, synthetics, and other blends. Gabardine is durable, tends not to wrinkle and drapes well. It is used for tailored clothing, dresses, shirts, straight skirts, trousers, jackets, coats, waistcoats and suits.

PROPERTIES

- CHARACTER: Firm, twill weave with a nice drape.
- WEAVE: Twill.
- WEIGHT: Medium.
- SPECIAL CONSIDERATIONS: Works for all seasons. Requires some patience when sewing; watch for puckering at the seams. Gabardine is also difficult to press.

WORKING WITH

- TO CUT: Use sharp scissors or a rotary cutter and mat.
- HANDLING FOR SEWING: Moderately easy to sew with, however, fabric can be difficult to ease around curves and seams tend to pucker - clipping seam allowances will help.
- NEEDLES: Universal H or Sharp HJ, sizes 70/10–90/14.
- THREAD: All-purpose cotton or wool.
- STITCH LENGTH: 2.5–3mm.
- SEWING MACHINE FEET: Standard.
- INTERFACING/LINING: Line jackets and tailored garments with cotton batiste, voile, organza, chiffon or China silk.

CARE

- WASHING: Dry-clean or hand wash. Do not wring or twist out water; gently squeeze instead.
- DRYING: Dry-clean or air-dry.
- IRONING: Medium heat and steam. Seams should be pressed open with a small drop of water in the seam, over a seam roll or seam stick. Press on the wrong side of the fabric, using little weight. When pressing on the right side, use a pressing cloth. If fabric is over-pressed and shines, hold a steam iron 1cm from the fabric to revive.
- SHRINKAGE: Moderate.

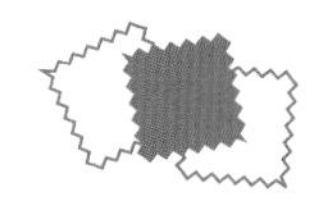

MELTON

Melton is a thick, heavy, felted wool with a visible nap. When sewing, you may keep the napped surface on the outside of your garment or choose to keep it inside, depending on your preference. Melton is water and wind resistant, making it ideal for heavy trench coats and pea coats.

Sewing with the fabric can be difficult and requires gumption from you and your machine (low-end machines may not be up to the challenge). Before starting your project, read up on alternate methods for creating seams – abutted (or 'butted') seams are ideal, since standard seams tend not to lie flat and can be bulky. Abutted seams are just as they sound – fabric edges are butted up next to each other, without any overlay, and sewn with a flatlock, zigzag or other stitch. This eliminates any bulk at the seams. Practise sewing a few times on fabric scraps before tackling your garment.

PROPERTIES

- CHARACTER: Thick, heavy felted wool with a napped surface.
- WEAVE: Felted.
- WEIGHT: Heavy and extremely thick.
- SPECIAL CONSIDERATIONS: Difficult to sew with. Requires a quality machine that is up to the task.

WORKING WITH

- TO CUT: Large, sharp scissors.
- HANDLING FOR SEWING: Abutted seams are ideal.
- NEEDLES: Universal H, sizes 80/12–100/16.
- THREAD: All-purpose polyester or cotton.
- STITCH LENGTH: 3–3.5mm.
- SEWING MACHINE FEET: Standard, straight stitch or Teflon.
- INTERFACING/LINING: None; fabric is stable on its own.

CARE

- WASHING: Dry-clean or hand wash.
- DRYING: Dry-clean or air-dry.
- IRONING: Use medium heat and steam, which helps considerably when pressing seams. For best results, use another piece of wool as your underlying surface, place your fabric on top of that with the right side face down, then sandwich it with another wool pressing cloth on top.
- SHRINKAGE: Moderate.

MERINO

Merino wool comes from the fur of merino sheep. One of the softest wools available, it can be woven or knit into fabric. It is often used in high-end athletic clothing as it breathes well and, like most wool, has wonderful wicking abilities. The wool draws moisture away from the skin and into the fabric, though the fabric itself may feel dry. It is anti-microbial, which means it inhibits the growth of bacteria on the fabric, and is also hypoallergenic.

Merino is sometimes blended with polyester, cashmere and silk to create fabric that is ultra-smooth and very soft. The fabric is used for lightweight knit garments, jumpers and socks. Like most wool, merino will shrink when washed, but no more than a typical cotton garment.

PROPERTIES

- CHARACTER: One of the softest wools available.
- WEAVE: Plain or knit.
- WEIGHT: Lightweight to medium.
- SPECIAL CONSIDERATIONS: Wonderful wicking abilities.

WORKING WITH

- TO CUT: Use sharp scissors or a rotary cutter and mat.
- HANDLING FOR SEWING: Sews similar to knits.
- NEEDLES: Universal H or Sharp HM, sizes 70/10 or 80/12.
- THREAD: Lightweight all-purpose polyester or cotton.
- STITCH LENGTH: 2mm.
- SEWING MACHINE FEET: Standard or straight stitch.
- INTERFACING/LINING: Optional.

CARE

- WASHING: Dry-clean, machine wash or hand wash.
- DRYING: Dry-clean or air-dry.
- IRONING: Use medium heat and steam.
- SHRINKAGE: Moderate.

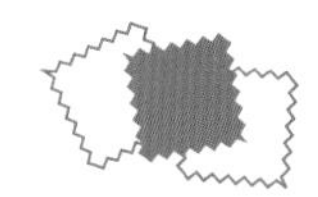

MOHAIR

The most common of the hair fibre textiles, mohair is warm and durable. Not to be confused with Angora rabbit fur, this wool comes from the Angora goat. The wool is silky soft and spun into yarn that can be knit or woven. Sometimes it is blended with other fibres to give the fabric the same lustre and sheen that mohair exhibits. The fabric holds dye well and is typically seen in solid colours and sometimes woven plaids. Mohair is a wonderful choice for fitted garments such as suits, skirts, coats and jackets.

PROPERTIES

- CHARACTER: Silky, soft, with a sheen.
- WEAVE: Plain.
- WEIGHT: Lightweight to medium.
- SPECIAL CONSIDERATIONS: Very warm without adding bulk, however the hairs in the fabric can be irritating to people with pet dander allergies. Line garments with a thin cotton or silk.

WORKING WITH

- TO CUT: Use sharp scissors or a rotary cutter and mat. Use with-nap layout when cutting pattern pieces.
- HANDLING FOR SEWING: Lift your presser foot periodically to help the fabric relax. In fabrics where hair fibres line the surface, sew in the direction of the pile.
- NEEDLES: Universal H, sizes 60/8 or 70/12.
- THREAD: All-purpose polyester or cotton.
- STITCH LENGTH: 2–3mm.
- SEWING MACHINE FEET: Standard, straight stitch, roller or walking.
- INTERFACING/LINING: Line jackets and tailored garments with cotton batiste, voile, organza, chiffon or China silk.

CARE

- WASHING: Dry-clean or hand wash. Read manufacturer's care instructions.
- DRYING: Dry-clean or air-dry.
- IRONING: Always test-press first. For best results, use another piece of wool as your underlying surface, place your fabric on top of that with the right side of the fabric facing down, then sandwich it with another wool pressing cloth on top. Use medium heat and steam.
- SHRINKAGE: Moderate.

SERGE

Serge is a resilient, twill-woven, sturdy fabric that drapes well and looks great on a variety of body types. Like wool challis, it's a dream to work with. It comes in a variety of weights (for a variety of climates), tends not to wrinkle and presses well. It's typically used for military uniforms and suits and can sometimes be costly. While wool serge was developed in Europe in the sixteenth century, silk serge actually dates further back to the eighth century. Silk serge is more fragile than wool and is commonly used for jacket linings.

PROPERTIES

- CHARACTER: Sturdy wool with a diagonal twill weave and little drape.
- WEAVE: Twill.
- WEIGHT: Medium to heavy.
- SPECIAL CONSIDERATIONS: Quality serge garments can last a lifetime.

WORKING WITH

- TO CUT: Use sharp scissors or a rotary cutter and mat.
- HANDLING FOR SEWING: Easy to sew.
- NEEDLES: Universal H, size 80/12.
- THREAD: All-purpose polyester or cotton.
- STITCH LENGTH: 2–2.5mm.
- SEWING MACHINE FEET: Standard.
- INTERFACING/LINING: Optional. Sew-in or fusible interfacings and lightweight linings.

CARE

- WASHING: Dry-clean or hand wash. Read manufacturer's label.
- DRYING: Dry-clean or air-dry.
- IRONING: For best results, use another piece of wool as your underlying surface, place your fabric on top of that with the right side face down, then sandwich it with another wool pressing cloth on top. Use medium heat and steam.
- SHRINKAGE: Moderate.

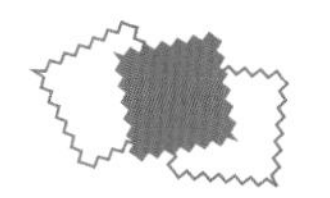

TARTAN

Tartan is the well-known colourful fabric used for Scottish and Irish kilts. It was worn by Celtic tribes, and ancient examples of tartan fabrics have been excavated in central Europe, Scandinavia and China. Tartan is typically a twill weave, with various coloured threads woven at right angles to each other to create intersecting lines of varying widths and shades. It can be woven with any fibre and comes in many weights, although wool is the most common choice. Wool tartan is used for kilts, scarves, shawls, wraps, jackets and some home furnishings.

DID YOU KNOW?

Over many centuries, different tartan patterns and colours developed in different regions of Scotland. Around the time of the Battle of Culloden in 1746, tartans began to signify particular clans and family names. In 1815 Scotland organised a registration process for tartans, which continues today.

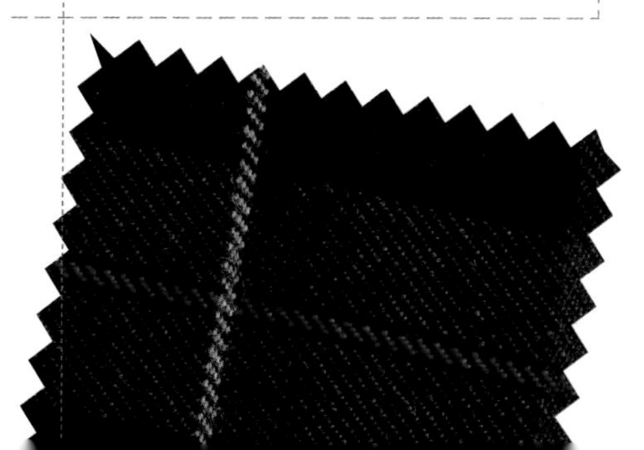

PROPERTIES

- CHARACTER: Colourful plaid, typically used for kilts.
- WEAVE: Twill.
- WEIGHT: Medium.
- SPECIAL CONSIDERATIONS: Comes in varying weights and fibres, though wool is most common.

WORKING WITH

- TO CUT: Use sharp scissors or a rotary cutter and mat.
- HANDLING FOR SEWING: Easy to sew.
- NEEDLES: Universal H of Sharp HJ, sizes 70/10–90/14.
- THREAD: All-purpose polyester or cotton.
- STITCH LENGTH: 2.5mm.
- SEWING MACHINE FEET: Standard.
- INTERFACING/LINING: Line jackets and tailored garments with cotton batiste, voile, organza, chiffon or China silk.

CARE

- WASHING: Dry-clean or hand wash.
- DRYING: Dry-clean or air-dry.
- IRONING: Use medium heat and steam. For best results, use another piece of wool as your underlying surface, place your fabric on top of that with the right side face down, then sandwich it with another wool pressing cloth on top.
- SHRINKAGE: Moderate.

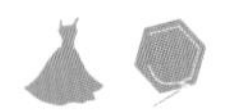

TWEED

Tweed encompasses a large group of rough, woollen, medium-weight fabrics. Most tweeds are twill woven, but patterns can vary greatly with the favourites being houndstooth, striped, tartan and herringbone. With a looser weave than most wools, tweed is flexible yet durable, and is very comfortable to wear. It is used for trousers, skirts, jackets, coats, suits, scarves, wraps, luggage and even shoes. Most tweeds are 100 per cent wool, but when blended with silk the fabric is lightweight and often used for women's summer jackets.

DID YOU KNOW?

It's not entirely clear how the name tweed came about. It may relate to twill, and it's likely the name came from the River Tweed on the Scottish border, which was once a textile centre for wool and tweed production.

PROPERTIES

- CHARACTER: Loose twill weave with varying patterns (herringbone, houndstooth, stripes and tartans are common favourites).
- WEAVE: Twill.
- WEIGHT: Medium.
- SPECIAL CONSIDERATIONS: Flexible and comfortable to wear.

WORKING WITH

- TO CUT: Use sharp scissors or a rotary cutter and mat.
- HANDLING FOR SEWING: Easy to sew.
- NEEDLES: Universal H or Sharp HJ, sizes 70/10–90/14.
- THREAD: All-purpose polyester or cotton.
- STITCH LENGTH: 2–2.5mm.
- SEWING MACHINE FEET: Standard or straight stitch.
- INTERFACING/LINING: Line jackets and tailored garments with cotton batiste, voile, organza, chiffon or China silk.

CARE

- WASHING: Dry-clean or hand wash.
- DRYING: Dry-clean or air-dry.
- IRONING: Use medium heat and steam. For best results, use another piece of wool as your underlying surface, place your fabric on top of that with the right side face down, then sandwich it with another wool pressing cloth on top.
- SHRINKAGE: Moderate.

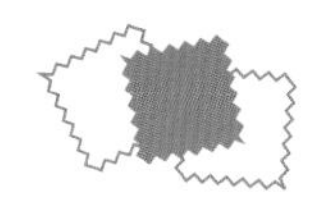

WOOL DOUBLE CLOTH

Double cloth, sometimes called double weave, is a reversible fabric made of two separately woven layers that are joined together by small interconnecting stitches. Unlike double-faced fabric (double-layered fabric that looks the same on both sides and cannot be separated), double cloth layers can be separated with a slight tug. The two layers are often entirely different weaves, designs and/or colours, which makes double cloth the ideal fabric for a unique reversible coat or winter skirt - you end up with two skirts in one!

To sew with double cloth, the layers are pulled apart slightly at the edges, making it possible to sew separate and hidden seams. Double cloth is typically made of wool and wool blends and ranges from lightweight to heavy. Other uses include dresses, capes, tote bags and scarves.

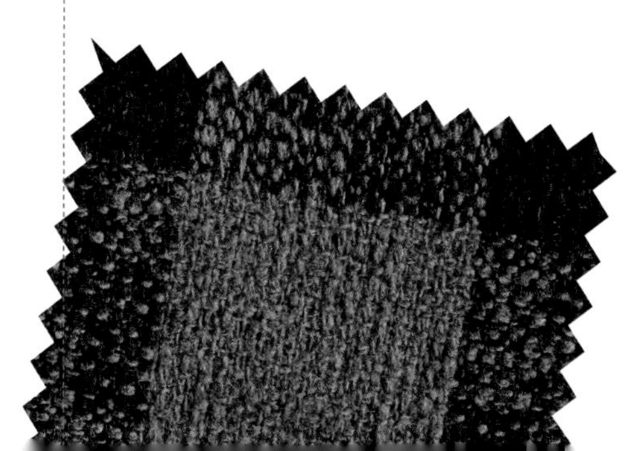

PROPERTIES

- CHARACTER: Two separate layers of woven fabric joined with small interconnecting stitches. The two sides often look different from each other.
- WEAVE: Plain.
- WEIGHT: Lightweight to heavy.
- SPECIAL CONSIDERATIONS: Works well for reversible garments.

WORKING WITH

- TO CUT: Use sharp scissors or a rotary cutter and mat. Use with-nap layout when cutting pattern pieces.
- HANDLING FOR SEWING: Pull layers apart at the edges to sew separate, hidden seams.
- NEEDLES: Universal H and Sharp HM or HJ, sizes 70/10–90/14.
- THREAD: All-purpose polyester or cotton.
- STITCH LENGTH: 2–3mm.
- SEWING MACHINE FEET: Standard or straight stitch.
- INTERFACING/LINING: None needed; the two layers work as a lining itself.

CARE

- WASHING: Dry-clean.
- DRYING: Dry-clean.
- IRONING: Use medium heat and steam. A wool pressing cloth is recommended.
- SHRINKAGE: Fabric may be pre-shrunk using steam from an iron or by sending it to the dry-cleaners.

WOOLLEN

Woollen fabrics are created from short wool fibres that are under 8cm/3in long. They have been carded or pulled straight out from the wool, before the longer fibres are then combed and used for worsted wool. When spun and woven, these short fibres create a unique hairy surface on the fabric. Woollens are soft with a rough texture, and, compared with the smoother-surfaced worsted wools, are easier to sew and cost less, although they can easily pill and snag. Woollens are best used for trousers, skirts, jackets, coats, luggage and shoes. Fabrics in the woollen family include tweed, melton, textured wools and some flannels.

PROPERTIES

- CHARACTER: Slightly hairy surface.
- WEAVE: Twill or plain.
- WEIGHT: Medium to heavy.
- SPECIAL CONSIDERATIONS: Easy to sew and less expensive than worsted.

WORKING WITH

- TO CUT: Use sharp scissors or a rotary cutter and mat.
- HANDLING FOR SEWING: Easy to sew, but can pill and snag.
- NEEDLES: Universal H or Sharp HJ, sizes 70/10–90/14.
- THREAD: All-purpose polyester or cotton.
- STITCH LENGTH: 2–2.5mm.
- SEWING MACHINE FEET: Standard or straight stitch.
- INTERFACING/LINING: Sew-in interfacing. Line jackets and tailored garments with cotton batiste, voile, organza, chiffon or China silk.

CARE

- WASHING: Dry-clean or hand wash.
- DRYING: Dry-clean or air-dry.
- IRONING: Use medium heat and steam. For best results, use another piece of wool as your underlying surface, place your fabric on top of that with the right side face down, then sandwich it with another wool pressing cloth on top.
- SHRINKAGE: Moderate.

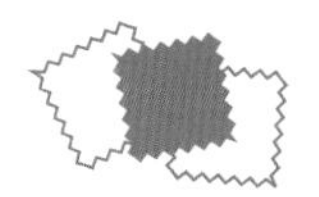

WORSTED

While woollens are made from short, carded fibres, worsted wool goes through a longer refining process to produce a smooth and lustrous finish. Once wool has been carded, the longer fibres are then combed and spun, and the resulting yarn is tightly woven into worsted fabric. Though worsteds cost slightly more than woollens, they are more durable, look wonderful on tailored garments, rarely snag and press well. They have a slight shine, are a lighter weight fabric compared to woollens and are best used for tailored garments, trousers, skirts, dresses, waistcoats, jackets and coats. Fabrics in the worsted family include gabardine, serge, tartan, wool challis and worsted flannel.

PROPERTIES

- CHARACTER: Smooth lustrous surface.
- WEAVE: Twill or plain.
- WEIGHT: Light to medium.
- SPECIAL CONSIDERATIONS: More expensive and difficult to sew with compared to woollens, but they press and drape well.

WORKING WITH

- TO CUT: Use sharp scissors or a rotary cutter and mat. Use with-nap layout when cutting pattern pieces, though the nap may not be obvious.
- HANDLING FOR SEWING: Use wide, 2.5cm seam allowances so they press and lay flat.
- NEEDLES: Universal H or Sharp HJ, sizes 70/10 or 80/12.
- THREAD: All-purpose polyester or cotton.
- STITCH LENGTH: 2–2.5mm.
- SEWING MACHINE FEET: Standard or straight stitch.
- INTERFACING/LINING: Sew-in interfacing. Line jackets and tailored garments with cotton batiste, voile, organza, chiffon or China silk.

CARE

- WASHING: Dry-clean or hand wash.
- DRYING: Dry-clean or air-dry.
- IRONING: Use medium heat and steam. For best results, use another piece of wool as your underlying surface, place your fabric on top of that with the right side face down, then sandwich it with another wool pressing cloth on top.
- SHRINKAGE: Moderate.

LINEN: An Overview

Linen is easily one of my favourite fabrics. It sews well, gives garments a casual, breezy look and it gets more comfortable with every wash. Yes, it wrinkles easily, but the crumpled look only adds to the fabric's character. Linen has a wide range of uses, from clothing to home furnishings, bed sheets and even lampshades. Simply put, linen is timeless and classic.

Linen is a natural fabric, made from the fibres of the flax plant. The tedious manufacturing process that goes into producing linen makes it an expensive fabric, though not as costly as silk. Higher-quality linen should be free from any slubs or knots, and if cost is a concern, less expensive linen blends (sometimes called linen-like or linen-look) are available. These aren't quite as soft as the real thing, but still have the classic linen charm.

Linen is easy to sew with – making it a wonderful choice for beginners – although it can fray excessively and shrinks easily. When folded for long periods of time, the fibres tend to break and the fabric loses colour in the creases, so it's always best to hang linens rather than fold them.

PRODUCTION & PROCESSES

Manufacturing linen is very labour-intensive. The process requires hand picking the flax plant and then tediously sorting the fibres, which is what makes the fabric costly compared with cotton. The best linen in the world comes from Western Europe, with major producers in Ireland, Italy and Belgium. Some bulk manufacturing is done in Eastern Europe and China, though the quality is not as high as that from the leading producers.

Linen comes from fibres found in the stalks of flax plants. When harvested correctly, the flax stalks are picked by hand and cut very close to the root. They are then put through a retting process, where bacteria breaks down the stalk fibres. The optimal method of retting is done in a natural water bath to reduce damaging the stalks, as is common with chemical retting. Once the fibres are softened, they are crushed and sorted according to length and size. The fibres are then spun together and woven or knit into cloth.

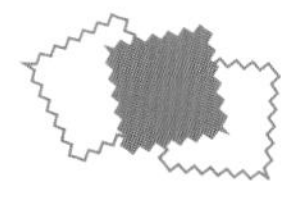

ORGANIC & FAIR TRADE

Organic linen is made from flax plants that are grown free from pesticides and fertilisers. There are many products on the market today labeled 'organic' or 'eco-friendly', however some of these textiles are a blended mix of linen and other fibres. Generally, a fabric cannot be labelled 'linen' or 'pure linen' unless it is 100 per cent linen.

USES

When choosing fabric for your project, select an appropriate weight. Heavier linen works well for garments such as drawstring trousers, skirts, shorts and bags, while lightweight and sheer linen is suitable for blouses, summer dresses, camisole tops and wraps. A thin cotton lining is recommended for sheer garments. Linen can also be used for napkins, tablecloths, bedding, sheets, towels, aprons and some lampshades.

CHARACTERISTICS

- Very comfortable to wear.
- Feels softer with every wash.
- Ideal for breezy summer clothing.
- Easy to sew.
- Frays excessively.
- Shrinks easily.
- Absorbs water well.
- Dries quickly.
- Can look shiny when over-pressed.
- Wrinkles easily.
- Blends well with other natural and synthetic fibres.
- Will lose colour where creases are left for extended periods of time.

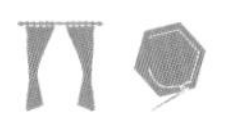

DAMASK and VENISE

Damask is a type of weave commonly used with linen textiles. Woven on a Jacquard loom, the fabric has a patterned image on one side and an inverse image on the other. Fabrics can be monochromatic (a single colour) or woven from multiple shades of yarn and sometimes made from silk fibres as well. Designs range from leaves and plants to Asian-inspired images, geometric shapes and ornate curved spades. The name damask comes from the city of Damascus, Syria, which, during the Middle Ages, was a hot spot for the manufacturing and trading of this type of woven textile.

Venise is a type of damask linen specifically characterised by large floral designs. Its name derives from the sixteenth-century Italian painter, Veronese. Venise is associated with high society and is often used for fine tablecloths and runners.

DID YOU KNOW?

Damask was originally produced as a rich silk fabric, often incorporating gold or silver threads in its design. The modern fabric is available in linen, cotton, worsted wool and man-made fibres.

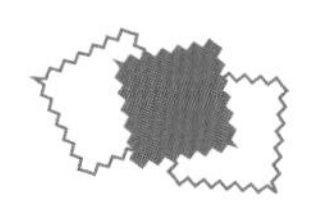

PROPERTIES

- CHARACTER: Patterned image on one side and an inverse image on the other.
- WEAVE: Damask; woven on a Jacquard loom.
- WEIGHT: Light to medium.
- SPECIAL CONSIDERATIONS: Fabric has two 'right' but opposite sides, which gives you more design options.

WORKING WITH

- TO CUT: Use sharp scissors or a rotary cutter and mat.
- HANDLING FOR SEWING: Easy to sew.
- NEEDLES: Universal H or Sharp HJ, sizes 70/10 or 80/12.
- THREAD: All-purpose polyester or cotton.
- STITCH LENGTH: 2–2.5mm.
- SEWING MACHINE FEET: Standard.
- INTERFACING/LINING: None.

CARE

- WASHING: Machine wash. Linens will soften with each wash, so if you prefer a stiffer finish it's best to dry-clean your garments. Either way, it's important to pre-shrink fabric before sewing, since linen shrinks considerably.
- DRYING: Air-dry or normal tumble dry.
- IRONING: Use high heat and steam. A pressing cloth is recommended when ironing on the right side or the fabric may shine.
- SHRINKAGE: Moderate to high; approximately 20 per cent.

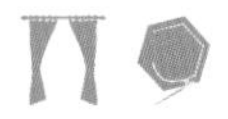

LOOSELY WOVEN

Loosely woven linens are typically plain woven with a wide amount of space between each yarn, which gives the fabric a loose and airy feel. Loosely woven linen is very absorbent and dries quickly, but is prone to excessive fraying, so when pre-washing fabrics, overlock around the edges or stitch the ends together to reduce the fray. Loosely woven linen is used for garments, aprons, bags, kitchen linens and art projects.

Though not typically found in everyday fabric shops, it's likely that you've stumbled upon the following loosely woven linens in their various forms:

BIRD'S EYE: Characterised by a recurring pattern on the right side that resembles small bird's eyes. It is typically used for nappies and sanitary towels.

HUCKABACK: Woven in towel lengths, typically ranging from 40 to 60cm wide. It is often blended with cotton fibres and sometimes has a damask weave or a small dotted pattern on top. Huckaback is used for tablecloths, tea towels and embroidery.

ART LINEN: Has a tight weave of hand-twisted yarns, giving it a very smooth surface and making it ideal for art canvases. After being stretched on a wooden frame, the linen is primed with gesso (a plaster-like paint) to create an absorbent surface for the paint to adhere to. Linen is smoother and finer than cotton canvas and usually costs more.

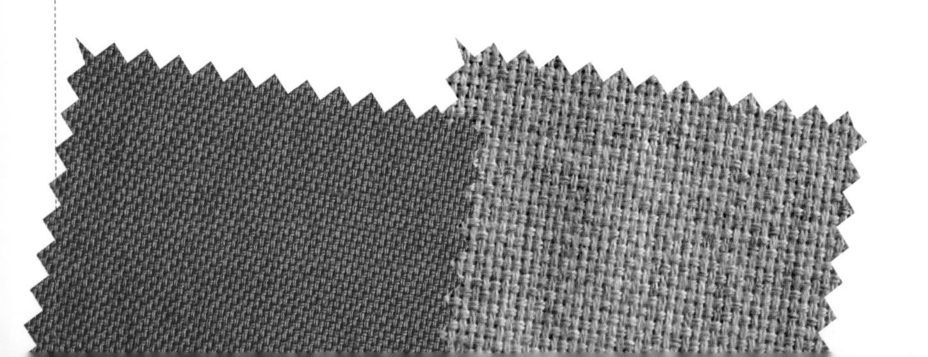

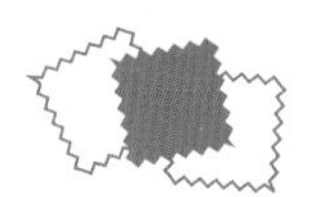

PROPERTIES

- CHARACTER: Very loose plain weave.
- WEAVE: Plain.
- WEIGHT: Medium to heavy.
- SPECIAL CONSIDERATIONS: Can fray excessively. When pre-washing fabrics, overlock around the edges or stitch the ends together to reduce the fray. Trim cut edges of pattern pieces with pinking shears. Finish off seams with an overlocker or zigzag stitch.

CARE

- WASHING: Machine wash. Linens will soften with each wash. If you prefer a stiffer finish it's best to dry-clean your garments.
- DRYING: Air-dry or normal tumble dry.
- IRONING: Use a high heat and steam.
- SHRINKAGE: Moderate to high; approximately 20 per cent.

WORKING WITH

- TO CUT: Use sharp scissors or a rotary cutter and mat.
- HANDLING FOR SEWING: Easy to sew.
- NEEDLES: Universal H or Sharp HJ, sizes 70/10 (lightweight fabrics) or 90/14 (heavy fabrics).
- THREAD: All-purpose polyester or cotton.
- STITCH LENGTH: 2–2.5mm.
- SEWING MACHINE FEET: Standard.
- INTERFACING/LINING: None.

HANDY HINT

Got a beautiful piece of linen in need of a project? Stretch the fabric over a simple handmade wooden frame - stapling the fabric to the backside of the frame - and you have a new piece of artwork to hang on the wall. You can let the print of the fabric shine as its own work of art, or, if that feels too plain, consider painting or stenciling a simple design over the top.

PLAIN WOVEN

Most linen fabrics fall into the plain woven category. They are often a solid colour, come in a wide spectrum of shades and range from very lightweight to heavy. Heavier linen works well for bags and bottom garments, such as drawstring trousers, skirts and shorts. Lightweight and sheer linen is suitable for blouses, summer dresses, camisole tops and wraps. A thin cotton lining is recommended for sheer garments.

Plain-woven linen is not limited to garments; different varieties have other common uses:

BUTCHER'S LINEN: This fabric is stiff and heavy, making it ideal for butcher's aprons.

CAMBRIC: This is the most lightweight and sheer of the plain-woven linens. Cambric is best used for doilies, handkerchiefs, dress collars (usually with added trim or lace), lingerie and lightweight or sheer summer dresses and tops.

CRASH: Sometimes referred to as Russian Crash or Crash Suiting, this linen is coarse and similar to towelling. It is used for table linens, runners, towelling, suiting and needlework.

GLASS TOWELLING: Found in checked and striped patterns of red on white or blue on white, this linen is ideal for drying dishes and glasses because it does not leave lint behind. Compared with damask linen, glass towelling has a more open weave of twisted yarns, making it more water absorbent as well.

HOLLAND: Used for window treatments and lampshades, Holland linen has a sizing layer of oil and starch over the top to keep light from peering through the plain weave.

PILLOWCASE LINEN: A soft, bleached linen used primarily for pillowcases.

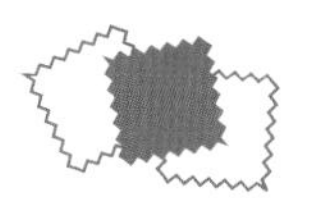

SHEETING: A heavier linen that is used for bed sheets. It is typically wider than your standard shop-size bolts, giving you more fabric to work with. It can also be used for garments.

TOWELLING: This is a general term given to all linen fabric - whether heavy or light, woven loose or tight - that is used to make towels. Linen towelling is very absorbent and dries quickly, and since linen softens with every wash, towelling is the perfect way to use this fibre.

PROPERTIES

- CHARACTER: Plain-woven linen in varying weights.
- WEAVE: Plain.
- WEIGHT: Light to heavy.
- SPECIAL CONSIDERATIONS: Though wrinkling is normal, long-term creases will break down the flax fibres and cause the creased areas to lose colour and turn white. It's best to hang linens rather than fold them. Linen also frays easily and will soften with each wash. Holland linen should not be washed as the starchy finish will wear off.

WORKING WITH

- TO CUT: Use sharp scissors or a rotary cutter and mat.
- HANDLING FOR SEWING: Easy to sew. Can fray excessively. When pre-washing fabrics, overlock around the edges or stitch the ends together to reduce the fray. Trim cut edges of pattern pieces with pinking shears. Finish off seams with an overlocker or zigzag stitch.
- NEEDLES: Universal H or Sharp HJ, sizes 70/10 (lightweight fabrics) or 90/14 (heavy fabrics).
- THREAD: All-purpose polyester or cotton.
- STITCH LENGTH: 2–2.5mm.
- SEWING MACHINE FEET: Standard.
- INTERFACING/LINING: Line lightweight linen garments with cotton batiste or voile.

CARE

- WASHING: Machine wash. Linens will soften with each wash. If you prefer a stiffer finish, it's best to dry-clean your garments. Either way, it's important to pre-shrink fabric before sewing, since linen shrinks considerably.
- DRYING: Air-dry or normal tumble dry.
- IRONING: Use high heat and steam. A pressing cloth is recommended when ironing on the right side or the fabric may shine.
- SHRINKAGE: Moderate to high; approximately 20 per cent.

SUSTAINABLE FABRICS: An Overview

When the industrial revolution hit in the eighteenth century, the manufacturing of textiles grew by leaps and bounds. The cultivation of cotton was improved, factories popped up in major cities and machinery made mass-production of fabrics a possibility. These new machines were improving the human way of life, but little thought was placed on the long-term effects they might have on the planet and its ecosystems. It would take over a hundred years before people started worrying about the environment and discussing more ecologically sustainable ways to produce materials.

Today, the terms 'green' and 'sustainable' are part of our everyday vocabulary. In a nutshell, they mean supporting environmentally friendly products and processes over those that pollute the environment. In the textiles world, the green movement has led to the production of sustainable fabrics that leave the least amount of impact on our environment. Fabrics such as hemp, bamboo, organic cotton and organic wool are produced by methods that reduce the use of chemicals, eliminate waste into the air and water, allow fabrics to biodegrade and provide healthy environments for livestock and workers. Some organic methods use natural enzymes to break down plant fibres rather than chemical processes, and organic wool production limits the number of sheep that can graze in a given pasture to ensure that animals are healthy and well cared for.

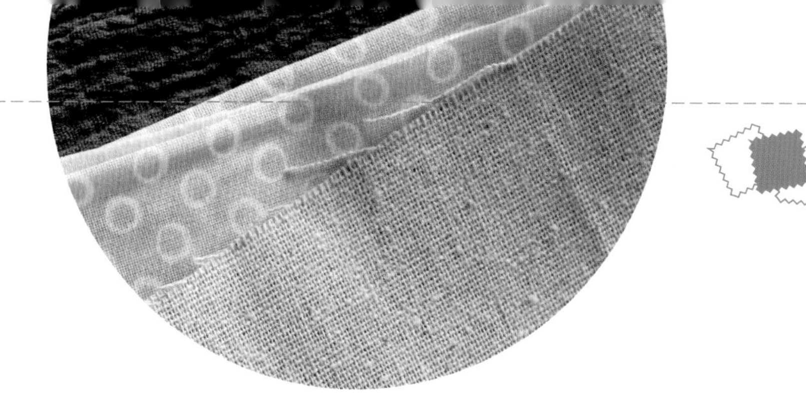

PRODUCTION & PROCESSES

The move towards truly sustainable fabrics is a slow process. It's easy to want to feel good about our impact on the environment, but when money comes into the equation, many manufacturers take the most cost-effective route. This means using pesticides and chemical processes, which are less expensive than sustainable and organic methods but have long-term negative effects on the land and air. Additionally, many cotton farmers and garment workers in the developing world suffer poor working conditions and are paid very low wages. Some manufacturers have switched to fair trade methods, paying workers more for their labour and limiting work hours to more realistic timeframes. New organic fabric companies are popping up every year and are slowly making names for themselves in the retail world.

Certification processes for sustainable fabrics are very drawn-out and can be costly. Governing bodies such as the International Federation of Organic Agriculture Movements (IFOAM) and the Global Organic Textile Standard (GOTS) help regulate the processes in which organic fabrics are made. Farmers and manufacturers must meet strict guidelines before receiving the official 'organic' stamp of approval. The following questions must be answered by organic fabric producers:

Are plants free from pesticides and chemicals? What are the methods and working conditions used for harvesting? Do livestock have room to roam and are conditions humane? Also, what is the output and waste created from the manufacturing of a textile? And finally, are the fabrics biodegradable or reuseable? Don't assume that your fabric has met all these criteria. Always double-check the label to check that it is eco-friendly.

USES

Organic cottons and wools have the same uses as traditional fabrics and should be sewn using the same methods outlined in this book. Fabrics such as hemp and bamboo have their own unique properties and in this section we'll discuss these fabrics and their many uses.

CHARACTERISTICS

- Fabrics are free from the chemicals typically used in textile production.
- Animals used for wool are fed organic food and are raised in organic conditions.
- Farmers and manufacturers typically engage in fair trade practices.
- Fabrics are high-quality and well-made.
- Some fabrics are biodegradable.
- Most plant-fibre fabrics soften when laundered.
- Some fabrics are very water absorbent and dry quickly.

BAMBOO

Bamboo is a plant-fibre fabric made from the pulp of bamboo grass. The fibres are highly absorbent, have great wicking abilities and accept dye well. Bamboo fabric has a smooth surface and can feel very soft, making it a good alternative for people with wool and hemp allergies. Bamboo is insulating in the winter but keeps you cool in the summer, and also has antibacterial qualities that reduce odour-causing bacteria growing on the skin. Simply put, bamboo is a versatile fabric that can be used for a wide range of garments including dresses, skirts, blouses, shirts, shorts, trousers, bags, lightweight jackets and wraps, as well as home furnishing items.

PROPERTIES

- CHARACTER: Very soft; can feel similar to rayon.
- WEAVE: Plain.
- WEIGHT: Light to medium.
- SPECIAL CONSIDERATIONS: Highly absorbent; great wicking abilities; dyes well; softer and cooler than cotton, linen and hemp.

WORKING WITH

- TO CUT: Use sharp scissors or a rotary cutter and mat.
- HANDLING FOR SEWING: Easy to sew.
- NEEDLES: Universal H, sizes 70/10 or 80/12.
- THREAD: All-purpose polyester or cotton.
- STITCH LENGTH: 2–2.5mm.
- SEWING MACHINE FEET: Standard.
- INTERFACING/LINING: Optional.

CARE

- WASHING: Machine wash.
- DRYING: Air-dry or normal tumble dry. Remove from the dryer when slightly damp to reduce wrinkling.
- IRONING: Medium heat and steam.
- SHRINKAGE: Minimal.

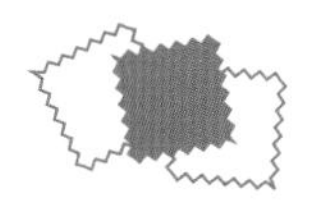

BURLAP and HESSIAN CLOTH

Hessian cloth, referred to as burlap in the US, is a very coarse, loosely woven fabric made of jute or hemp. It is stiff yet bendable, with small rough hairs covering the surface. Because of its durability and open weave, burlap is often used to make storage bags for transporting food and grains. The loose weave allows air to flow through, reducing the spoilage of fruits and vegetables. Burlap is not limited to storage, however, and can also be used to create summer tote bags, interesting wall coverings or perhaps a rugged window treatment.

PROPERTIES

- CHARACTER: Coarse, loosely woven, stiff fabric; typically light brown/tan in colour.
- WEAVE: Plain.
- WEIGHT: Medium to heavy.
- SPECIAL CONSIDERATIONS: Burlap frays very easily.

WORKING WITH

- TO CUT: Use sharp scissors or a rotary cutter and mat.
- HANDLING FOR SEWING: Easy to sew. Treat it just like a heavier-weight cotton or linen.
- NEEDLES: Universal H, sizes 70/10–90/14.
- THREAD: All-purpose polyester or cotton.
- STITCH LENGTH: 2–2.5mm.
- SEWING MACHINE FEET: Standard.
- INTERFACING/LINING: Optional.

CARE

- WASHING: Machine wash, though burlap may lose some stiffness with laundering.
- DRYING: Air-dry or normal tumble dry.
- IRONING: Use high heat and steam.
- SHRINKAGE: Moderate.

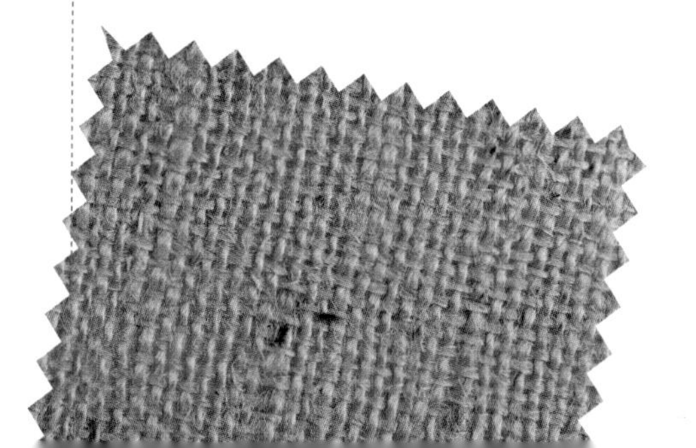

HEMP

Hemp is an eco-friendly plant-fibre fabric that is similar to linen. It softens with each wash and is easy to sew with, yet wrinkles less than linen and is more absorbent. Hemp breathes well and is very comfortable to wear. It comes in varying weights and can be used for loose dresses, skirts, blouses, shirts, waistcoats, jackets and trousers.

Although the term 'hemp' often conjures images of the drug, marijuana, hemp fibres and fabric are far from harmful. In fact, the positive impact of hemp production is quite astounding. The plant can be grown at a rapid rate in many climates and requires very little water. It also acts as a natural weed suppressor, replenishing the surrounding soil with minerals while cleaning toxins from the ground. Hemp has many uses beyond textiles and can also be found in concrete, paper, rope and even fuel.

PROPERTIES

- CHARACTER: Plain woven in varying weights; similar to linen.
- WEAVE: Plain.
- WEIGHT: Light to heavy.
- SPECIAL CONSIDERATIONS: Hemp can fray easily and will soften with each wash.

WORKING WITH

- TO CUT: Use sharp scissors or a rotary cutter and mat.
- HANDLING FOR SEWING: Easy to sew. Can fray excessively. When pre-washing fabrics, overlock around the edges or stitch the ends together to reduce fraying. Trim cut edges of pattern pieces with pinking shears. Finish off seams with an overlocker or zigzag stitch.
- NEEDLES: Universal H or Sharp HJ, sizes 70/10 (lightweight fabrics) or 90/14 (heavy fabrics).
- THREAD: All-purpose polyester or cotton.
- STITCH LENGTH: 2–2.5mm.
- SEWING MACHINE FEET: Standard.
- INTERFACING/LINING: Line lightweight hemp garments with cotton batiste or voile.

CARE

- WASHING: Machine wash. Hemp will soften with each wash. If you prefer a stiffer finish it's best to dry-clean your garments.
- DRYING: Air-dry or normal tumble dry.
- IRONING: Use high heat and steam.
- SHRINKAGE: Moderate to high.

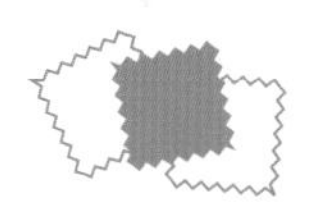

ORGANIC COTTON

In order for cotton fabric to be deemed organic, it must be produced with cotton grown free from pesticides, herbicides, insecticides and fertilisers. When cotton is produced traditionally, the amount of chemicals used account for almost 20 per cent of the world's agriculture pesticides. These pesticides pollute our air, water and can even irritate our skin. Another concern is the issue of the human working environment. Many cotton farmers and garment workers in the developing world suffer poor working conditions and are paid very low wages. There are thousands of deaths a year as a result of pesticide poisoning in developing nations. In response to this, some farmers and garment manufacturers have switched to organic and fair trade methods.

The certification of cotton is a drawn-out process with very strict guidelines. Governing bodies, such as the Global Organic Textile Standard (GOTS) must approve every single step, starting with the land the cotton is grown on (the soil used must be three years removed from any type of chemicals and pesticides). Farmers must keep strict production records detailing their methods used, and they must also be ready for periodic inspections from regulating bodies. Approvals are also needed for methods of transporting the cotton to a mill, weaving the cotton into fabric, bleaching, dyeing and eventually printing. All of these check-points ensure that organic cotton is as environmentally friendly as possible, yet they also increase the fabric's price-tag. As the 'green' movement goes forwards, organic cotton and other certified fibres may become more commonplace and potentially reduce the cost for the consumer.

Organic cotton fabrics are sewn just as you would sew traditional cottons. Refer to the Cotton chapter for detailed sewing information (see pages 12–51).

ORGANIC WOOL

When wool is produced traditionally, livestock may be subject to synthetic pesticides, hormones, genetic engineering and non-organic food, so methods for producing wool that are less harmful to the environment has become a concern for consumers. The certification of organic wool can vary from country to country, however the International Federation of Organic Agriculture Movements (IFOAM) is recognised by 116 countries as being the umbrella organisation for others to fall under.

In the UK, the Soil Association has a list of requirements for wool fabric to be certified as organic. In addition to being void of the traditional pesticides and hormones listed above, livestock used for organic wool must graze on land that is large enough to accommodate the number of animals.

Organic wool fabrics are soft, textured, warm and versatile. Refer to the Wool chapter for detailed sewing information (see pages 82–105).

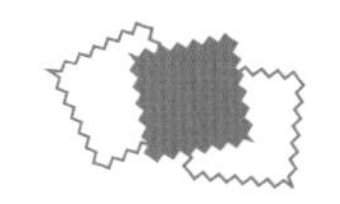

TENCEL

Tencel is the registered name for the fabric Lyocell, which is made from wood pulp cellulose (the structural component in plants and trees). It is an eco-friendly alternative to polyester, nylon, rayon and cotton, and can be knit or woven. The production of Tencel involves non-toxic solvents, does not require bleaching and does not release chemical by-products into the air. However, the wood fibres in Tencel fabric are difficult to dye, which sometimes encourages manufacturers to use chemical treatments that are not environmentally friendly; check the fabric bolt for organic certification. Tencel is comfortable to wear, easy to clean and has properties similar to cotton.

PROPERTIES

- CHARACTER: Feels similar to cotton and rayon; may be knit or woven.
- WEAVE: Plain woven or knit.
- WEIGHT: Lightweight to medium.
- SPECIAL CONSIDERATIONS: Tencel has properties similar to cotton. It has little elasticity and will shrink.

WORKING WITH

- TO CUT: Use sharp scissors or a rotary cutter and mat.
- HANDLING FOR SEWING: Easy to sew. Hold fabric taut with both hands while sewing.
- NEEDLES: Universal H or Sharp HJ, sizes 70/10 or 80/12.
- THREAD: All-purpose polyester or cotton.
- STITCH LENGTH: 2–2.5mm.
- SEWING MACHINE FEET: Standard.
- INTERFACING/LINING: Optional; fusible or sew-in interfacing.

CARE

- WASHING: Machine wash.
- DRYING: Air-dry or low tumble dry. Remove from the dryer when slightly damp to reduce wrinkling.
- IRONING: Medium heat with a damp cloth and steam.
- SHRINKAGE: Moderate.

MANUFACTURED FIBRES: An Overview

It's often said that imitation is the best form of flattery, and in the textiles world, that statement is a fact. With all of the wonders that cotton and wool exhibit, it's only logical that we would use science to develop synthetic fibres that mimic and exceed what natural fibres can offer. These manufactured fibres are often durable, strong, wrinkle-free, retain shape and drape beautifully. Their development has transformed the fashion world, and it's often easier to find synthetic versions of silk in your fabric shop than it is to find the real thing! Of course, cost and manufacturing are big factors, and if it's easier to produce, it's often easier to sell.

But Mother Nature is still queen, and playing copycat comes at a cost. Their strengths aside, many manufactured fibres are also highly flammable, don't breathe well, create static cling and pill. They may be wonder fabrics, but they don't have the same allure as good-quality cotton lawn or nubby dupioni silk.

PRODUCTION & PROCESSES

Manufactured fibres are typically broken down into two categories:

- **SYNTHETIC:** created from petroleum, gas, plastics and liquid chemicals
- **MAN-MADE:** created from wood pulp and plant cellulose

SYNTHETIC

Most synthetic fabrics were developed in the mid-1900s and are today manufactured around the globe. They are inexpensive to produce and are often blended with natural fibres for added comfort and ability. They include acrylic, nylon and polyester.

MAN-MADE

Man-made fibres were developed in the late 1800s and are another inexpensive alternative to natural fibre production. They are not considered synthetic, but since they are manipulated to mimic natural fibres they fall in the manufactured category. Man-made fibres are created from wood and plant cellulose (the structural component in plants and trees). Pulp and cellulose are ground up and mixed with sodium hydroxide, left to dry, and are then mixed with liquid chemicals and formed into filament strands. The strands are used to create yarn and, finally, fabric.

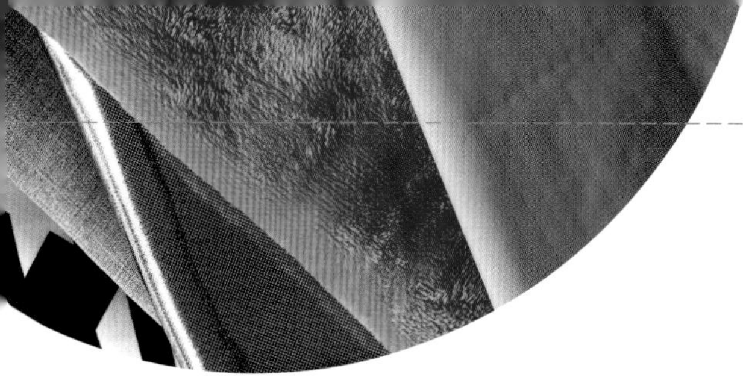

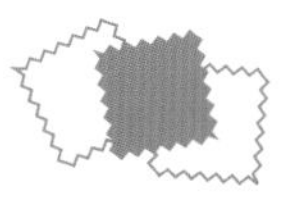

SUSTAINABILITY

Some claim that cotton is good for the environment and that polyester is bad. While polyester is made from plastics, which don't biodegrade, the belief that synthetic fibres are harming the environment is not always true, and when compared to cotton production, some studies have found that polyester may actually have a better impact on the environment. Today, new polyester is often recycled from existing polyester fibres, a process that requires very little water and leaves little waste behind. In the average household, care for polyester garments tends to use less energy, since polyester fabric doesn't need ironing and can be washed in cold water. As consumers, we can support these processes by upcycling, reusing clothing and recycling plastics.

Man-made fibres can also have a positive impact on the environment. Wood cellulose is often harvested using environmentally friendly methods, with pulp coming from closely managed forests (with reforestation programmes in place). Acetate can be biodegradable and sometimes composted, and most of the acetone used in the manufacturing process is recovered.

USES & SELECTING FABRICS

Since manufactured fabrics are meant to imitate natural fibres, their uses are virtually limitless. Synthetic and man-made fibres are used for all types of clothing, home furnishings, outdoor gear, shoes, luggage and accessories.

Many fabric shops have a wider selection of synthetics than they do of their natural fibre counterparts, and may employ their own labelling system, which makes it difficult to decipher what is 'charmeuse silk' versus what is 'nylon'. This book will help you to understand the properties of each so that you can make an educated decision when you get to the cutting counter.

CHARACTERISTICS

- Durable and strong.
- Wrinkle-resistant.
- Comfortable and economical.
- Drapes well and retains shape.
- Easy to care for.
- Easy to handle and sew.
- Very flammable; many fibres melt under an iron.
- Does not breathe well.
- Creates static cling.
- Pills.

ACETATE

Acetate is a man-made fabric created from wood pulp cellulose. The fabric is soft, luxurious and drapes well. In many ways, acetate mimics the look and feel of satin and charmeuse, but costs far less and is resistant to moths and wrinkles. On the other hand, it melts easily. Acetate fabric comes in many forms, from knitted jersey to brocade to all types of satin. In fact, acetate is often used in place of real silk fabrics for wedding gowns and formal attire, but one of the main uses of acetate is as a lining for jackets. The fabric does not absorb moisture easily, but when it does get wet, it dries quickly.

While not truly sustainable, the production of acetate fabric could be considered somewhat eco-friendly. The acetate process was first discovered in the late 1800s by drawing cellulose (the structural component in plants and trees) out of wood pulp and cotton. It was originally used to create plastics and film, but after experimentation in the 1920s, the fibres were spun into a continuous yarn and then turned into fabric. Wood pulp is typically harvested using environmentally friendly methods and comes from closely managed forests (with reforestation programmes in place). Acetate can be biodegradable and sometimes composted, and most of the acetone used in the manufacturing process is recovered. Acetate is therefore a wonderful choice for eco-sensitive consumers.

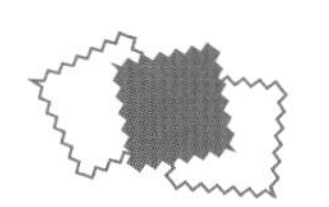

PROPERTIES

- CHARACTER: Looks and feels similar to silk satin and charmeuse.
- WEAVE: Plain, satin or knit.
- WEIGHT: Light to medium.
- SPECIAL CONSIDERATIONS: Resists wrinkles and drapes well, but can melt easily.

WORKING WITH

- TO CUT: Use sharp scissors or a rotary cutter and mat.
- HANDLING FOR SEWING: Sews similar to satin and taffeta.
- NEEDLES: Woven: Universal H or Sharp HJ. Knits: Universal H, Stretch HS, or Ballpoint H SUK.
  Sizes: 60/8–90/14 (varying from lightweight to heavy fabrics).
- THREAD: All-purpose polyester or cotton.
- STITCH LENGTH: 2.5–3mm.
- SEWING MACHINE FEET: Standard, straight stitch or roller.
- INTERFACING/LINING: Is often used as a lining itself.

CARE

- WASHING: Most acetate fabrics can be machine washed, however, consult the manufacturer's care instructions. When in doubt, dry-clean.
- DRYING: Air-dry, tumble dry, or dry-clean. Consult the manufacturer's care instructions.
- IRONING: Low dry heat, as acetate will melt under extreme heat. Use a pressing cloth and never iron directly on the fabric. Avoid steam and water, as they will spot the fabric.
- SHRINKAGE: Minimal.

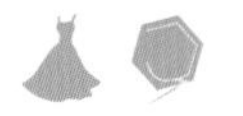

ACRYLIC

Acrylic is a soft, synthetic fabric that is warm without feeling bulky. It dyes, drapes and breathes well; it is also resilient, absorbs moisture, resists wrinkles and can be so soft that it is often used to replace cashmere. However, it can pill, it does not absorb moisture well, tends to absorb odours and can melt easily under high heat.

Acrylic comes in a variety of textures and weaves, and can be used to create knit fabrics, faux fur, wool replacements, felt and water-resistant fabrics. It is often used for dresses, skirts, sweatshirts, sleepwear, childrenswear, costumes and crafts.

Discovered by the DuPont chemical company in the 1940s, fabric fibres are made from the liquid chemical acrylonitrile and are then dry-spun or wet-spun to create yarn. These yarns are stretched and then knit or woven into fabric. While exposure to high levels of acrylonitrile can be toxic, small doses of the chemical break down quickly into the environment, so acrylic is often categorised as eco-friendly, although some people dispute that.

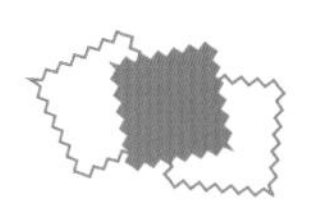

PROPERTIES

- CHARACTER: Soft and lightweight. Acrylic fabric is warm without being heavy.
- WEAVE: Plain or knit.
- WEIGHT: Light to medium.
- SPECIAL CONSIDERATIONS: Acrylic tends to dull scissors and needles quickly, so replace needles more frequently throughout your project.

WORKING WITH

- TO CUT: Use sharp scissors or a rotary cutter and mat.
- HANDLING FOR SEWING: Sews much like knits and woollen fabrics.
- NEEDLES: Woven: Universal H or Sharp HJ. Knits: Universal H, Stretch HS or Ballpoint H SUK.
  Sizes: 60/8–90/14 (varying from lightweight to heavy fabrics).
- THREAD: All-purpose polyester or cotton.
- STITCH LENGTH: 1.5–2.5mm.
- SEWING MACHINE FEET: Standard, straight stitch or roller.
- INTERFACING/LINING: Optional.

CARE

- WASHING: Machine wash.
- DRYING: Tumble dry on low heat.
- IRONING: Very low dry heat; a pressing cloth is recommended. Avoid steam and water, as they will spot the fabric.
- SHRINKAGE: Minimal.

LAMÉ

Lamé has a very individual look – it's a shiny, metallic fabric that drapes, glides and at times looks iridescent. Whether kitsch or classy, one thing is certain – lamé makes a statement. You'll find the synthetic fabric in a variety of colours, from gold to green to vibrant hot pink. Typically, lamé is a blend of metallic and natural fibres that are knit or woven (lightweight woven being the most common). Since wovens can feel scratchy to the skin, they are often lined with charmeuse, organza or synthetic silk. Some fabric shops carry stretch lamé, which is slightly thicker and softer on the wrong side.

Lamé is often used for theatrical costumes, variety show stage decorations, curtains, fancy dress costumes and other over-the-top looks. It can fray and snag easily, and the metallic fibres can dull your scissors and sewing needles.

HANDY HINT

Though more difficult to sew with than some other synthetics, woven and stretch lamé fabrics are a colourful choice for kids' costumes. The flashy fabric can work well as a billowy princess gown, superhero cape or a funky leotard (using stretch lamé). Line woven lamé with simple acetate or polyester fabric or it will feel scratchy against the skin.

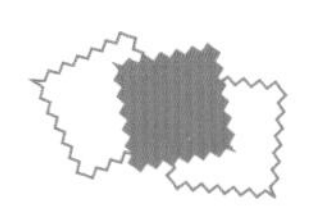

PROPERTIES

- CHARACTER: Lightweight metallic fabric. It is available in a variety of colours, but typically comes in silver, gold and copper.
- WEAVE: Plain.
- WEIGHT: Lightweight.
- SPECIAL CONSIDERATIONS: Woven lamé can be difficult to sew with. It can feel scratchy, frays and snags easily, and the metallic fibres can dull your scissors and sewing needles.

WORKING WITH

- TO CUT: Use sharp scissors or a rotary cutter and mat.
- HANDLING FOR SEWING: To avoid excessive fraying, do not cut the fabric until you are ready to sew. Use weights when cutting out patterns and use pins only in the seam allowances. Change needles frequently to avoid snagging the fabric.
- NEEDLES: Woven: Universal H or Sharp HM or HJ.
  Knits: Stretch HS.
  Sizes: 60/8–70/10.
- THREAD: Lightweight all-purpose polyester or,cotton.
- STITCH LENGTH: 2–2.5mm.
- SEWING MACHINE FEET: Standard, straight stitch or roller.
- INTERFACING/LINING: Some lamé can be scratchy and irritating to the skin. Line garments with a thin layer of silk charmeuse, organza or China silk.

CARE

- WASHING: Dry-clean or hand wash. Consult the manufacturer's care instructions.
- DRYING: Dry-clean or air-dry. Consult the manufacturer's care instructions.
- IRONING: Very low dry heat. A pressing cloth is recommended. Avoid steam and water, as they will spot the fabric. Lamé becomes damaged with improper pressing, so always test the fabric first.
- SHRINKAGE: Minimal.

MICROFIBRE

Microfibre fabrics are made from very fine synthetic fibres such as polyester, rayon, acrylic and nylon. They typically look and feel similar to suede, but can also resemble leather, velvet and chiffon. The discerning factor between microfibre and other synthetic fabrics is that the fibres are so small that they produce a tightly woven or knit fabric that measures less than 1 denier.

Microfibre is very popular when it comes to home decorating and upholstery. It is fairly easy to clean, slow to absorb liquids and resists wear, although it's not without faults. The processes used to create microfibres are not eco-friendly, so this should be a consideration for eco-conscious consumers when purchasing fabrics.

Aside from upholstery, microfibre fabrics can also be used for garments such as trousers, shorts, skirts, jackets, raincoats and other casualwear.

DID YOU KNOW?

Think of the last sofa you sat on. Was it soft and velvety? Smooth like suede? Did your spilled drink wipe up fairly quickly? Yes? Then it's likely you lounged on microfibre. In fact, it's difficult these days to find sofas, chairs and ottomans that are not made from such fabrics. Microfibre is very durable, comfortable and child friendly.

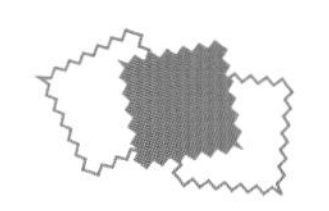

PROPERTIES

- CHARACTER: Typically soft like suede but can also resemble leather, velvet and chiffon.
- WEAVE: Knit or woven.
- WEIGHT: Light to medium.
- SPECIAL CONSIDERATIONS: The processes used to create microfibres are not eco-friendly and often pollute the environment.

WORKING WITH

- TO CUT: Use sharp scissors or a rotary cutter and mat.
- HANDLING FOR SEWING: Microfibres will dull your scissors and rotary cutter quickly. Fabric pens are useful for tracing patterns, but may leave permanent marks on the fabric; tailor's chalk is a better option. Always use a new needle when starting your project.
- NEEDLES: Universal H or Sharp HM or HJ, sizes 60/8 and 70/10.
- THREAD: Lightweight all-purpose polyester or cotton.
- STITCH LENGTH: 1.5–2mm.
- SEWING MACHINE FEET: Standard, straight stitch or roller.
- INTERFACING/LINING: Lightweight sew-in or fusible interfacing.

CARE

- WASHING: Machine wash. Washing will soften and relax the fabric.
- DRYING: Normal tumble dry.
- IRONING: Low dry heat. A pressing cloth is recommended. Always test press on a scrap of fabric.
- SHRINKAGE: Minimal.

MINKY

Minky fabric is an ultra soft imitation of mink fur (one of the softest animal furs). Created from microfibres, minky fabric is often used to make baby blankets and comes in a spectrum of colours and a variety of textures and patterns, from dots and lines to animal prints. Minky is an ideal choice for baby projects such as toys, blankets, quilt backings and clothing.

PROPERTIES

- CHARACTER: Ultra soft and plush; feels similar to cashmere and real mink fur. Very smooth on the wrong side.
- WEAVE: Woven with pile.
- WEIGHT: Medium.
- SPECIAL CONSIDERATIONS: Minky leaves fuzzy debris behind, so clean your scissors, needle plate and bobbin case often.

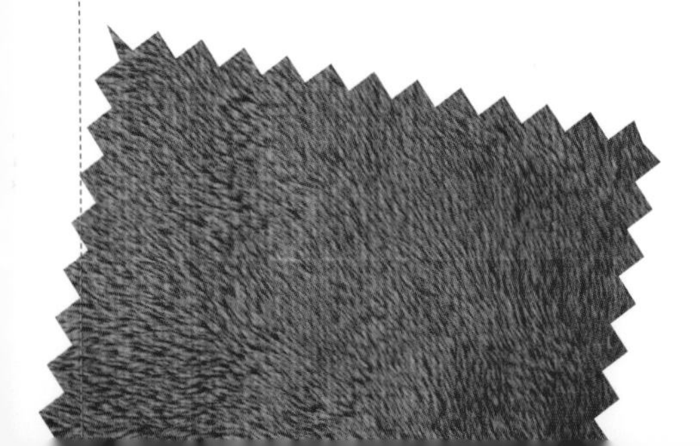

WORKING WITH

- TO CUT: Use sharp scissors or a rotary cutter and mat. Use with-nap layout when cutting pattern pieces.
- HANDLING FOR SEWING: Test your stitching before starting a project. When you can, sew in the direction of the nap. To avoid slipping, pin your fabrics well (pins will not damage the fabric). When sewing with two different fabrics, keep the minky layer on the bottom as it will feed better.
- NEEDLES: Universal H or Sharp HM or HJ, sizes 70/10 and 80/12.
- THREAD: All-purpose polyester or cotton.
- STITCH LENGTH: 2.5–3mm.
- SEWING MACHINE FEET: Standard, straight stitch or walking foot.
- INTERFACING/LINING: Satin or charmeuse are often used as a lining to create plush baby blankets.

CARE

- WASHING: Machine wash.
- DRYING: Normal tumble dry.
- IRONING: Low heat and steam. Place a towel down on your ironing surface, then place the fabric on top with the pile facing down and iron on the underside.
- SHRINKAGE: Very minimal.

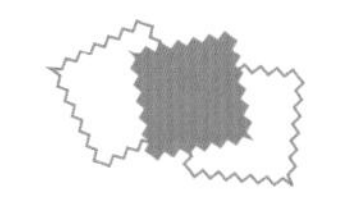

NYLON

Nylon is a lightweight, durable, synthetic fabric made from petroleum products. It was developed by the DuPont company in the 1930s as a replacement for silk. Nylon comes in a variety of weights and colours, and can be knit or woven. It can be as sheer as tights and chiffon, or as tightly woven as water-resistant tent fabric. This wonder fabric is used for dresses, blouses, cagoules, rain ponchos, casualwear, swimwear, leotards and jackets.

HANDY HINT

Fabrics such as ripstop nylon don't fray, and using them will save time when sewing. Check the fabric bolt or run your finger over the cut fabric edge to see if it starts to fray. Online shops tend to have the best selection of non-fray nylons.

PROPERTIES

- CHARACTER: Very durable and strong, typically lightweight.
- WEAVE: Woven or knit.
- WEIGHT: Lightweight to medium.
- SPECIAL CONSIDERATIONS: Woven nylons will fray. Nylon can pill and retain static electricity.

WORKING WITH

- TO CUT: Use sharp scissors or a rotary cutter and mat. Nylon will dull scissors and needles quickly.
- HANDLING FOR SEWING: Always start with a fresh needle and change throughout your project.
- NEEDLES: Woven: Universal H or Sharp HM or HJ.
  Knits: Stretch HS or Ballpoint H SUK.
  Sizes: 60/8–90/14 (varying from lightweight to heavy fabrics).
- THREAD: All-purpose polyester or cotton-covered polyester.
- STITCH LENGTH: 2.5–3mm.
- SEWING MACHINE FEET: Standard, straight stitch or walking foot.
- INTERFACING/LINING: Varies depending on fabric weight and garment design.

CARE

- WASHING: Machine wash.
- DRYING: Normal tumble dry.
- IRONING: Always test press. Use a low dry heat. A pressing cloth is recommended.
- SHRINKAGE: Minimal.

POLYESTER

Polyester is likely the most popular synthetic fabric of our time. It's often slippery with a bit of sheen and is wrinkle-free, durable, strong, resists mildew, dries quickly, retains shape well and doesn't shrink.

Developed in Britain in the 1940s, polyester is made from synthesised polymers (molecules with the highest molecular weight and a long repeating chain of smaller monomers). Sometimes referred to as PET (polyethylene terephthalate), it can be found in many everyday items, such as bottles and other plastics. When used as a fabric, polyester can be knit or woven, and is often blended with other natural fibres to create a variety of weights. Polyester is versatile, inexpensive and readily available. It is used for all types of clothing - casualwear, dressy designs, suits, jackets, skirts, trousers, shorts and cagoules - as well as bedding and home furnishings.

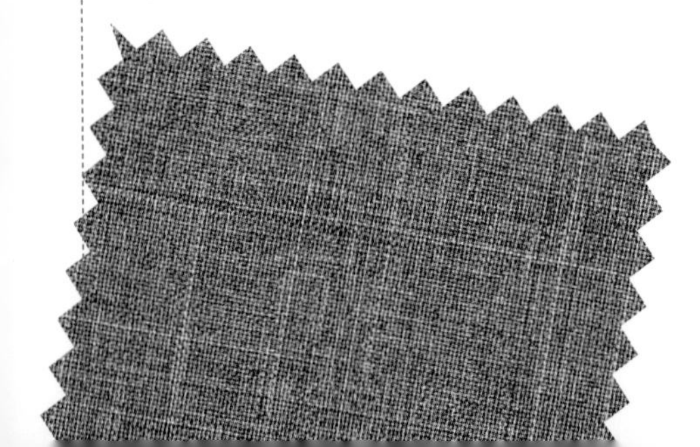

PROPERTIES

- CHARACTER: Slippery with a bit of shine.
- WEAVE: Woven or knit.
- WEIGHT: Lightweight to heavy.
- SPECIAL CONSIDERATIONS: Polyester is wrinkle-free, durable, strong, resists mildew, dries quickly, retains shape well and doesn't shrink.

WORKING WITH

- TO CUT: Use sharp scissors or a rotary cutter and mat.
- HANDLING FOR SEWING: Synthetic fibres tend to dull needles and scissors, so change sewing needles frequently.
- NEEDLES: Woven: Universal H or Sharp HM or HJ.
  Knits: Universal H, Stretch HS, or Ballpoint H-SUK.
  Sizes: 60/8–90/14 (varying from lightweight to heavy fabrics).
- THREAD: All-purpose polyester or cotton-covered polyester.
- STITCH LENGTH: 2.5–3mm.
- SEWING MACHINE FEET: Standard, straight stitch or walking foot.
- INTERFACING/LINING: Varies depending on fabric weight or garment design.

CARE

- WASHING: Machine wash.
- DRYING: Normal tumble dry.
- IRONING: Always test press. Use a low dry heat.
- SHRINKAGE: Minimal to none.

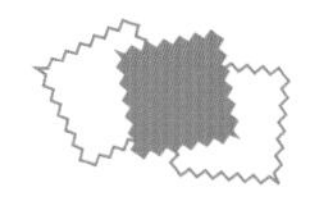

RAYON (Viscose)

Like acetate, rayon (also known as viscose rayon) is a man-made fibre created from wood pulp cellulose. Developed in the late 1800s as an alternative to silk, rayon is versatile, absorbent, inexpensive, colours well and drapes beautifully. On the down side, it doesn't age well, fades, creates static electricity, pills and shrinks. Although it is sometimes given a bad reputation for being cheap, rayon is a beautiful textile. It works well for dresses, skirts, blouses, lingerie, jackets and suits, and also works well for linings.

PROPERTIES

- CHARACTER: Slippery and lightweight. Drapes beautifully.
- WEAVE: Woven or knit.
- WEIGHT: Light to medium.
- SPECIAL CONSIDERATIONS: Versatile and absorbent but pills and doesn't age well.

WORKING WITH

- TO CUT: Use sharp scissors or a rotary cutter and mat.
- HANDLING FOR SEWING: Synthetic fibres tend to dull needles and scissors.
- NEEDLES: Woven: Universal H or Sharp HJ. Knits: Universal H, Stretch HS, Ballpoint H SUK. Sizes: 60/8–90/14 (varying from lightweight to heavy fabrics).
- THREAD: All-purpose polyester or cotton.
- STITCH LENGTH: 2.5–3mm.
- SEWING MACHINE FEET: Standard, straight stitch or roller.
- INTERFACING/LINING: Is often used as a lining itself.

CARE

- WASHING: Most rayon fabrics can be machine-washed, but consult the manufacturer's care instructions. When in doubt, dry-clean.
- DRYING: Air-dry, tumble dry, or dry-clean. Consult the manufacturer's care instructions.
- IRONING: Medium dry heat. Use a pressing cloth and never iron directly on the fabric. Ironing the fabric may cause shine. Avoid steam and water, as they will spot the fabric.
- SHRINKAGE: Moderate.

PART TWO:
KNIT FABRICS

An Overview

I would say that at least 60 per cent of my wardrobe is made up of knit clothing. Why? Because knit items are comfortable and casual; they can be dressed up or down, are inexpensive and they stretch. Knit fabrics can be used to make leggings, casual dresses, swimsuits and the perfect V-neck T-shirt. If you've had a fear of sewing with knits, then it's time to put those days behind you – just pick up an old T-shirt or a metre of jersey knit and see where it takes you!

PRODUCTION & PROCESSES

Knit fabrics are created in much the same way as a hand-knitted scarf – with yarns linked together by connecting loops using needles – but the yarns are much more narrow than those used to create a jumper. Look closely at a T-shirt and you'll see that it is comprised of tiny loops and ribs. Industrial knitting machines are used to create two types of knit fabrics: weft or warp. Weft knitting uses one continuous yarn with machines running horizontally across the fabric, and warp knitting involves multiple needles and runs vertically. Weft knits, such as jersey and interlock, are more commonly used for sewing and fashion than warp knits, such as tricot and raschel.

Knits are made from all types of fibres including natural, man-made and other blends. They vary in weight and elasticity and are produced globally. Concerns over organic processes and fair trade issues relate back to the fibre content of the fabric.

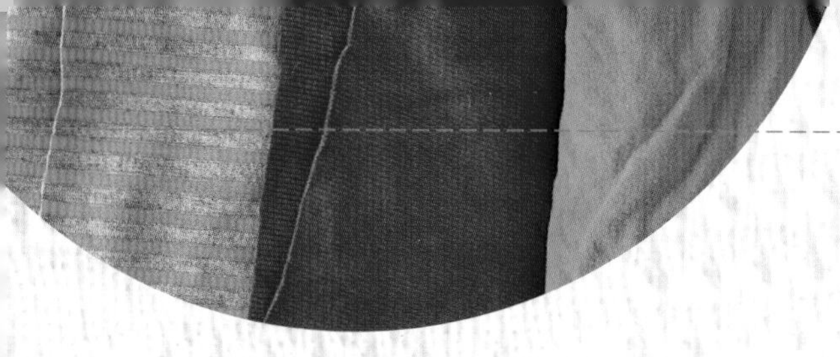

Fashion 

Home furnishing 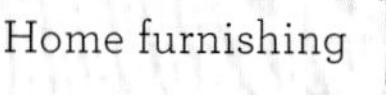

Craft/Misc 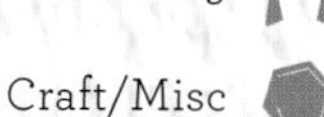

USES & SELECTING FABRICS

Knit fabrics are extremely versatile and can be used to create all types of garments as well as bags, bed sheets and other home furnishing items.

Different knit fabrics have distinct characteristics, so when making a selection it's important to bear these unique behaviours in mind. While knits are known for stretching, some have very little stretch, such as double-knit fabric, and are known as 'stable knits'. Stretchy knits are known as 'unstable knits' and can be categorised even further into two-way or four-way stretch (depending on how many directions the fabric will stretch). Elastane is an amazing unstable, four-way stretch knit, which can stretch up to seven times its length and bounce right back to its original shape, making it the perfect choice for swimsuits and leotards. This section outlines the most commonly used knit fabrics, with details on what makes each one unique.

CHARACTERISTICS

- Wide range of elasticity.
- Categorised as 'Stable' or 'Unstable', and two- or four-way stretch.
- Very comfortable to wear.
- Easy to care for.
- Versatile.
- Some knits retain shape well.
- Some knits curl up at the edges.
- Fabric is easily damaged by seam-ripping.
- Fabrics are knit from all types of fibres.

DOUBLE KNIT

Double knit is a double-faced, thick and stable knit fabric that retains shape well but has little stretch. With two faces, there is no 'wrong' side to the fabric. The textile is knit with a set of double needles to create two layers of fabric that are joined by interlocking stitches. Found in a variety of fibres (wool, cotton, rayon and polyester), double-knit is a heavy fabric that works well for jackets, coats, cardigans, tunic tops, trousers, skirts and hats.

PROPERTIES

- CHARACTER: Double-faced/reversible, thick knit.
- WEIGHT: Heavy.
- STABILITY: Stable knit with little to no stretch.
- SPECIAL CONSIDERATIONS: Double knit has little stretch, which makes it easier to sew with compared to other knits. It also retains shape well.

WORKING WITH

- TO CUT: Use sharp scissors or a rotary cutter and mat.
- HANDLING FOR SEWING: Let the machine feed the fabric naturally; do not pull, tug or stretch the fabric.
- NEEDLES: Universal H, sizes 70/10–90/14.
- THREAD: All-purpose polyester or cotton.
- STITCH LENGTH: 2.5–3mm.
- SEWING MACHINE FEET: Standard or straight stitch.
- INTERFACING/LINING: Fusible or sew-in interfacings for garment details, collars, etc. Knit fabric lining is optional.

CARE

- WASHING: Consult the manufacturer's care instructions. Some natural fibres should be dry-cleaned and some synthetics can be machine washed.
- DRYING: Consult the manufacturer's care instructions.
- IRONING: Use medium heat and steam.
- SHRINKAGE: Minimal to moderate, depending on the fibre content (cotton double knit will shrink more than polyester).

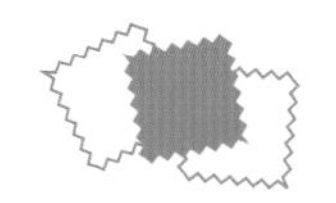

FLEECE

Fleece is an extremely soft knit fabric with fuzzy pile on one or both sides that mimics the fleece of a sheep or goat. It is a versatile fabric and comes in a wide range of colours and prints. Typically knitted with polyester or a blend of natural/synthetic fibres, the wool-like fabric has wonderful wicking abilities, making it ideal for outdoor adventure clothing. Fleece is lightweight yet warm, and it is also inexpensive, readily available and easy to sew with. Fleece fabric can be broken down into the following categories:

LIGHTWEIGHT MICRO FLEECE: A thin fleece that is often fuzzy on both sides. It is used for lightweight jacket linings, leggings, scarves and shirts.

MEDIUM-WEIGHT POLARTEC: A popular choice for outdoor adventure gear. It's warm without being bulky, is fuzzy on both sides and can be worn in all seasons. It is used for hats, mittens, waistcoats, jackets, blankets and linings.

ANTI-PILL FLEECE: Has a finish on the right side of the fabric that prevents it from pilling and balling up over time, as many inexpensive fleeces have a tendency to do. It's worth the extra investment, since a pilling fleece can spoil the time and effort that's gone into your project.

SWEATSHIRT FLEECE: Smooth on one side with a fuzzy nap on the other side. It comes in many weights, colours and prints. When used for sweatshirts and jackets, it's typically paired with knit ribbing for the cuffs and waistband. ▶

HANDY HINT

Although it may not always seem like it, fleece does have a right and wrong side and the nap has a specific direction, so it's important to determine these characteristics before cutting and sewing or you may end up with a garment that looks mismatched. With printed fleece, the more vibrant side is typically the right side, and with solids the wrong side usually looks denser, like wool felt. If you're uncertain, wash and dry the fabric a few times and use the side that looks nicer as the right side. Before cutting, use erasable chalk to mark the wrong side of the fabric with an 'X'.

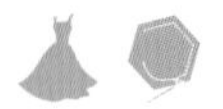

FLEECE continued

PROPERTIES

- CHARACTER: Extremely soft pile on one or both sides.
- WEIGHT: Light to medium.
- STABILITY: Stable knit with minimal stretch.
- SPECIAL CONSIDERATIONS: Easy to sew; great for beginners. Fleece doesn't fray, so edges can be left raw and unfinished.

WORKING WITH

- TO CUT: Sharp scissors work best. If fabric is thick, cut through one layer at a time. Use with-nap layout when cutting pattern pieces.
- HANDLING FOR SEWING: Mark the wrong side of the fabric with chalk to help identify each side when sewing. When you can, sew in the direction of the nap or pile. Let the machine feed the fabric naturally; do not pull, tug or stretch the fabric.
- NEEDLES: Universal H or Stretch HS, sizes 70/10–90/14.
- THREAD: 100 per cent polyester.
- STITCH LENGTH: 3–4mm.
- SEWING MACHINE FEET: Standard, straight stitch, roller or embroidery foot.
- INTERFACING/LINING: None.

CARE

- WASHING: Machine wash in cool water.
- DRYING: Normal tumble dry. Do not dry-clean.
- IRONING: The fabric can melt under heat. Use low heat, steam and a pressing cloth.
- SHRINKAGE: Minimal to none.

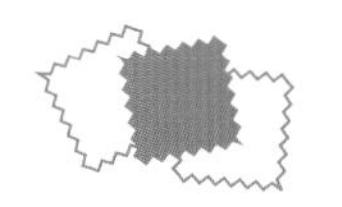

INTERLOCK

Interlock is easily one of the most common knit fabrics used by home and industrial sewers. As the name implies, interlock is made of interlocking stitches to create a double-sided fabric (similar in concept to double-knit, but not as thick and with more stretch).

Interlock is easy to print on and the double-face makes it easy to sew, since there's no wrong or right side. It can be made from wool, cotton, silk, polyester and nylon, with cotton and polyester being the most common. Polyester interlock will pill with time and washing, though it is very accessible and costs less than cotton. Interlock is used for all types of clothing: shirts, skirts, dresses, tunic tops, casualwear, leggings, trousers, shorts, sleepwear, hats and childrenswear.

PROPERTIES

- CHARACTER: Double-sided knit with two 'right' sides. Not as thick as double-knit but heavier than jersey.
- WEIGHT: Light to medium.
- STABILITY: Stable knit with minimal two-way stretch.
- SPECIAL CONSIDERATIONS: A very easy knit to sew with; great for beginners.

WORKING WITH

- TO CUT: Use sharp scissors or a rotary cutter and mat. Fabric does not curl at the edges but will lay flat.
- HANDLING FOR SEWING: Don't pull, tug or stretch the fabric; let the machine feed the fabric naturally.
- NEEDLES: Universal H, Ballpoint H-SUK, Stretch HS, sizes 70/10–90/14.
- THREAD: All-purpose polyester or cotton.
- STITCH LENGTH: 2.5–3mm.
- SEWING MACHINE FEET: Standard or Teflon.
- INTERFACING/LINING: Lightweight fusible or sew-in interfacings. Knit fabric lining is optional.

CARE

- WASHING: Machine wash (cotton and polyester), dry-clean (wool and silk).
- DRYING: Tumble dry (cotton and polyester), dry-clean (wool and silk).
- IRONING: Medium to high heat and steam.
- SHRINKAGE: Fabric will shrink according to fibre content (i.e. cotton will shrink more than polyester).

JERSEY KNIT

Next to interlock, jersey is the other most common knit fabric when it comes to sewing and fashion. It is a plain, single-knit fabric with moderate stretch, and the edges curl up to the right side, which makes it easy to identify the right and wrong side. The fabric is made entirely of purl stitches, so the right side is very smooth and the back looks like a tightly knitted jumper of miniature purl stitches. Jersey can be made from wool, cotton, silk, polyester and nylon, but cotton is the most accessible of the fibre options. Wool is warm, but the more inexpensive fabrics can feel itchy. Polyester will pill with time and washing, and silk is the most expensive jersey, but drapes nicely. Jersey can be used to make T-shirts, skirts, dresses, leggings, trousers, shorts, hats, childrenswear and pretty much anything else you can think of!

PROPERTIES

- CHARACTER: Single knit with narrow lengthwise ribs.
- WEIGHT: Light to medium.
- STABILITY: Unstable knit with two-way and sometimes four-way stretch.
- SPECIAL CONSIDERATIONS: Jersey stretches less than most other knits, unless it is blended with elastane.

WORKING WITH

- TO CUT: Use sharp scissors or a rotary cutter and mat. Fabric will curl up to the right side at the edges.
- HANDLING FOR SEWING: Don't pull, tug or stretch the fabric; let the machine feed the fabric naturally.
- NEEDLES: Universal H, Ballpoint H-SUK, Stretch HS, sizes 70/10–90/14.
- THREAD: All-purpose polyester or cotton.
- STITCH LENGTH: 2.5–3mm.
- SEWING MACHINE FEET: Straight stitch or Teflon.
- INTERFACING/LINING: Lining is optional; lightweight fusible or sew-in interfacings work best.

CARE

- WASHING: Machine wash (cotton and polyester), dry-clean (wool and silk).
- DRYING: Tumble dry (cotton and polyester), dry-clean (wool and silk).
- IRONING: Medium to high heat and steam.
- SHRINKAGE: Fabrics will shrink according to fibre content.

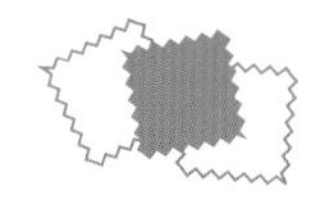

PIQUÉ

Piqué is used to make the quintessential polo shirt. Similar to woven piqué, knit piqué has a raised diamond or waffle-like effect on the surface. It has little stretch and is typically made from cotton. It is used for polo shirts, polo dresses, tops and other breathable knit garments.

PROPERTIES

- CHARACTER: Diamond or waffle-like effect on the fabric's surface.
- WEIGHT: Light to medium.
- STABILITY: Stable with little stretch.
- SPECIAL CONSIDERATIONS: Can be sewn in a similar way to wovens.

WORKING WITH

- TO CUT: Use sharp scissors or a rotary cutter and mat.
- HANDLING FOR SEWING: Easy to sew.
- NEEDLES: Universal H, size 70/10 or 80/12.
- THREAD: All-purpose polyester or cotton.
- STITCH LENGTH: 2.5–3mm.
- SEWING MACHINE FEET: Standard or straight stitch.
- INTERFACING/LINING: Lightweight fusible or sew-in interfacings. Knit fabric lining is optional.

CARE

- WASHING: Machine wash.
- DRYING: Normal tumble dry or air-dry.
- IRONING: Medium to high heat and steam.
- SHRINKAGE: Moderate.

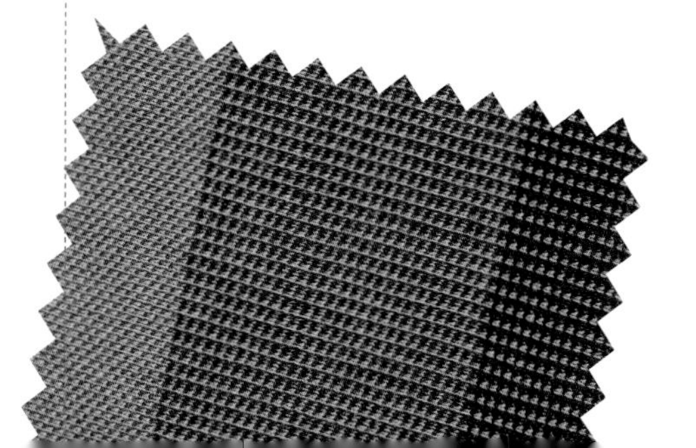

POINTELLE

Pointelle is a soft, lightweight, ribbed knit fabric with dainty cut-out patterns on the right side. The delicate fabric is created by unlooping certain stitches into small recurring shapes such as diamonds, flowers or zigzag formations. Pointelle is cute, feminine and used for baby clothing, pyjamas, camisole tops, T-shirts and some lightweight dresses.

PROPERTIES

- CHARACTER: Soft knit with dainty cut-out patterns on the right side.
- WEIGHT: Light.
- STABILITY: Unstable knit with two-way stretch.
- SPECIAL CONSIDERATIONS: Fabric will curl up to the right side at the edges.

WORKING WITH

- TO CUT: Use sharp scissors or a rotary cutter and mat.
- HANDLING FOR SEWING: Don't pull, tug or stretch the fabric; let the machine feed the fabric naturally.
- NEEDLES: Universal H, Ballpoint H-SUK, Stretch HS, sizes 70/10–90/14.
- THREAD: All-purpose polyester or cotton.
- STITCH LENGTH: 2.5–3mm.
- SEWING MACHINE FEET: Straight stitch or Teflon.
- INTERFACING/LINING: Lightweight fusible or sew-in interfacings. Knit fabric lining is optional.

CARE

- WASHING: Machine wash.
- DRYING: Tumble dry.
- IRONING: Medium to high heat and steam.
- SHRINKAGE: Fabrics will shrink according to fibre content (i.e. cotton will shrink more than polyester).

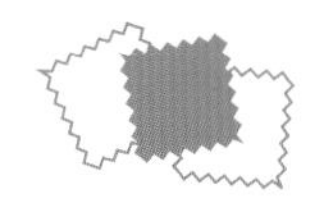

RASCHEL

Raschel is a stable knit polyester fabric that resembles hand-knitted or crocheted fabric or lace. Designs are typically machine knit and range from large ornate florals to small geometric patterns. Like hand-crocheted blankets, raschel is a very porous fabric with visible holes, so garments often require an undershirt or semi-attached lining. Appropriate designs include tunic tops, cardigans, jackets and dresses.

PROPERTIES

- CHARACTER: Hand-crocheted look.
- WEIGHT: Light to medium.
- STABILITY: Stable with little to no stretch.
- SPECIAL CONSIDERATIONS: The fabric has little to no stretch and pills over time.

WORKING WITH

- TO CUT: Use sharp scissors or a rotary cutter and mat.
- HANDLING FOR SEWING: As you sew, raise the presser foot periodically to allow the fabric to relax. A roller foot will help prevent snags in the fabric.
- NEEDLES: Universal H, size 80/12 or 90/14.
- THREAD: All-purpose polyester or cotton.
- STITCH LENGTH: 2.5–3mm.
- SEWING MACHINE FEET: Standard, roller or straight stitch.
- INTERFACING/LINING: Porous fabric designs require an undergarment or semi-attached lining.

CARE

- WASHING: Machine wash or dry-clean.
- DRYING: Normal tumble dry, air-dry or dry-clean.
- IRONING: Medium to high heat and steam.
- SHRINKAGE: Moderate.

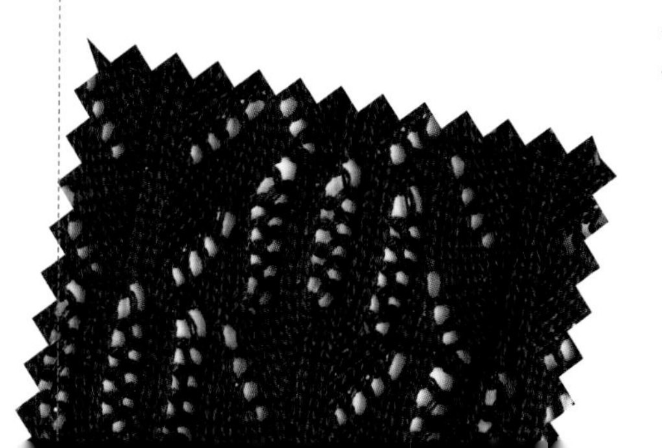

RIBBING

Ribbing is a knit fabric with long vertical ribs. The ribs give it plenty of room to expand and contract, which is why it is often used for T-shirt collars, cuffs and form-fitting clothes such as vests. The ribs can be one-by-one, with one rib on the surface and one underneath, or two-by-one, with one rib on the surface and double the rib space underneath, which gives each rib a more exposed look. Just like jersey, the fabric curls up at the edges on the right side, but there is really no right or wrong side to ribbing (unless you are using two-by-one ribbing and prefer the single ribs to pop outwards). Aside from trims, ribbing can also be used for turtlenecks, T-shirts and beanies.

PROPERTIES

- CHARACTER: Expandable knit with long vertical ribs.
- WEIGHT: Light to medium.
- STABILITY: Unstable with two-way stretch.
- SPECIAL CONSIDERATIONS: Though the edges will curl up to the 'right' side, there is generally no 'wrong' side to the fabric.

WORKING WITH

- TO CUT: Use sharp scissors or a rotary cutter and mat.
- HANDLING FOR SEWING: Don't pull, tug or stretch the fabric; let the machine feed the fabric naturally.
- NEEDLES: Universal H, Ballpoint H-SUK, Stretch HS, sizes 70/10–90/14.
- THREAD: All-purpose polyester or cotton.
- STITCH LENGTH: 2.5–3mm.
- SEWING MACHINE FEET: Straight stitch or Teflon.
- INTERFACING/LINING: None.

CARE

- WASHING: Machine wash.
- DRYING: Normal tumble dry.
- IRONING: Medium to high heat and steam.
- SHRINKAGE: Moderate.

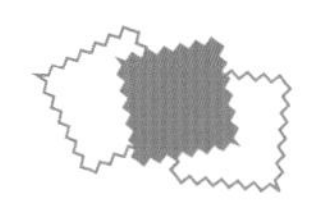

SPANDEX (Elastane) and LYCRA

Elastane, also commonly referred to as Lycra (a trade name), or spandex in the US, is hands-down the most elastic fabric available. Developed in the late 1950s by DuPont, elastane is a synthetic wonder. It can stretch up to seven times its length and then bounce back to its original shape. When added to cotton, wool, nylon and polyester, the result is an extremely stretchy fabric that is ideal for swimsuits, dancewear, leggings, lingerie, ice skating costumes and ski clothing. Elastane is often added in small amounts to woven fabrics for added comfort and stretch, but in the textiles world, the term elastane typically refers to stretchy knit fabric.

HANDY HINT

Many sewers are terrified by the notion of sewing their own swimsuit, but it's not as difficult as you might think. Using a ball or stretch needle, swimwear elastic and a little trial and error, you can transform Lycra into your very own custom-made swimsuit.

PROPERTIES

- CHARACTER: Extremely stretchy.
- WEIGHT: Light to medium.
- STABILITY: Unstable with four-way stretch.
- SPECIAL CONSIDERATIONS: Elastane should never be bleached as bleach will break down the fibres.

WORKING WITH

- TO CUT: Use sharp scissors or a rotary cutter and mat.
- HANDLING FOR SEWING: Synthetic fibres will dull your needle and scissors, so change needles frequently. Zigzag stitches will give more stretch to your seams. Seam ripping will damage the fabric, so it's best to pre-test patterns and to sew carefully.
- NEEDLES: Stretch HS or Ballpoint H-SUK, sizes 70/10–90/14.
- THREAD: 100 per cent polyester.
- STITCH LENGTH: 2–2.5mm.
- SEWING MACHINE FEET: Standard or roller.
- INTERFACING/LINING: None.

CARE

- WASHING: Machine wash.
- DRYING: Normal tumble dry.
- IRONING: Test press first. Low to medium heat without steam.
- SHRINKAGE: Moderate (cotton and wool), minimal (nylon).

SWEATER KNITS

Sweater knit fabrics are sold by the metre in varying weights, patterns and colours. They look just like knitted jumpers, and are ideal for loose-fitting designs such as dresses and tunic tops. Bear in mind that sweater knit fabric frays at the edges and that hems are difficult to finish, so ribbing or woven cotton fabrics are a nice way to create cuffs and hems that enclose ravelling edges.

PROPERTIES

- CHARACTER: Fabric that looks like a knitted jumper.
- WEIGHT: Light to medium.
- STABILITY: Unstable with two-way stretch.
- SPECIAL CONSIDERATIONS: Fabric is difficult to work with and frays easily at the edges. Unravelling edges and hems can be finished off with knit ribbing or woven cottons.

WORKING WITH

- TO CUT: Use sharp scissors or a rotary cutter and mat.
- HANDLING FOR SEWING: Do not stretch the fabric as you sew; let the machine feed it through. Zigzag stitches will give more stretch to your seams. Seam ripping will damage the fabric, so it's best to pre-test patterns and sew carefully.
- NEEDLES: Universal H, Stretch HS or Ballpoint H-SUK, size 70/10 or 90/14.
- THREAD: 100 per cent polyester.
- STITCH LENGTH: 2–2.5mm.
- SEWING MACHINE FEET: Roller or walking foot.
- INTERFACING/LINING: Lining is recommended for wool or fabrics that are itchy.

CARE

- WASHING: Hand wash or dry-clean.
- DRYING: Dry-clean or air-dry by laying flat.
- IRONING: Using low to medium heat and steam depending on fibre content. Test press first and use a pressing cloth.
- SHRINKAGE: Moderate.

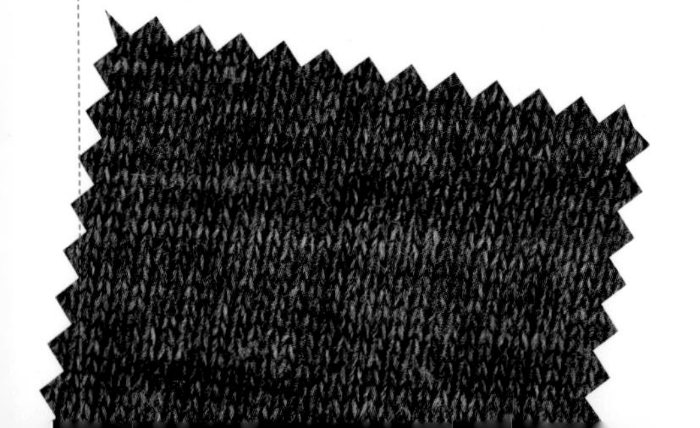

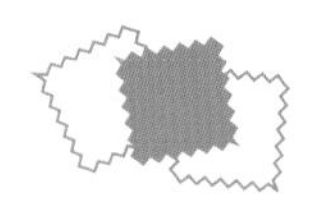

THERMAL KNITS

Thermal knits are primarily used for undergarments, long underwear and long-sleeve thermal shirts in a variety of colours. Thermal fabric is characterised by its waffle weave, which is visible on the surface. Made from cotton, wool, synthetics or blended fibres, the waffle pattern works well as a winter fabric, creating small pockets of air between the fabric and the skin to wick sweat away from the body. Thermal knit is a great choice for shirts, pyjamas, leggings and long underwear.

PROPERTIES

- CHARACTER: Unique waffle weave.
- WEIGHT: Light to medium.
- STABILITY: Unstable knit with two-way stretch.
- SPECIAL CONSIDERATIONS: Will curl up to the right side when cut.

WORKING WITH

- TO CUT: Use sharp scissors or a rotary cutter and mat.
- HANDLING FOR SEWING: Don't pull, tug or stretch the fabric; let the machine feed the fabric naturally.
- NEEDLES: Universal H, Ballpoint H-SUK, Stretch HS, sizes 70/10–90/14.
- THREAD: All-purpose polyester or cotton.
- STITCH LENGTH: 2.5–3mm.
- SEWING MACHINE FEET: Straight stitch or Teflon.
- INTERFACING/LINING: Lining is optional; lightweight fusible or sew-in interfacings work best.

CARE

- WASHING: Machine wash.
- DRYING: Tumble dry.
- IRONING: Medium to high heat and steam.
- SHRINKAGE: Fabrics will shrink according to fibre content (i.e. cotton will shrink more than polyester).

TRICOT

Tricot (pronounced tree-ko) is a lightweight knit fabric that is typically used for lingerie, nightgowns and garment linings. It can be made from almost any synthetic or natural fibre and is often blended with elastane for added stretch. The knit pattern found on tricot is unique, and features small vertical ribs on the front side of the fabric and horizontal ribs running across the back. Tricot is easy to sew with, yet snags easily and can cling. Do not pre-wash tricot fabric, as the edges will curl up significantly, making it difficult to cut and sew.

PROPERTIES

- CHARACTER: Lightweight knit with vertical ribs on the front side and horizontal ribs on the back.
- WEIGHT: Lightweight.
- SPECIAL CONSIDERATIONS: Tricot is easy to sew with, but it stains easily, snags and can cling.

WORKING WITH

- TO CUT: Use sharp scissors or a rotary cutter and mat.
- HANDLING FOR SEWING: The fabric will curl up at the edges on the right side of the fabric. Zigzag stitches will give more stretch to your seams. Seam ripping will damage the fabric, so it's best to pre-test patterns and sew carefully.
- NEEDLES: Universal H, Stretch HS or Ballpoint H-SUK, size 60/8 or 70/10.
- THREAD: 100 per cent polyester.
- STITCH LENGTH: 2–2.5mm.
- SEWING MACHINE FEET: Roller or straight stitch.
- INTERFACING/LINING: Is often used as a lining itself.

CARE

- WASHING: Machine wash.
- DRYING: Normal tumble dry.
- IRONING: Low dry heat.
- SHRINKAGE: Minimal to moderate.

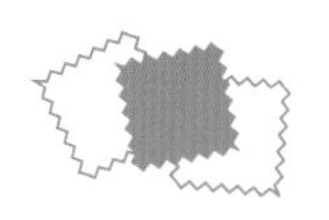

VELOUR

Velour, sometimes referred to as stretch velour, is a knit fabric with a plush pile, meant to mimic velvet. The fabric can be knit in any fibre, but is typically made from synthetic polyester, poly blends and microfibres. Velour appears kitsch when compared to real velvet, but its soft drape also makes it ideal for comfy tunic tops, leggings, tracksuits, costumes, home furnishing items and some upholstery. Velour is inexpensive and is much easier to sew with than real velvet.

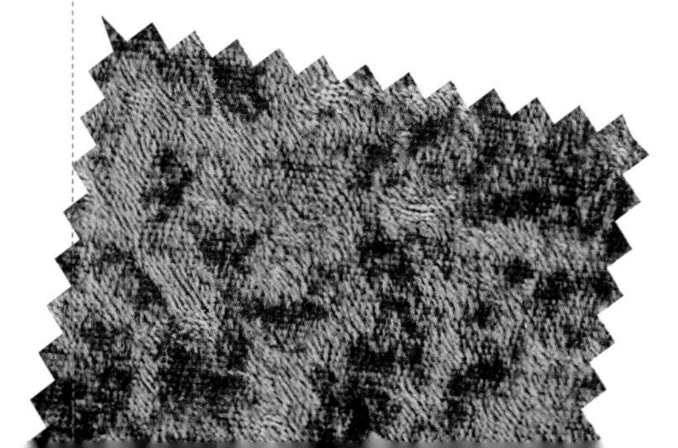

PROPERTIES

- CHARACTER: Stretch knit with a plush, velvet-like pile on top.
- WEIGHT: Lightweight to medium.
- STABILITY: Unstable with two-, sometimes four-way stretch.
- SPECIAL CONSIDERATIONS: Can look cheap and kitsch.

WORKING WITH

- TO CUT: Use sharp scissors or a rotary cutter and mat. Use with-nap layout when cutting pattern pieces.
- HANDLING FOR SEWING: Do not stretch the fabric as you sew; let the machine feed it through. Zigzag stitches will give more stretch to your seams. Seam ripping will damage the fabric, so it's best to pre-test patterns and sew carefully.
- NEEDLES: Universal H, Stretch HS or Ballpoint H-SUK, sizes 60/8 or 70/10.
- THREAD: 100 per cent polyester.
- STITCH LENGTH: 2–2.5mm.
- SEWING MACHINE FEET: Roller or straight stitch.
- INTERFACING/LINING: Tricot knit lining when needed.

CARE

- WASHING: Machine wash.
- DRYING: Normal tumble dry.
- IRONING: Low heat.
- SHRINKAGE: Minimal to moderate.

PART THREE:
SPECIALITY FABRICS

An Overview

When we talk about fabrics we are generally referring to wovens and knits, but textiles can be created in other ways too. Animal skins, furs, plastics, vinyl and rubber are interesting resources, some of which have been used for centuries for both fashion and utility.

FAIR TREATMENT

Owning a coat made from animal fur was once considered a ticket to high society. Today, however, the use of animal furs and skins in fashion is the subject of an ongoing debate. Is it cruel? Do you live in an environment where animal furs are necessary for winter protection? If the animal is already being used as a meat source, shouldn't we use the skin as well? Or are animals simply being raised for their wonderful leathers? Such questions should be answered on an individual basis, as the debate over leather use weighs out equally on both sides of the argument. When it comes to the use of real animal furs, however, many people deem their usage cruel since most of these animals are raised solely for their furs. In response to this, many manufacturers and retailers have adopted a fur-free policy, and as a result, an array of synthetic furs, faux leathers and pleathers are readily available in the marketplace and continue to improve in quality and style. There is also a big movement towards upcycling old leather and furs from worn bags and jackets to create new items, which is a wonderful way to extend the lives of such valuable textiles.

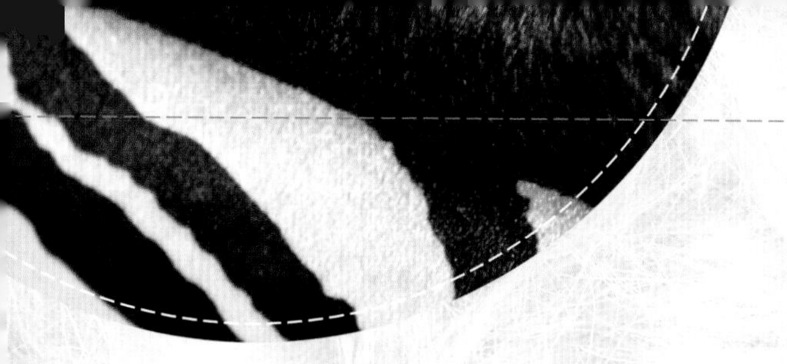

Fashion

Home Furnishing

Craft/Misc.

ENVIRONMENTAL IMPACT

Aside from the debate on the treatment of animals, there is also discussion over which textiles are more environmentally friendly – real leather and furs or imitation pleather and faux furs. It would seem logical that leather, which is a product of nature, would leave a smaller footprint on the environment. However, a great deal of chemicals and acids are used in the tanning process to extend the life of the hide and keep it from rotting over time. Extended exposure from these chemicals may have a harmful impact on the air and water. Some manufacturers engage in more environmentally friendly tanning processes, beginning with raising cattle in organic conditions, then using vegetable products, salts and plant-based dyes for the tanning.

Faux furs, pleather, oilcloth and other plastic-based textiles have come a long way from their original manufacturing days. Some faux furs are made from organic cottons, while some are made from polyester. And while polyester is generally not biodegradable, many synthetic textiles today are recycled from existing fibres, a process that requires very little water and leaves little waste behind.

USES

Sewing with specialty fabrics offers a myriad of project ideas: leather, pleather, vinyl and oilcloth can be used to make bags, purses, totes, belts, shoes and accessories; faux furs can add the perfect trim to a winter coat, specialty fabrics can be used to make elegant dresses and gowns; and neoprene is perfect for wetsuits, orthopedic braces, cup holders and laptop cases. Sewing with these fabrics requires a few tricks, but they are easy enough to tackle and will greatly expand your sewing knowledge.

EMBELLISHED FABRICS

(Beaded, Embroidered and Sequined)

Embellished fabrics are knit or woven and come in a variety of weights and textures, but they all have one thing in common - embellishments. Whether simple or ornate, beaded or embroidered, these embellished elements give that special touch. Speciality fabrics are often used for evening gowns, bridal dresses, jackets, clutches, purses and trims.

Beads and sequins are typically sewn, glued or fused to the fabrics. They can be applied individually or in a long chain - if you happen to snag a chain of sequins be aware that the entire line may unravel, leaving an unwanted gap in your gorgeous gown.

Embroidery is a decorative top stitch sewn with a variety of threads or ribbons, and is sometimes coupled with beads, sequins or other embellishments.

PROPERTIES

- CHARACTER: Knit or woven fabric embellished with beads, sequins or embroidery.
- WEIGHT: Light to heavy.
- SPECIAL CONSIDERATIONS: Minimal designs that allow the embellished fabric to be the main feature work best.

WORKING WITH

- TO CUT: Use sharp scissors or a rotary cutter and mat.
- HANDLING FOR SEWING: To avoid fraying or sequins and beads unravelling, do not cut the fabric until you are ready to sew. Sequins and beads should be removed from the seam line before sewing. Once cut, handle the fabric as little as possible. Because the metal used for sequins is soft and pliable, sequined fabrics and trims can be sewn by machine, although the fabric will dull your sewing needle quickly. Change your needle frequently and work slowly to avoid mistakes. Removing stitches can be difficult and can leave unwanted holes in the sequins.

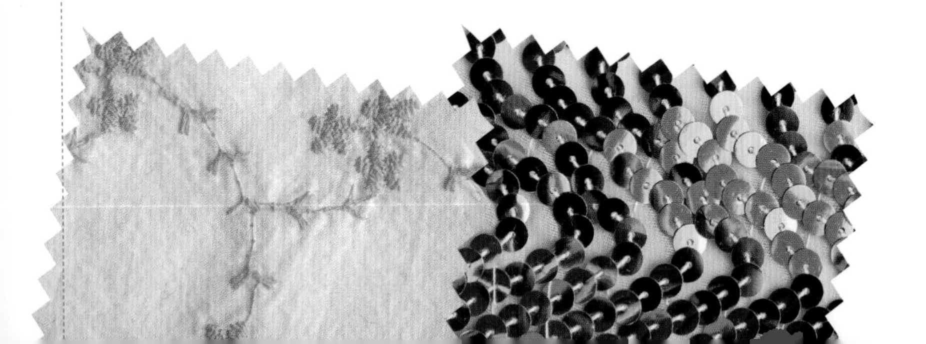

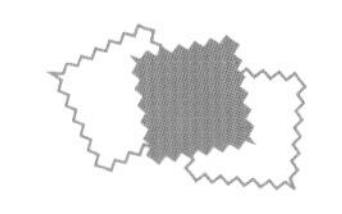

FAUX FUR

Since the beginning of time, animal furs and hides have been used for clothing and protection. Although originally used for necessity and utility, over time, animal furs came to be seen as chic, elegant and luxurious. Today, the use of real fur is controversial, and many retailers have taken a pledge to adopt 'fur-free' policies and use faux fur instead. Though imitation furs may not look and feel as 'real' when compared to actual animal furs, styles and quality are improving, and they're a more humane and cheaper alternative when a furry look is desired.

Animal fur differs from hair fibre textiles in that the fur is still attached to the animal skin or leather. Faux fur mimics this idea with a stiff cotton or synthetic backing and one of two furry pile weights on top: soft low-pile rayon, and stiffer long-pile polyester. ▸

- NEEDLES: Universal H, Sharp HM and HJ, or Stretch HS (depending on the base fabric), sizes 60/8–90/14.
- THREAD: All-purpose polyester or cotton.
- STITCH LENGTH: 2–2.5mm.
- SEWING MACHINE FEET: Standard or straight stitch.
- INTERFACING/LINING: Lining is recommended to reduce scratchy seams.

CARE

- WASHING: Dry-cleaning is recommended. Some specialty fabrics should be hand washed. Consult the manufacturer's care instructions.
- DRYING: Dry-clean or air-dry. Consult the manufacturer's care instructions.
- IRONING: Always test press, as the recommended heat will vary depending on the fabric's fibre content. A pressing cloth is recommended when ironing on the right side of the fabric. When ironing on the wrong side, use a towel as your ironing surface and place the fabric over it, face down. This will protect the embellishments as you press.
- SHRINKAGE: Varies depending on the fabric.

FAUX FUR (continued)

SEWING TIPS

- Find the natural direction in which the fur lies down and make sure the hairs hang properly. For instance, if you're making a waistcoat, the hairs should hang down towards your feet.
- Comb any tangles out of the fur.
- Draw all pattern markings on the wrong side of the fur with tailor's chalk or a fabric pen.
- To reduce bulk in your garment, try using abutted (or 'butted' seams). Fabric edges are butted up next to each other and often sewn together with flatlock or zigzag stitching. Standard seams will also work but seam allowances should be trimmed with scissors or hair clippers when you have finished sewing.
- When necessary, hand-sew pieces together using a glover's needle and thimble.
- Short-hair furs are easier to work with but should be handled in a similar manner as long-hair furs.
- Faux furs will often leave a cloud of small hairs all over the work room, under your sewing machine needle plate and sometimes in your mouth. Clean up often to reduce the mess.
- Always test-sew on a scrap piece first.

PROPERTIES

- CHARACTER: Synthetic mesh backing with synthetic animal hair and fur on the surface.
- WEIGHT: Medium to heavy.
- SPECIAL CONSIDERATIONS: Requires some patience when sewing.

WORKING WITH

- TO CUT: Sharp scissors or razor blade when needed.
- HANDLING FOR SEWING: See Sewing Tips.
- NEEDLES: Sharp HM or HJ, Jeans/Denim H–J, or Leather HLL or NTW, sizes 70/10 to 90/14.
- THREAD: All-purpose polyester.
- STITCH LENGTH: 2.5–4.0mm.
- SEWING MACHINE FEET: Roller or Teflon.
- INTERFACING/LINING: Lining recommended for all outerwear.

CARE

- WASHING: Machine or hand wash.
- DRYING: Air-dry.
- IRONING: Do not iron.
- SHRINKAGE: Minimal to none.

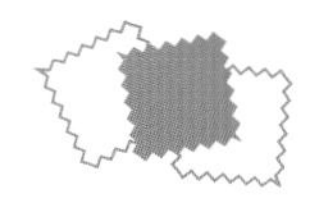

FAUX SUEDE

Faux suede is made from polyester. It is available at a fraction of the cost of real animal hides, and is much easier to care for. Faux suede doesn't fray, has no obvious grain line and is usually machine washable. It comes in two weights - soft or firm - and is used for jackets, skirts, casualwear, bags, shoes and home furnishings.

PROPERTIES

- CHARACTER: Soft leather-like feel, similar to real suede.
- WEIGHT: Medium to heavy.
- SPECIAL CONSIDERATIONS: Faux suede is much easier to care for than real suede and costs considerably less.

WORKING WITH

- TO CUT: Rotary cutter and mat work best; scissors will work as well.
- HANDLING FOR SEWING: Faux suede is hard to ease and shape into armholes and other curved areas. Use the strength of both hands to work the fabric in place. Simple garment designs are recommended.
- NEEDLES: Leather HLL or NTW, Sharp HM or HJ, sizes 70/10–90/14.
- THREAD: All-purpose polyester.
- STITCH LENGTH: 2.5–3mm.
- SEWING MACHINE FEET: Roller or Teflon.
- INTERFACING/LINING: Lining recommended for all outerwear.

CARE

- WASHING: Most faux suedes are machine washable. Washing and drying will soften the fabric and create a better drape. Consult the manufacturer's care instructions.
- DRYING: Tumble dry. Consult the manufacturer's care instructions.
- IRONING: Low dry heat. A pressing cloth is recommended. Faux suede is sensitive to a hot iron, so always test press.
- SHRINKAGE: Moderate.

LEATHER, SUEDE and ANIMAL SKINS

Leather is the topside of the animal skin and suede (which is typically softer) is the underside. 'Animal skin' is a general term used for skins and hides from animals such as cows, alligators, crocodiles, ostriches, snakes, lizards, stingrays, eels and kangaroos. Skins and hides come in varying weights, can be soft or rough, and come in a wide range of colours. There are a variety of faux leather and faux suede fabrics available as alternatives to real animal skins, and because these fabrics are made from synthetic fibres they tend to be easier to sew.

Leather and suede are used for purses, handbags, jackets, wallets, belts, coats, waistcoats, trousers, skirts, gloves, shoes, accessories and furniture upholstery.

SEWING TIPS

- Leather is sold by the square metre or square foot rather than the metre or yard. Some shops sell scrap pieces, which are ideal for testing or for making simple leather accessories.
- Leather does not have a grain, but stretches less in the length of a hide than the width.
- The centre of a skin is typically the most attractive part of the hide (if there is a visible pattern).
- When sewing, use a sharp or leather needle. Universal needles will work as well, but leather needles help the fabric move more smoothly as you sew.
- Needles will pierce and cut through the leather as you sew. A longer stitch is recommended, as small stitches may cause the leather to tear.
- Avoid using a walking foot as this can scratch the skin.
- Hold pieces of leather together with paper clips or small clamps, since sewing pins will leave holes.
- When using thick leathers or skins, sew with abutted (or 'butted') seams. Fabric edges are

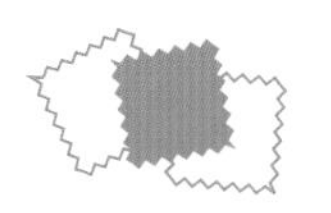

- butted up next to each other and are often sewn together with flatlock or zigzag stitching.
- When necessary, hand-sew pieces together using a plain stitch, feather stitch or zigzag stitch. A glover's needle and thimble are helpful.
- Always test-sew on a scrap piece first.

PROPERTIES

- CHARACTER: Can be rough, supple or soft.
- WEIGHT: Medium to heavy.
- SPECIAL CONSIDERATIONS: Sewing with leather requires patience. Leather and skins are sold by the square metre or square foot.

HANDY HINT

Re-purposed leather is an inexpensive and environmentally friendly alternative to purchasing new leather. Use leather from an old bag, a belt or a torn coat to create new items.

WORKING WITH

- TO CUT: Use sharp scissors or a rotary cutter and mat.
- HANDLING FOR SEWING: Refer to the above tips.
- NEEDLES: Leather HLL or NTW, Sharp HM or HJ, sizes 70/10–90/14.
- THREAD: All-purpose polyester; the tannin in leather may cause cotton thread to rot.
- STITCH LENGTH: 2.5–4mm.
- SEWING MACHINE FEET: Roller or Teflon.
- INTERFACING/LINING: Lining is recommended for all outerwear.

CARE

- WASHING: Dry-clean.
- DRYING: Dry-clean.
- IRONING: Medium dry heat. Use a paper bag as a pressing cloth. Press and lift as you go to avoid stretching the skin.
- SHRINKAGE: Leather may shrink when wet.

NEOPRENE

Neoprene is a synthetic rubber material that is form-fitting and resilient. The fabric is suitable for underwater gear that requires flexibility, buoyancy and a waterproof seal, which makes it perfect for wetsuits. When water soaks into a neoprene wetsuit, it is actually trapped between the fabric and the wearer's skin. Body heat warms the trapped water, which means that the wearer can stay warm in cold water for long periods of time. Neoprene is also used to make knee pads, orthopedic braces, mouse pads, insulated can holders and stretchable laptop cases, as it provides padding, protection and insulation from the bumps and moisture that a travelling laptop will encounter. Neoprene comes in a variety of foam styles and densities, ranging in thickness from 1.5–7mm.

SEWING TIPS

- Neoprene is typically sold by the metre, in sheets or on rolls.
- Overlock and flatlock seams are recommended and require an overlocker or serger.
- With standard machines, larger needles, longer stitches and zigzag stitches work best.
- Gluing your seams before sewing will ensure a waterproof seal and make your garment stronger. Use a neoprene sealer such as McNett's Aquaseal.
- Taping seams ensures additional waterproof protection. After seams are glued and sewn, apply heat-sealable tape such as Melco or Bemis across the top of the seam.
- Bind edges with a strip of stretchy Lycra or fold-over elastic.

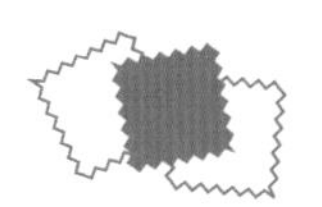

PROPERTIES

- CHARACTER: Stretchy, bouncy, rubber-like fabric.
- WEIGHT: Lightweight to medium.
- SPECIAL CONSIDERATIONS: An overlocker or serger is recommended.

WORKING WITH

- TO CUT: Use sharp scissors or a rotary cutter and mat.
- HANDLING FOR SEWING: Refer to the above tips.
- NEEDLES: Universal H or Stretch HS, size 80/12 or 90/14.
- THREAD: 100 per cent all-purpose polyester or nylon.
- STITCH LENGTH: 3–4mm, typically a zigzag stitch.
- SEWING MACHINE FEET: Roller.
- INTERFACING/LINING: None.

CARE

- WASHING: Machine wash in warm water.
- DRYING: Air-dry.
- IRONING: Not necessary.
- SHRINKAGE: None.

OILCLOTH

Similar in character to laminated cotton, oilcloth is actually a vinyl fabric on the top, bonded and supported with a woven cotton mesh on the back. With roots in the fishing and sailing industry, the fabric was originally made from oil-infused canvas, spawning the name 'oilcloth'. It is water-resistant, slightly stiff and the surface can be wiped clean.

Oilcloth comes in a variety of colours and patterns, although options tend to be limited. It is harder to sew with than laminated cotton, but costs half the price and both sides of the fabric are waterproof, making it ideal for beach bags and totes. It is also used for tablecloths, place mats, aprons, accessories and home furnishing projects. It should be noted that in the US, the Consumer Product Safety Improvement Act of 2008 (CPSIA) prohibits the use of oilcloth in baby bibs and toys for children under the age of 12. This is due to the level of phthalate softener in the PVC vinyl, which oilcloth is made from.

SEWING TIPS

- Pins will leave holes, so only pin in the seam allowance.
- Needles actually pierce through the fabric as you sew. A longer stitch is recommended, as small stitches may cause the cloth to tear.
- Use the strength of both arms when sewing around curves.
- The fabric doesn't fray, so you don't have to worry about unfinished seams.
- Like vinyl, oilcloth has a tendency to stick under your presser foot when sewing. Here are three different ideas to combat sticking:
  1. Sandwich the fabric with a piece of tissue paper on the top and bottom. When you're done sewing, carefully tear the tissue paper away.
  2. Apply masking tape to the bottom of your presser foot and to the top of your machine plate. This helps the fabric glide through more smoothly.
  3. Use a non-stick, Teflon or roller foot.

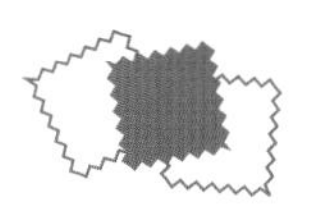

PROPERTIES

- CHARACTER: Vinyl on top with a bonded cotton mesh on the back; stiff but pliable.
- WEIGHT: Medium.
- SPECIAL CONSIDERATIONS: The fabric is stiff and can be difficult work with. In the US, the CPSIA prohibits the use of oilcloth for baby bibs and toys.

WORKING WITH

- TO CUT: Use sharp scissors or a rotary cutter and mat.
- HANDLING FOR SEWING: Refer to the Sewing Tips.
- NEEDLES: Universal H or Sharp HM and HJ, size 80/12 or 90/14.
- THREAD: All-purpose polyester or cotton.
- STITCH LENGTH: 3–4mm.
- SEWING MACHINE FEET: Non-stick, Teflon or roller.
- INTERFACING/LINING: None.

CARE

- WASHING: Oilcloth can be wiped clean using a warm, soapy sponge and then dried off with a soft cloth or sponge. Machine washing is not recommended.
- DRYING: See above.
- IRONING: When purchasing online, oilcloth will often arrive in the post with folded creases. These can be easily removed by laying the cloth flat in a warm place. As the oilcloth softens, use your hands to smooth out any creases. Once the fabric is smooth, keep it rolled or hung up. Oilcloth should never be ironed.
- SHRINKAGE: None.

HANDY HINT

If your kitchen stools or patio chairs need a face-lift, why not re-cover them with oilcloth? Using the old covers as a pattern, you can easily make your furniture childproof - sticky prints and spilled drinks can be wiped up without sacrificing one ounce of style.

VINYL, FAUX LEATHER and PLEATHER

Vinyl is a synthetic fabric that imitates leather, and is sometimes referred to as faux leather or pleather. Vinyl doesn't breathe well and is typically used for home furnishings and upholstery rather than clothing, but it can be used for crafts and to make accessories such as belts, bags, wallets and other leather-like items.

Vinyl comes in varying weights and colours, and is typically found in the upholstery section of a fabric shop on large rolls. Some vinyl has soft backings and other vinyl is rough. Clear vinyl is wrapped with a layer of tissue paper in between to keep it from sticking to itself, which can come in very handy when sewing as a way to prevent the fabric from sticking to your presser foot. Since vinyl is a plastic, it has a tendency to crack over time, so when storing, it's best to keep vinyl rolled up rather than folded.

SEWING TIPS

- Pins will leave holes, so only pin in the seam allowance.
- Needles actually pierce through the fabric as you sew. A longer stitch is recommended, as small stitches may cause the fabric to tear.
- When sewing around curves, use the strength of both arms.
- The fabric doesn't fray so you don't have to worry about unfinished seams.
- Like oilcloth, vinyl has a tendency to stick under your presser foot when sewing. Here are three different ideas to combat sticking:
    1. Sandwich the fabric with a piece of tissue paper on top and bottom. When you're done sewing, carefully tear the tissue paper away.
    2. Apply masking tape to the bottom of your presser foot and to the top of your machine plate. This helps the fabric glide through more smoothly.
    3. Use a non-stick, Teflon or roller foot.

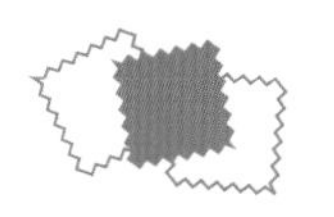

PROPERTIES

- CHARACTER: Plastic-like, pliable fabric that mimics leather.
- WEIGHT: Medium to heavy.
- SPECIAL CONSIDERATIONS: The fabric is stiff to work with and can stick to the presser foot.

WORKING WITH

- TO CUT: Use sharp scissors or a rotary cutter and mat.
- HANDLING FOR SEWING: Refer to the Sewing Tips.
- NEEDLES: Universal H or Sharp HM and HJ, sizes 80/12–100/16.
- THREAD: All-purpose polyester or cotton.
- STITCH LENGTH: 3–4mm.
- SEWING MACHINE FEET: Roller or Teflon.
- INTERFACING/LINING: None.

CARE

- WASHING: Vinyl can be wiped clean using a warm, soapy sponge and then dried off with a soft cloth or sponge. Machine washing is not suggested.
- DRYING: See above.
- IRONING: When purchasing online, the fabric will often arrive in the post with folded creases. These can be easily removed by laying the cloth flat in a warm place. As the vinyl softens, use your hands to smooth out any creases. Once the fabric is smooth keep it rolled or hung up. Vinyl should never be ironed.
- SHRINKAGE: None.

PART FOUR:
BLENDED FABRICS

An Overview

If the finest relationships bring out the best in each individual, then blended fabrics are the perfect marriage. Blended fabrics are a mix of various fibres combined together to create a stronger, more versatile fabric than either fibre would be on its own.

Blended fabrics can be a natural/ natural fibre combination, such as cotton and wool, or a synthetic/ natural combination, like the very popular poly cotton. Some combinations are more evenly spread, in a 40/60 per cent combination, while other blends are minimal, like cotton with 2 per cent elastane. Even that tiny bit of elastane improves the fabric's ability to stretch, exceeding cotton's primary abilities. This section walks you through the most common blends available on the market today and their ideal uses.

PRODUCTION & PROCESSES

Fabrics are often blended for added strength and ability, but they also cut back on manufacturing costs. Linen production is tedious and costly, but a linen/rayon blended fabric requires less linen fibres and can be produced and sold at a cheaper price. Even small amounts of an added fibre can reduce costs while staying true to the main fabric's properties.

To create blended fabrics, two or more fibres are blended together in the yarn-spinning process and are then knit or woven into fabric. Blended textiles are created worldwide and are readily available in most fabric shops.

Fashion 

Home furnishing

Craft/Misc.

USES & SELECTING FABRICS

Blended fabrics can be used for almost anything, since they combine and replace other fabrics. When selecting a fabric for your next project, consider your needs, the cost of the fabric and what added benefits you'd like in your garment. Do you want a bit of stretch in your trousers for added comfort? Is 100 per cent wool too pricey for your budget? Grab a 50 per cent wool blend and it may give you the same look. With so many fabrics and blends available, it's a buyer's market.

CHARACTERISTICS

- Stronger than fibres would be on their own.
- More economical.
- Easy to care for.
- Easy to handle and sew.

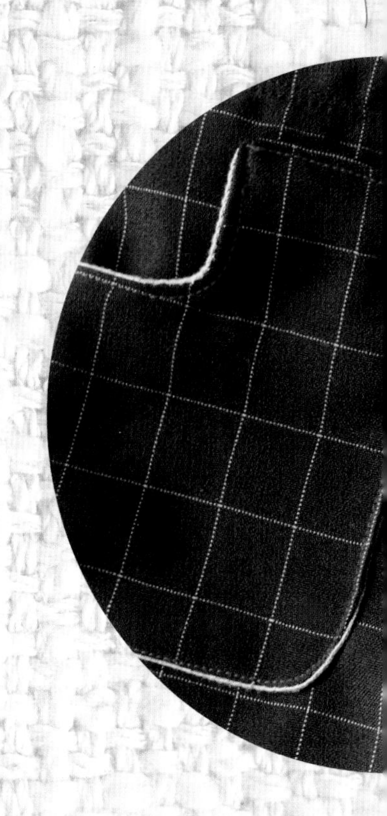

LINEN BLENDS:
Linen/Silk and Linen/Rayon

LINEN/SILK, LINEN/RAYON: Linen is a natural, soft, breezy fabric created from flax plant fibres. It is classic and timeless, but the manufacturing processes to produce linen are tedious and the fabric frays, shrinks and wrinkles easily. Blending linen with other fibres tends to reduce the amount of wrinkling and improves the fabric's drape. The most common blends are linen/silk and linen/rayon (a man-made fibre). Blends can be knit or woven depending on weave and weight, and they should be sewn according to their core fabrics (linen, silk, etc.), as outlined in this book. Most linen blend fabrics can be machine washed, but consult the manufacturer's care instructions for details. Linen blends are used for a variety of clothing, bags and home furnishing projects.

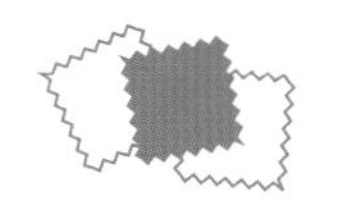

OTHER BLENDS:

Nylon/Acetate and Rayon/Cotton

NYLON/ACETATE: Nylon is a lightweight, durable, synthetic fabric made from petroleum products. Acetate is a strong, durable, man-made fibre created from wood pulp cellulose, and is often used to replace silk. When the two fibres are blended together, the fabric is more absorbent than either fibre is on its own. Nylon/acetate can be knit or woven, and depending on the weave and weight, should be sewn similar to nylon or acetate, as outlined in this book. Most fabrics can be machine washed, but consult the manufacturer's care instructions for more details. When in doubt, dry-clean. Nylon/acetate blends are used for dresses, wedding gowns, blouses, shirts and linings.

RAYON/COTTON: Rayon is a man-made fibre created from wood pulp cellulose. It is versatile, absorbent, inexpensive, dyes well and drapes beautifully; however, it doesn't age well and can pill. Cotton is a natural fibre known for being cool, comfortable and breathable, but it wrinkles and shrinks easily. When the two fibres are blended together, the resulting fabric typically has a soft, fuzzy surface. It is very wearable, comfortable and washes well. Rayon/cotton blends can be knit or woven, and depending on the weave and weight, should be sewn in a similar way to rayon or cotton, as outlined in this book. Rayon/cotton blends are used for dresses, skirts, blouses, shirts and all types of casualwear.

POLYESTER BLENDS:
Polyester/Cotton and Polyester/Ramie

Polyester is a strong synthetic fibre that retains shape and resists wrinkling, however it doesn't breathe well and can melt under high temperatures. When blended with natural fibres, the fabric tends to keep polyester's positive attributes, while gaining new abilities. Poly blends can be knit or woven, and depending on weave and weight should be sewn in a similar way to their core fabrics (polyester or cotton, etc.), as outlined in this book.

POLYESTER/COTTON: Cotton is a natural fibre known for being cool, comfortable and breathable, but it can wrinkle and shrink easily. Poly cotton is a versatile fabric that is available in most fabric shops. It is cool and light, washes well, doesn't tend to shrink and wrinkles far less than standard cotton. On the other hand, poly cotton is known to pill easily, which may deter people from sewing with it. It is used for all types of clothing.

POLYESTER/RAMIE: Ramie is made from plant fibres that are native to Eastern Asia. It is soft, cool, eco-friendly and comfortable to wear, but just like linen, can wrinkle excessively and is costly to produce. Polyester blended with ramie creates a fabric that is easy to care for and doesn't tend to wrinkle. It is comfortable to wear and is used for all types of clothing.

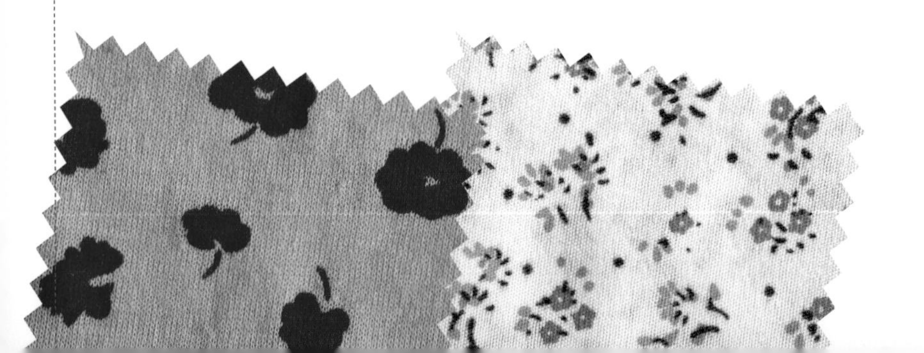

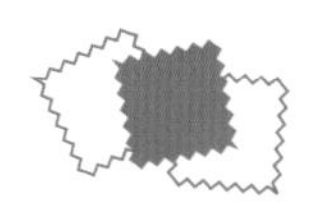

WOOL BLENDS: Wool/Cotton, Wool/Silk, Wool/Nylon and Wool/Synthetics

Wool is a natural, versatile, insulating fabric with wonderful wicking abilities, but it can shrink easily when wet and often requires extra care when pressing and cleaning. Blending wool with other fibres brings out its strengths and improves its weaknesses. Blends can be knit or woven, and depending on the weave and weight, should be sewn in a similar way to their core fabrics (wool, cotton, silk, etc.), as outlined in this book. Always check the manufacturer's care instructions before washing wool-blended fabrics.

WOOL/COTTON: Cotton is a natural fibre known for being cool, comfortable and breathable, but it wrinkles and shrinks easily. When blended with wool, the fabric performs better, is often lighter in weight (similar to cotton), is more comfortable and is easier to care for. Wool/cotton blends are used for all types of clothing.

WOOL/SILK: Silk is a natural fibre cultivated from silkworm cocoons. Silk fabrics are strong, absorbent, warm yet lightweight and very elegant; however, manufacturing silk is tedious and fabrics are costly. Blending silk with wool results in a medium-weight silky fabric with a textured surface. The fabric is used for casualwear, dresses and men's ties. Unfortunately, wool/silk blends can still be pricey.

WOOL/NYLON: Nylon is a lightweight, durable, synthetic fabric made from petroleum products. It doesn't press well and can fray easily, but when blended with wool the combination is softer and more absorbent and durable. The fabric is used for all types of clothing.

WOOL/SYNTHETICS: Synthetics are imitation fibres created by chemical processes. They are often strong, durable, resistant to wrinkles and don't tend to shrink; however, they perform poorly under high temperatures and don't have the same rich feel as natural fabrics. Blending wool with synthetic fibres creates a fabric that possesses wonderful draping and tailoring abilities. The fabric is often used for men's and women's suits and coats.

PART FIVE:
PATTERNED FABRICS

An Overview

So far we've covered natural fibre fabrics, man-made fabrics, wovens, knits and a range of other options, but there's one category left to discuss - a group of fabrics that would individually fall into any of the aforementioned categories, but collectively have one unique characteristic - patterns.

You might assume that patterned fabrics would be limited to cotton, but the range of prints is infinite. This section explores the most popular patterned fabrics and offers suggestions for their uses. Each fabric should be sewn according to its fibre content, which is always listed on the fabric bolt in the shop or can be determined with a burn test.

PRODUCTION & PROCESSES

Patterned fabrics can be made from all types of fibres in a variety of ways, and the processes for creating patterns vary as well. Some patterns are actually woven into the fabric itself, such as wool houndstooth or silk brocade. Batik fabrics are created with a wax-resist dyeing method, while discharge dyeing uses bleach to remove colour in a recurring pattern. The most common method for creating patterns is direct printing on to the fabric itself, using silkscreens, stencils and engraved plates to apply dye to the fabric in a systematic method using powerful machinery. The invention of the roller printer in 1783 industrialised this process, making it possible to print six colours at once.

If you're up for the challenge, you may enjoy printing your own fabric at home. Simple DIY screen-printing kits allow you to paint a permanent image on to your fabric multiple times, and are available in most craft shops and online. Direct-to-Garment printing (DTG) is another at-home method, which uses inkjet printers and fabric sheets to digitally print on to fabric. There are also online companies (such as Spoonflower.com) that will print small amounts of original fabric for you. Of course, if you're just not ready to invest in printing equipment, you can cut out and create a one-time screen-

Fashion

Home furnishing

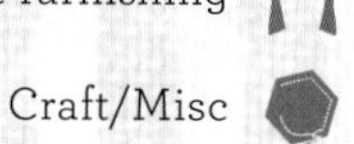

Craft/Misc

printed image for a T-shirt, bag, or baby romper suit – the poor-man's version of screen-printing and a craft that's easy to get addicted to!

ORGANIC

Though you may buy a shirt made from organic cotton fabric, it's important to consider whether the printing processes were organically achieved as well. With traditional printing methods, some chemicals are released as by-products into the environment. Over time, these toxins have damaging effects on air and water. With organic printing, manufacturers use solvent-free, water-based dyes that don't contain toxins. The dyes are vibrant and permanent and leave little impact on the environment.

USES

Patterned fabrics can be used for all types of garments and projects. It's important when selecting a print to remember the scale of the fabric's pattern. For instance, if you're making a detailed shirt with many seams, stay away from fabrics with large patterns. A better use for a large print would be a set of curtains or a gathered skirt that would show off the printed pattern.

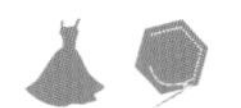

ARGYLE

The Argyle pattern originated in Scotland and dates back to at least the seventeenth century. It is created when diamond shapes are arranged in a diagonal chequerboard pattern. Some diamonds are coloured, while others are left in an outlined shape. The pattern is layered, recurring and symmetrical. When seen on jumpers and socks, the Argyle pattern is typically knitted into the garment itself. When found on cotton it is usually printed on to the fabric. Argyle comes in an assortment of colours and patterns and can be made in any fibre, but is most typically seen in cotton, wool or synthetics.

USES

Argyle can look up-market when used on jumpers and knitted vests, trousers or as a purse lining. It can also be very playful when used on a pair of knee-high socks, a T-shirt or a knitted headband.

BATIK

Authentic batik is an Indonesian design achieved using a wax-resist dyeing method, where wax is used to resist, or hold back, the dye in certain areas of the textile in order to create a pattern. Similar in tradition to tartan wool, batik patterns are specific to the different regions from which they derive, and often tell a story about family, nature and everyday life. Patterns range from stripes and diamonds to more tie-dyed effects. Some patterns are symmetrical and others are more chaotic, which adds to the fabric's character. Today, batiks are commercially printed and are sold in most fabric shops.

USES

Batik fabric is most commonly used for quilting and to make beach sarongs. The woven fabric is very lightweight, dries quickly and wraps easily around the waist. In Indonesia, batik is sometimes used as a headdress. It can also be used to make shirts, skirts, ties, scarves and accessories.

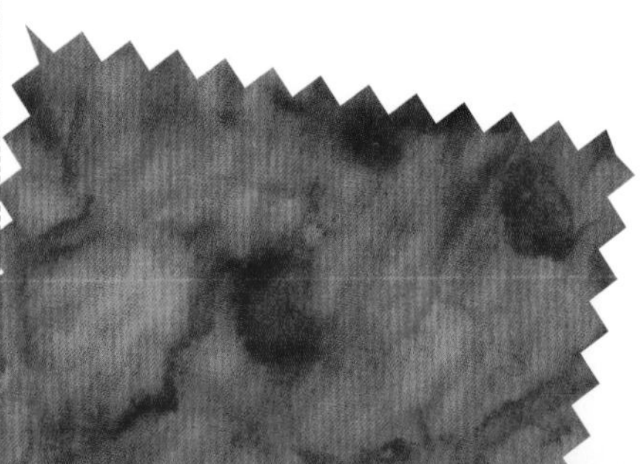

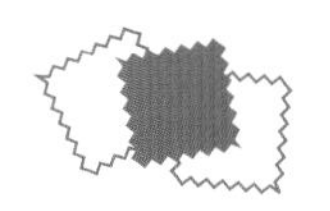

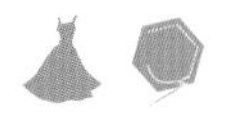

CALICO

In the UK, calico is a plain-woven cotton fabric, but in the US it is a simple cotton fabric with very small flowers, stars or miniature shapes printed on to the surface. Typically used for quilting, fabric shops often have walls of calico prints that are categorised according to colour. When examined closely, you can decipher the patterns and shapes, but from afar the fabric resembles one main colour, which is why they work well for mixing and matching on quilts.

USES

In addition to quilting, calico is used for children's bedding, childrenswear, small sewing projects and crafts.

CAMOUFLAGE

Once used solely for military purposes, camouflage has trickled its way into casual streetwear. Camouflage is characterised by large splotches of three different colours, intended as a way for soldiers to blend into their surroundings. Today, you'll find camouflage fabrics in black/grey tones, the standard brown/tan/olive green, and even in orange/grey and pink shades.

USES

Knit or woven in cotton and synthetics, camouflage is typically used for T-shirts, skirts, trousers, jackets, sweatshirts and all types of military gear. It is readily available in most fabric stores.

CHEVRON

Chevron is the official word used for the V shape of a military badge, but in the fashion world it has morphed into a highly popular printed fabric, with a recurring V pattern connected together in a zigzag formation. The zigzag pattern can be wide or thin, and is typically two-toned with white contrasted next to a colour.

USES

Most chevron prints come in varying weights of cotton and tend to be used for home furnishings and accessories; they are ideal for chic curtains and throw cushions. Chevron can also be used for skirts and dresses.

DAMASK

While damask was once considered an old-fashioned, stuffy textile from the Baroque period, it has made a trendy comeback. Now you'll find it everywhere, from wallpaper to buttons and purses. A damask pattern typically has recurring geometric shapes and curved spades. The style is very ornate and detailed.

USES

Damask is usually printed on woven cotton and can be used for blankets, bedding, quilts, bags, purses, accessories and skirts.

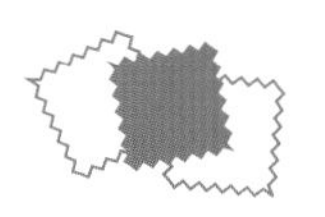

GINGHAM

Gingham is a quintessential summer fabric. From barbeque napkins and tablecloths to summer dresses, gingham checks are a popular choice. Patterns are woven or printed, and typically start with a solid coloured background and a contrasting colour with parallel stripes running both vertically and horizontally across the fabric. Where the stripes intersect, a chequerboard effect occurs. Some gingham checks are small, some are large and some come in multiple colours. Quality gingham is woven on cotton and has reversible sides. Polyester and nylon versions cost half as much, but are not as high quality and can snag under your sewing needle.

USES

Colours are usually bold and bright, but also come in pastel shades. They can be used for all types of projects and garments. Uses include shirts, dresses, scarves, children's clothing, linings, home furnishings, bedding, napkins, tablecloths and curtains.

HEATHER

A heathered pattern features scattered white specks throughout the fabric. The yarns are knit or woven in an interlocking pattern using varying shades of the same colour, with white as a contrasting colour. Heathers come in all shades, with grey and tan knits being the most common.

USES

Heather knits are perfect for comfortable T-shirts, tracksuit bottoms, pyjamas, dresses, skirts and sweatshirts.

HOUNDSTOOTH

Houndstooth is a two-toned broken checked pattern. Finer houndstooth is woven with wool, but today you'll find it printed on cotton, corduroy and even fleece. Traditional checks are small-scale and found in muted tones of brown and black. Trendy houndstooth patterns have large-scale checks, sometimes in bright flashy colours, such as hot pink with black.

USES

Traditional uses include tailored trousers and coats, waistcoats, purses, bags, bow ties and scarves. More trendy uses include dresses, skirts, leggings, T-shirts, shoes, bedding and home furnishing items.

IKAT

Similar to batik, ikat is an Indonesian fabric that uses a resist-dyeing method to create interesting shapes and designs. With ikat, dye is applied to the thread before the fabric is woven, unlike batik, where it is dyed afterwards. Double-ikat means that both the weft and the warp have been dyed. Ikat designs are usually geometric, jagged or blurred-looking, with diamonds, triangles and misshapen ovals. Most ikat fabrics look the same on both sides and there is no 'wrong' side to the fabric. Thai ikat fabrics are woven on smaller looms, typically 86–99cm/34–39in wide.

USES

Ikat is used for dresses, skirts, wraps and some home furnishing items.

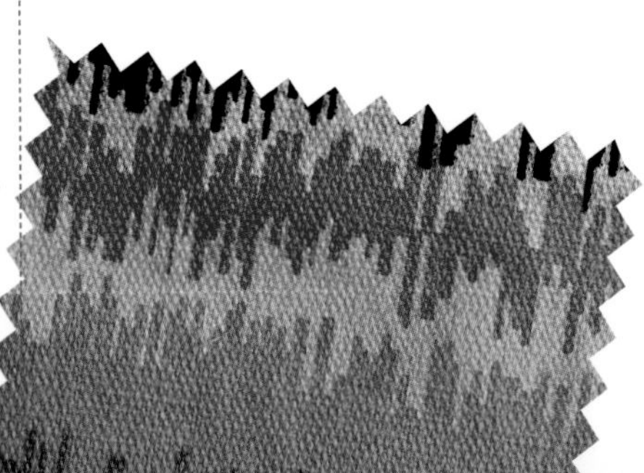

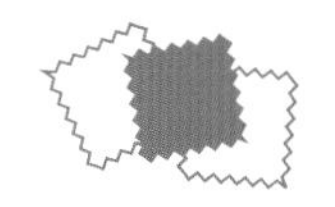

MADRAS

Madras is a lightweight colourful fabric with mismatched squares of plaid. It is bright, fun and often used for summer clothing. Originally, Madras fabrics were not colourfast, meaning they faded and bled with each wash. Some people enjoy the colour-changing look, but today, colourfast fabrics make it easier to wash Madras with the rest of your laundry load.

USES

Madras is used for all types of breezy, summer clothing, including shorts, trousers, dresses, capri pants, skirts, shirts and bags. It is typically 100 per cent cotton, shrinks easily and is carried in some fabric shops.

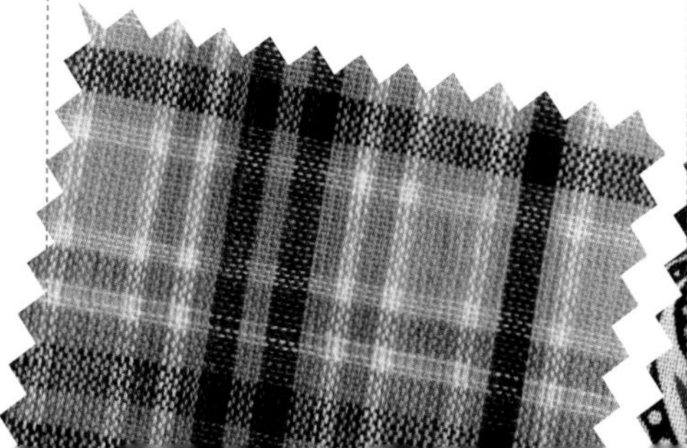

PAISLEY

Paisley is an ornate pattern that looks like a teardrop of water with a curve at the end. Some paisley fabrics are outlined with scallops, zigzags or multiple borders. Patterns can be overly busy and fussy or minimal and spread out. Fabrics are made from all fibres and come in a variety of colours. Though the pattern originated in India, paisley got its name from the Scottish town of Paisley, where it was manufactured in the early 1900s.

USES

Paisley is most commonly used for men's ties, scarves and handkerchiefs, but is also used for shirts, dresses, handbags, purses, shoes and all types of home furnishings.

PLAID (Tartan)

Tartan is a fabric woven with criss-crossed threads in multiple colours and varying widths. It comes in a spectrum of colours and fibres, with cotton and wool being the most common. Originating in Scotland, tartan is used for kilts and other traditional clothing.

USES

Traditionally, you'll find tartan patterns on wool scarves, men's ties and expensive purses. Tartan can be used for almost anything: shirts, dresses, skirts, childrenswear, bags and home furnishings.

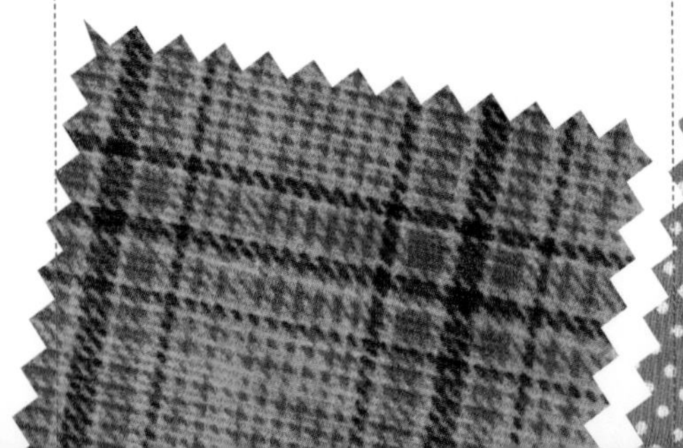

POLKA DOT

Easily one of the most favoured patterned fabrics, polka dot patterns feature recurring symmetrical dots of even space and size. Dots can be big and bold or small and far apart, but one thing is certain: the pattern is cute, colourful and used by people of all ages. If you think the name originated from the polka dance, you're partially right. It doesn't have any association with the dance as a metaphor for pattern or design, but since the two rose in popularity at the same time, the polka dot fabric adopted the polka dance name.

USES

Polka dot fabrics have a wide range of uses, and are suitable for all types of clothing, including aprons, swimsuits, accessories, bags and purses. They are also a good choice for bedding, home furnishings and crafts.

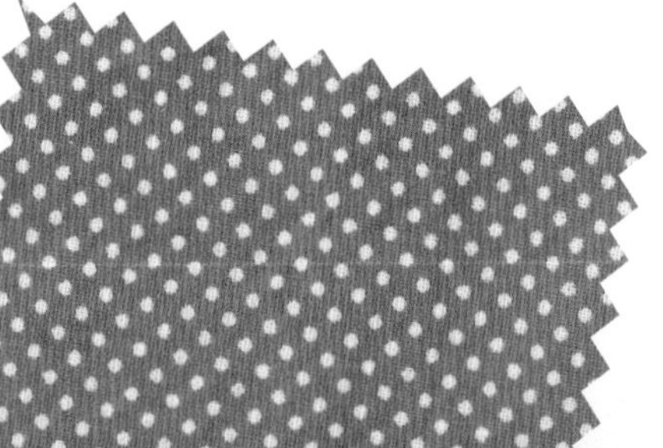

STRIPES

Striped patterns have parallel lines that run either vertically or horizontally across the fabric. Stripes can be evenly spaced, spread out, vary in widths and come in a range of colours. Ticking is a specific type of striped fabric, similar in weight to denim, with vertical blue, black or red lines on a light coloured background. Like polka dots, stripes are a classic favourite and add a great design element to any project. When used on garments, horizontal stripes can accentuate curves, while vertical stripes used on trousers, coats and blazers can make the wearer look slimmer.

USES

Striped fabric can be used for virtually any project. Stripes look good on all types of clothing, accessories, bags, upholstery, home furnishings, crafts, shoes, hats and well… anything else you can think of.

TOILE

Toile, the French word for 'cloth', is often thought of as a white fabric with printed red or blue images of vintage farm scenes and people. It's considered 'shabby chic', and is often used for upholstery, wallpaper and home furnishings. But toile is not limited to farm scenes – the fabric also encompasses leisurely beach or town scenes, and can feature mythological figures, cars, buildings and animals. Unusual toile patterns are found in some online boutique shops and antique shops, although they're quite hard to come by.

USES

Toile is primarily used for home furnishings and upholstery, but can also be used for bags and some clothing.

NOTIONS and TOOLS

We love fabric. We love its lustre, beauty and unique personality. It's pretty to look at, soft to touch and irresistible to collect. But the fact remains – fabric is simply fabric until we do something with it. When fabric is manipulated, cut, sewn, trimmed or buttoned together it takes on a new purpose. It can be transformed into a garment or accessory, going from pretty eye-candy to something utilitarian and fashionable. And all this is done with the aid of notions and tools.

I've been sewing since I was 10 years old, but only in my adult life did I truly start to understand what sewing notions and tools were and what they could be used for. Notions cover a wide range of accessories, from trims to fasteners, and there are also a wide variety of tools that can help the sewing process. Some tools are meant to deconstruct projects – such as seam rippers (used to rip apart mistakes) – but most help to construct, build and create. Most fabric shops have a dedicated notions and tools section that will surely get your creative wheels spinning.

This section is split into two parts – the first covers notions and the second part covers tools. Hopefully this section will demystify what notions and tools are so that you have a better understanding of how to use them in your sewing projects.

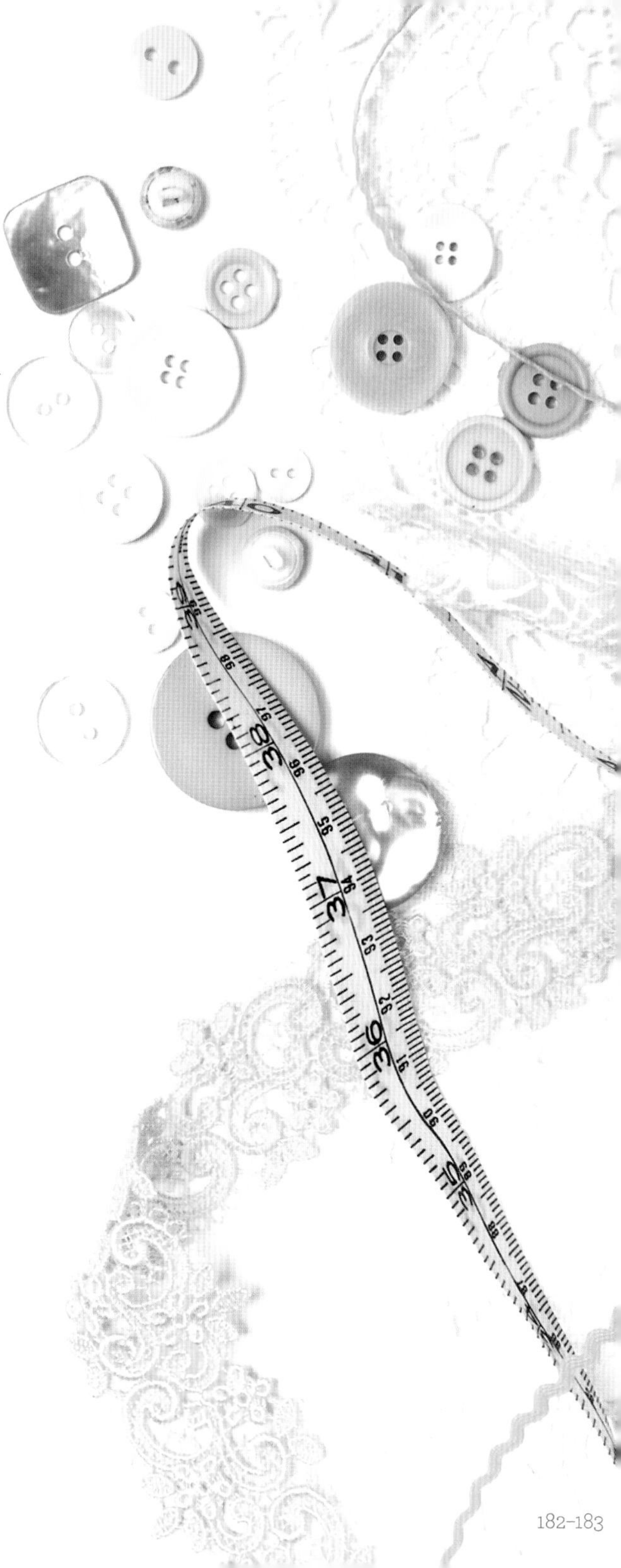

PART ONE: NOTIONS

PART TWO: TOOLS

APPLIQUÉ

FUSIBLE WEB

This double-sided web (known under the brand names HeatnBond® and Vilene Wonder Under/ Bondaweb) is the backbone of fabric appliqué. Sold in pre-cut packages or by the metre, fusible web is a synthetic clear fibre backed with paper that melts under the heat of an iron, fusing two pieces of fabric together. To apply the webbing, first pre-wash your fabric to remove any sizing or finishes that may interrupt the fusing process. Cut a piece of web slightly larger than the design/shape you wish to appliqué, and then iron the rough side of the web to the wrong side of your appliqué fabric, leaving the web's paper in place. Trace and cut out your design and, when you're ready, fuse it to another fabric (such as a T-shirt, bag or blanket), by peeling off the paper and ironing the appliqué design on the other fabric. Although the webbing will keep the fabric edges from fraying, most appliqués are finished off by hand or by using a zigzag machine stitch.

FREEZER PAPER

Similar to fusible web, freezer paper is a one-sided iron-on paper used for appliqué and screenprinting. Although freezer paper is a product more commonly used in the US to wrap cuts of meat, it has now become popular with crafters and sewers worldwide, and is especially helpful when creating appliqué with edges that are folded under rather than fused. First, the design element is cut out of freezer paper and ironed to the wrong side of the fabric. The fabric is cut approximately 0.5cm larger than the freezer paper and the edges of the fabric are then snipped close to the edge of the paper, especially in areas with a curve, and ironed over to give a crisp edge. The design is then machine or hand sewn to a quilt square (or other fabric), and finally, a small slit is cut in the back of the fabric to carefully pull the paper out. Freezer paper can also be used to create iron-on stencils.

TEMPLAR

Templar is a heat-resistant plastic used to create appliqué templates. It works well when ironing over fabric edges (similar to using freezer paper), and is removed before sewing the appliqué piece on to your fabric.

LACE

BATTENBURG

Battenburg is easy to create and is probably the most common lace around. It is a tape lace, which means pieces of fabric tape of even width are linked together with small lace stitches to create intricate designs.

BOBBIN

This lace is made by hand from many different threads that are attached to separate bobbins. To create the lace, pins are set in a pillow and threads are woven through the pins while the weaver holds the bobbins up above the design, working them over, under and around one another to create a detailed lace pattern.

NEEDLE

While a hand-sewing needle and thread is all that's needed to create this type of lace, the process is tedious and time-consuming. Designs can be simple or ornate, and are created by hand-sewing small stitches together (usually using a buttonhole stitch). While being worked, the design is attached with several stay-stitches on to a hard backing, such as card, which is eventually cut away from the finished design. The most prized antique laces often fall into this category.

CROCHET

This lace is typically made using fine crochet thread and a crochet hook. Similar to knitting, crocheting pulls loops of yarn through each other to create a textile; however, the single hook and stitches used in crocheting allow for more intricate designs in comparison to knitting.

CUTWORK

This is a type of needlepoint where small stitches are sewn on to a piece of fabric and then the fabric is cut away at certain points in the stitched design to create an open space, similar to eyelet fabric.

MACRAMÉ

Rather than weaving or sewing, macramé is made by tying knots in yarn or thread to create interesting designs. Although it isn't technically a type of lace, it does have lace-like characteristics. Macramé was very popular in the 1970s and was used to create wall hangings, trims, pot holders and other household items.

TATTING

Tatting is similar to macramé, as it uses knots to create lace-like designs, but also incorporates interlocking loops that are made using a tatting shuttle tool. Designs are typically used for doilies, shirt collars and trims.

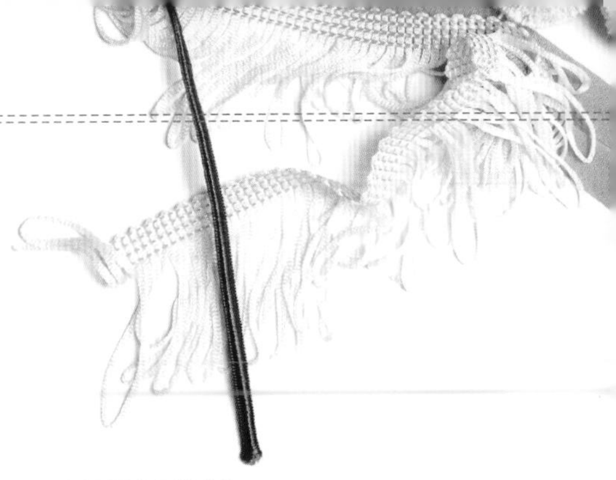

TRIMS

BIAS BINDING

This is a finishing tape that is often made of cotton or polyester-blend fabric. It is typically sandwiched and sewn over raw edges, such as the edge of a blanket or armholes on a shirt. Because it is cut on the bias (the diagonal of the fabric's grain), it has additional give and works well around curved areas. Pre-packaged bias binding is typically 2.5m/3yd in length, sold in various colours and widths (usually no more than 2.5cm/1in wide), and can be single or double-fold. With the use of a tool called a bias binding maker, you can easily make your own bias binding in any fabric print or fibre you like.

BRAID

Braid is typically a thick satin-soft trim that looks like it has been braided. It is often used in home furnishings for cushions and upholstery, and is sewn on top of the fabric. A braid presser foot helps guide the braid in a straight line as you sew, but isn't necessary.

CORDING

Similar to piping, cording is made by twisting two yarns together into a rope. It sometimes comes with an attached fabric lip, which makes it easy to sandwich and sew between two fabrics. A piping or zip presser foot will keep the cord tight next to the seam as you sew. The term welt cord refers to fabric-covered cord or piping.

FRINGING

Fringed trims have a stringy edge. Fringing can be an extension of the fabric itself, with the fabric edge cut into small strips, or it can be an applied trim with strings, cording, ribbons and beads hanging from an attached tape.
A popular trim in the 1920s, fringing is also seen in classic cowboy styles (such as leather fringe waistcoats), and is often used in home furnishings on cushions and lampshades. It can also add a unique finish to purses, hair accessories, dresses and skirts.

PIPING

Sometimes referred to as welt cord, piping is a fabric-covered cord with an extended fabric lip, which makes it easy to sandwich and sew between two fabrics. Larger piping is used around cushion edges, while smaller, skinnier piping is used for clothing, such as on the edge of a pocket, a shirt collar or for a pop of colour on decorative dress seams. Although piping is sold by the metre at most fabric shops, it's easy to make your own using simple shop-bought cord (which looks like cream-coloured rope) and your own bias binding. A piping or zip presser foot will keep the piping tight and next to the seam as you sew.

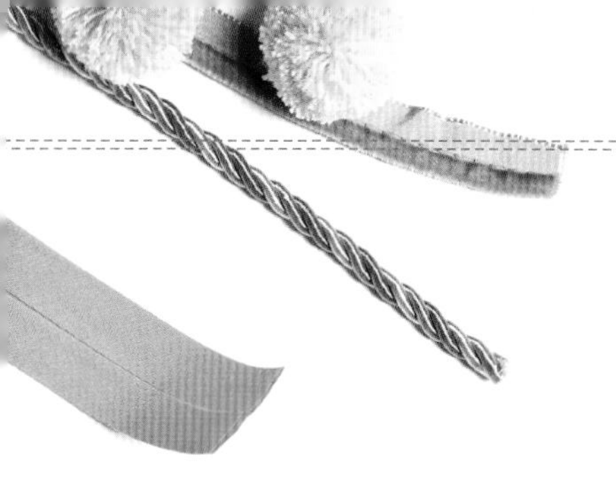

POM POM

This trim is cute, playful and works well for children's decor (it should not be used for baby items as it can be a choking hazard). It is made of a soft woven tape with small pom pom balls attached to create a fringe. It is easy to sew on top of a fabric using a standard presser foot.

QUILT BINDING

Similar to bias binding, this is used to bind the raw edges of a quilt or blanket. You can make your own with cotton, synthetic or satin fabric, or you can purchase pre-made packages. Shop-bought binding is typically 2.5m/3yd in length, comes in varying widths, in solid colours and is made of cotton or synthetic blends. Some quilt bindings have a ruffled edge with a double-fold lip on one side, allowing you to sandwich it over a blanket edge.

RICKRACK

This trim is cute and colourful. Made of polyester or cotton, rickrack is a zigzagged trim of small connected V-shapes. It comes in a wide range of colours and is sewn on top of fabric right down the middle. Polyester rickrack tends to curl up at the edges, while cotton lays flat. It is often used on the edges of skirts, bags, aprons and cushion covers; for crafts; and even for artwork and wall hangings.

RUFFLES

With a dainty and feminine look, ruffled trim is made by gathering fabric, ribbon or lace together. It can either be attached to fabric tape, which is then sewn to the edge of a clothing item, or the edges may be left raw and incorporated into the seam of a garment.

SEQUINS and BEADS

Sequined and beaded trims are usually a row of sequins or beads that are strung together and hung as a fringe, or woven with elastic on to a stretchy trim. Most sequins can be machine sewn, but beaded strands (unless attached to fabric tape) require hand stitching.

TWILL TAPE

This is a twill-woven ribbon that is made from different fibres, although cotton is the most common. It is soft, often solid in colour, sold by the metre, and comes in varying weights and widths. The look of twill tape is soft, natural and simple. It makes a wonderful tie, drawstring or ribbon, works well as an edging and is also used to make clothing labels. If you don't find a colour you like you can easily dye your own.

RIBBONS

ACETATE
This is a synthetic woven ribbon that can have a dull or shiny satin finish. It is usually stiff and creases when folded, which makes it suitable for paper crafts, gift wrapping and floral arrangements.

CHIFFON
This is a lightweight ribbon that is similar to chiffon fabric. Nicer chiffon ribbons feel soft and won't crease when folded, and others have a small metal wire lining the edge, making them easy to bend and shape into a large bow for furnishings or gift wrapping.

CLOTH
Cloth ribbons are made from woven cotton or synthetic blended fabrics. The quality of the ribbon depends on the quality of the cloth used.

GROSGRAIN
Grosgrain (pronounced 'grow-grain') is characterised by the vertical ribs found throughout the ribbon. It is durable, has a dull satin feel and works well for a variety of craft projects, hair bows and as a fabric trim.

JACQUARD
This is a very decorative ribbon that is woven on a jacquard loom. Designs usually involve multiple colours (sometimes metallic) and intricate patterns. Jacquard ribbons are more expensive than common acetate ribbons, but they have a unique character and can add a beautiful design element to a sewing project.

SATIN
Satin ribbons are made with a satin weave using polyester or acetate fibres, and can be shiny on one or both sides. Nicer ribbons are soft, drape well and don't crease when folded, making them ideal for sewn garments.

TAFFETA
Taffeta ribbon has the same crisp feel and iridescent look as taffeta fabric. The ribbon ends will fray easily, so it's best to cut them on an angle.

VELVET
Velvet ribbon has a soft plush pile on top, similar to velvet fabric. Most ribbons are made from synthetic fibres and some will bend more easily than others. Velvet ribbon adds a beautiful trim to clothing, baby items, bags, blankets and hats.

BUTTONS

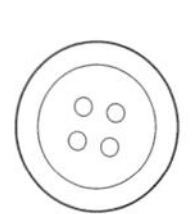

FLAT or SEW-THROUGH

These types of buttons are characterised by two or four holes punched out in the middle of the button. Whether sewn on by hand or machine, thread comes up through one hole and back down through another hole, attaching the button to the fabric or garment. Sew-through buttons are the most common type of button available.

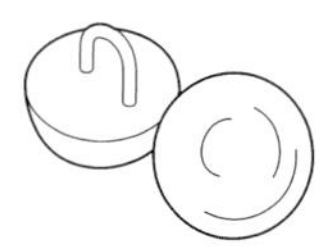

SHANK

Shank buttons are often decorative and come in all different shapes and colours. They don't have holes, but rather a plastic or metal shank loop attached to the back, which is where the thread passes through and attaches the button to the fabric. They shouldn't be used with delicate fabrics (unless reinforced with facing), as they may weigh down the fabric and cause it to droop. Shank buttons are sometimes paired with a corded loop rather than a buttonhole.

FABRIC

There are three types of fabric buttons:

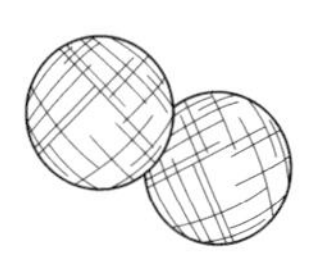

FABRIC-COVERED: These are typically made from lightweight metal and are composed of two pieces. The front of the button is covered with fabric and is then attached to the back piece, which holds the fabric taut. The entire button is attached to fabric through a back loop, similar to shank buttons.

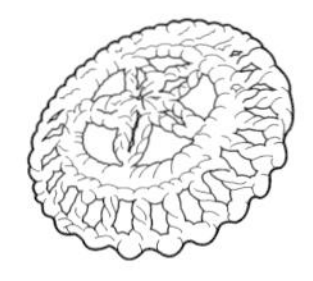

WORKED/CLOTH: Similar to fabric-covered buttons, these have an embroidered or crocheted pattern over the button form.

MANDARIN: Also known as Chinese knot or frog buttons. They are made of knotted strings and are sewn directly on to clothing. They don't require a buttonhole, but are connected by a corded loop attached to another piece of fabric.

FASTENERS

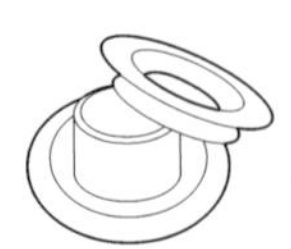

EYELETS and GROMMETS

Eyelets and grommets are metal rings, typically brass, that are sandwiched around a cut hole in a piece of fabric and then clamped together. These reinforced holes allow cord, rope, curtain rods or shoelaces to pass through. They come in a variety of sizes and are often sold with a simple attachment kit consisting of a metal rod that is placed over the eyelets and pounded with a hammer. More sophisticated kits come with a plier-like tool, but are only worth the investment if you plan on attaching a large number of grommets.

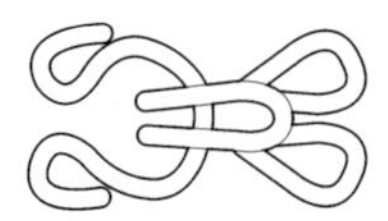

HOOK and EYE

These fasteners are similar to the buttons and loops often found on the back of a shirt or the waistline of a skirt; unlike buttons, they aren't meant to be seen. A hook and eye is made of two parts – a small metal hook that is attached to one side of the clothing and a small metal loop (or eye) that is attached to the other side (and usually hand sewn). The hook slips into the eye and fastens the two fabrics together.

SNAP FASTENERS

Next to buttons and zips, snap fasteners, or press studs, are one of the most common types of fasteners. Like grommets, they are made of two pieces – one piece has a small metal ball that snaps into a small metal hole in the other piece. When attached to fabric, it is easy to pull the fastener apart. Snap fasteners are commonly used for baby clothing, and in places where small fasteners are needed. Sizes and snap types vary, and while many need to be sewn on by hand, some are sold with a simple attachment kit consisting of a metal rod that is placed over the snaps and pounded with a hammer. More sophisticated kits come with a plier-like tool, but are only worth the investment if you plan on attaching a large number of fasteners. There are a few different types of snap fasteners available, including:

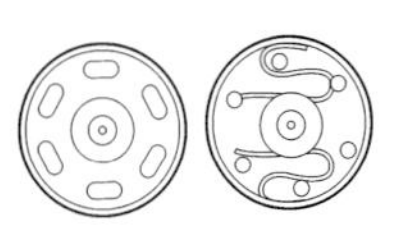

SEW-ON: These snap fasteners have small holes in the edges that allow you to hand sew the fastener on to the fabric.

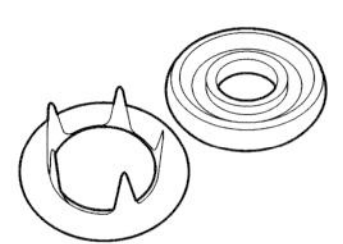

NO-SEW: These snap fasteners have cleat-like prongs on each side, which allow them to grab on to fabric. The fasteners are pounded using a small metal rod (sold with a snap kit) and a hammer. When using snap fasteners on lightweight fabrics, it's best to reinforce them with an additional piece of fabric, tape or interfacing so that the prongs don't snag the fabric when the fastener is pulled open.

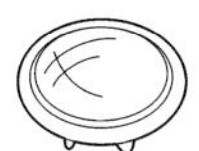

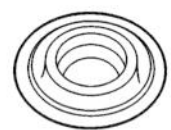

COVERED: Similar to covered buttons, these snap fasteners have fabric covering the visible side of the fastener. This is a clever way to match fasteners with the fabric of your garment or to give them a contrasting fabric look.

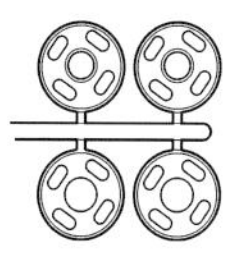

IRON-SAFE: These are heat-resistant snap fasteners made from nylon and are often clear.

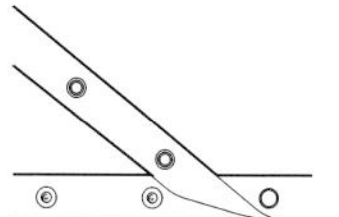

SNAP TAPE: Typically made of twill tape, snap tape has evenly spaced, pre-attached fasteners. It is easy to use, and the perfect way to fasten a baby sleeper, romper suit or child's shirt.

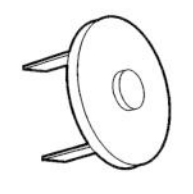

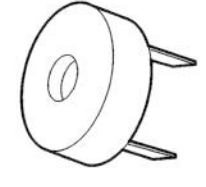

MAGNETIC: These are heavy duty snap fasteners that are often used for bags and purses and attach via a magnetic closure. Like no-sew snap fasteners, they have protruding prongs that are clamped on to fabric.

HOOK and LOOP

Commonly known under the trademark name Velcro, hook and loop is a stiff tape made of two layers: one side is covered with many rough hooks, while the other is covered with soft, hairy loops. Each side is attached to a piece of fabric (either by sewing or with sticky adhesive on the back of the tape). The two sides are then stuck together to create a fastener and can be pulled apart by hand when needed.

BUCKLES

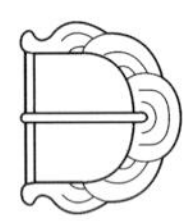

FASHION

These buckles are used on belts and bags. They're usually made of metal, with a centre bar and rod that pokes through a hole in the belt or strap, holding the two pieces of fabric together. Some fashion buckles are sold in large fabric shops, but you'll find a wider selection online.

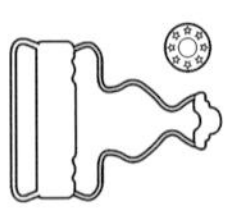

DUNGAREE CLIP

These are two-piece buckle sets used for dungarees. Usually made from metal or brass, the button piece is attached at the top of the bib and the buckle is threaded through the straps (which are usually adjustable in length). The buckle hooks on to the button and holds the trousers up.

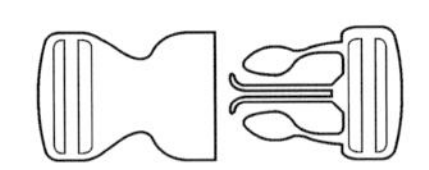

QUICK RELEASE

Sometimes called parachute buckles, these are typically made from plastic and consist of two parts – one side has two flexible teeth that push in and snap into the other side. Release buckles are paired with thick nylon webbing or tape.

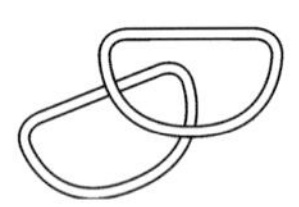

D-RINGS

Shaped like the letter D, these rings are used for luggage, bags, purses, outdoor gear, saddles and fashion. A strap is looped and sewn to the straight side of the ring, providing a reinforced opening for another strap to be looped through.

CENTRE RELEASE

Similar to quick release buckles, but instead of using two flexible teeth, the buckle is attached by a centre button that snaps in and releases.

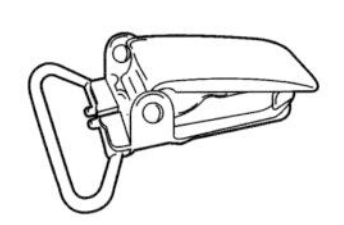

BRACES/MITTEN CLIPS

These are metal clips that are sewn to the end of a wide piece of elastic or a strap (as with braces) and then clamped on to a garment.

ELASTIC

TYPES of ELASTIC

WOVEN: This has visible crosswise ribs, is heavier than most elastics and is sometimes thick, making it ideal for heavyweight denim and home furnishing fabrics. It doesn't narrow when stretched, so can be used inside a casing or sewn directly to the fabric itself. It is typically made from polyester or nylon, and sometimes cotton.

KNIT: Typically made from polyester or nylon and feels soft and lightweight. It doesn't narrow when stretched, so can be used inside a casing or sewn directly to the fabric itself.

BRAID: Refers to fibres that have been braided around rubber strands. It is typically made from polyester or nylon, and sometimes cotton. It narrows and curls as it is stretched, which can be frustrating when used inside a waistband casing.

TRANSPARENT: Made from synthetic polyurethane and sometimes referred to as clear elastic. It stretches more than woven, knit or braid elastic, and is often used in swimsuits and dancewear.

ELASTIC VARIETIES

WAISTBAND: Can be made from any fibre and is used primarily for waistbands, with the elastic usually sewn into a casing. The most common widths are 2–2.5cm/¾–1in.

UNDERWEAR AND LINGERIE: This is sewn directly on to the garment. It is decorative, comes in various colours and is sometimes scalloped at the edges. Woven and knit elastics are the most common, as they don't narrow and curl when pulled tight.

FOLD-OVER ELASTIC (FOE): Soft and stretchy with one blunt/straight edge and often a scalloped edge on the other side. It is meant to be sandwiched or folded over raw edges and sewn into place. When sewn to non-stretchy fabrics, the elastic is stretched as you sew, so it is taut with the fabric and gathers up and springs back when you have finished sewing.

BABY: Very skinny elastic that is used for doll and baby clothing. It can be sewn directly on top of the fabric or pulled through a casing.

SWIMWEAR: Clear, transparent elastic. Not all transparent elastic is suitable for swimwear, however, so read labels carefully and make sure the elastic can withstand exposure to chlorine and salt water.

DRAWSTRING: Elastic with a drawstring attached. It is ideal for making pyjama bottoms and stringing through a waistband casing.

BUTTONHOLE: Has sewn buttonholes evenly spaced throughout. It is often used for adjustable waistbands.

CORDED: Very skinny elastic, similar to piping and cord trim. It is used for doll and baby clothing, home furnishings and crafts.

ZIPS

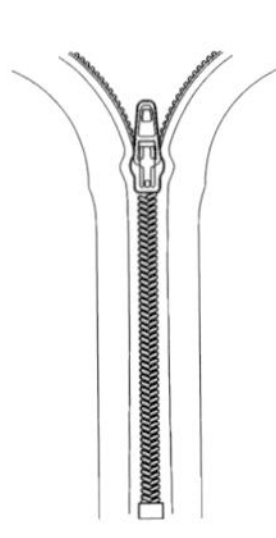

NYLON COIL

Nylon coil zips are the most common zips on the market, and are used for all types of projects. The teeth (or coils) are made from synthetic nylon and run up and down the zip with a slider in the middle. The zip has a small stopper at the bottom that keeps it from going any further.

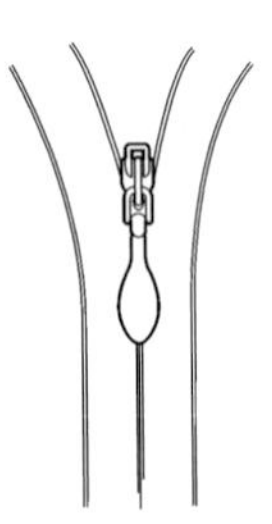

INVISIBLE

These zips, installed with an invisible zipper foot, have teeth that are hidden on the wrong side of the zip, making them invisible on the finished garment. Typically used for skirts and dresses, the only visible part, when sewn correctly, is the slider.

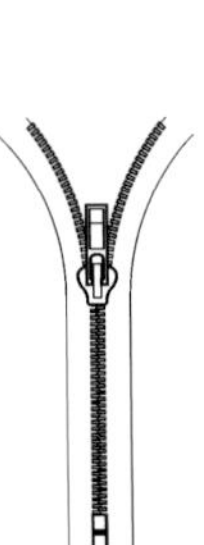

METAL TOOTH

These zips are similar to coil zips, but the teeth are made of metal. They are typically used for jeans and other trousers.

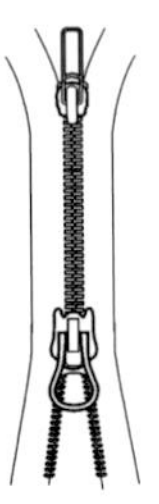

OPEN-ENDED/SPORT

These zips are typically made from nylon, but are open-ended on both sides, meaning they don't have a small stopper at the bottom. This makes them reversible and useable from both ends. Be careful not to zip the slider off before sewing it in place, as it will be difficult to place back on.

THREAD

ALL-PURPOSE

This is the most common type of thread and is made of cotton-wrapped polyester. The cotton provides strength, while the polyester adds a bit of stretch, making it the ideal thread for most projects.

100% POLYESTER

This has a bit of give to it and works well with stretch fabrics and knits.

100% COTTON

This is made from spun cotton filaments and is used for general sewing projects.

100% SILK

Strong thread made from silk filaments. It can be used to sew many fabrics, but is more pricey.

100% RAYON

This is a strong thread with a bit of shine. It is sometimes used for embroidery sewing.

100% NYLON

This is a synthetic thread that is very durable. It is sometimes clear or transparent.

MERCERISED COTTON

This is cotton thread that has been processed additional times for added lustre and strength.

METALLIC

Adds a decorative look to a project but should never be used as a construction thread, as it is not as strong as other standard threads. It is typically aluminium wrapped around cotton or polyester, and may dull your sewing needle quicker than other threads.

SPOOLED

Also known as serger or cone thread, this is 100% polyester thread wound on to a large spool. It is ideal for overlocking machines, since overlocking requires a great deal of thread, with three to four spools of the same thread colour used at one time. The large spool is difficult to use on a standard sewing machine unless you have a spool pin attached to your machine.

ELASTIC

Elastic thread is wound by hand on the bobbin, with standard thread used on the top of the sewing machine. When sewn, the stretchy thread gathers fabric up nicely, and only shows on the wrong side of the fabric.

DENIM JEANS

This is a durable, often yellow/mustard coloured thread used to sew denim jeans. It is sometimes sold pre-packaged rather than on the rack with other spools of thread.

PATTERN and PLANNING TOOLS

DRESSMAKER'S CARBON and TRACING PAPER

A useful pattern-making and planning material is carbon and tracing paper. Used for drawing or tracing patterns, these papers come in varying weights, colours and forms, such as:

DRESSMAKER'S CARBON PAPER: This comes in a variety of coours, including white, so it can be used with many different-coloured fabrics. The carbon paper is used to mark fabric in combination with a tracing wheel. The pattern piece is pinned to the fabric, then the tracing wheel is used to trace around the pattern, transferring the imprint of the marking side of the paper on to the wrong side of the fabric.
TRACING PAPER AND PATTERNED PAPER: These come on a roll and are typically white, brown, manila or dotted. They are similar to craft or butcher paper and are large enough that patterns can be drawn right on top.

LIGHTWEIGHT INTERFACING: Typically sewn into clothing or bags, lightweight interfacing also works well for tracing and cutting out patterns, as it doesn't crease or tear easily. You can use standard interfacing found in most fabric shops or buy industrial-sized pattern tracing interfacing on a roll.
SEPARATING TISSUE: This is used in cutting rooms to separate layers of fabric from each other. It is a lightweight tissue that comes in multiple colours, which helps with identifying bolts. It can also be used for tracing and drawing patterns.

DRESS FORMS

Sometimes referred to as sewing dummies and mannequins, dress forms are an imitation of the human body and come in all shapes and sizes. They are a perfect way to visualise your work in progress in three-dimensional form. This may be done by draping calico or other fabric over the form to see how it hangs and fits, and draping tape can be used to create a pattern on the form itself. Sometimes dress forms are used simply to display finished products.

Dress forms are made in general dress sizes, adjustable sizes or are custom-made to fit your exact size. They are typically made from fibreglass and have wire on the inside, a dense foam layer on top that gives a soft support and a fabric covering for pinning fabrics and patterns. Some forms have a linen or cotton fabric covering and others have a removable cover that can be sewn to fit your body and then pulled over the foam base. The type of sewing projects and body you're sewing for will determine the dress form needed. Here is a list of the most common varieties:

LADIES DRESS FORMS: These forms fit the female body and come in varying dress sizes. They typically don't have arms or legs, and some have wheels on the base for easy movement in a workroom.

MALE DRESS FORMS: These forms fit the male body and come in varying body sizes. They typically don't have arms or legs.

LADIES FULL-BODY FORMS: Forms with legs, but without arms.

LARGE WOMEN FORMS: Designed for larger body types.

JUNIOR FORMS: Meant for children's clothing. Some forms have legs but most don't have arms.

TROUSER FORMS: A pair of legs (from the hip down) with a hanging-style base.

ANTIQUE DRESS FORMS: Hollow forms made of wire. They are sometimes used as decorative pieces rather than as a working form.

DISPLAY DRESS FORMS: Used to display finished clothing. Some are made of quality products while others are simple plastic forms, such as a mannequin used in a retail shop window display.

MARKING TOOLS

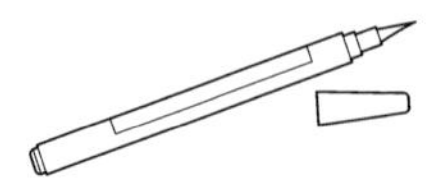

AIR-SOLUBLE PENS

These pens typically write in blue, pink or purple, and have ink that disappears within 24–48 hours as a result of being exposed to air. Projects should be sewn soon after they are marked, otherwise markings will begin to fade. Read the instructions carefully, as some inks may become permanent when ironed.

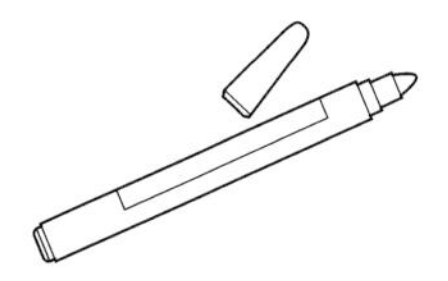

WATER-SOLUBLE PENS

These pens have blue, pink or purple ink that disappears when sprayed with water. Some pen markings can also be erased with the appropriate eraser pen. Water-soluble pens should only be used on fabrics that will not water spot or become ruined by exposure to water.

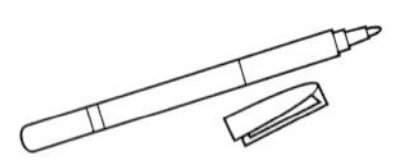

PERMANENT MARKERS

Permanent markers and other standard pens can be used for pattern drafting. However, because the markings are permanent, they should be drawn with confidence.

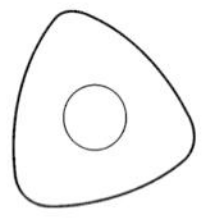

TAILOR'S CHALK and CHALK LINERS

Tailor's chalk can be used to mark on any fabric colour or fibre. Light-coloured chalks are ideal for use on dark fabrics (and vice versa), since the chalk shows up more easily.

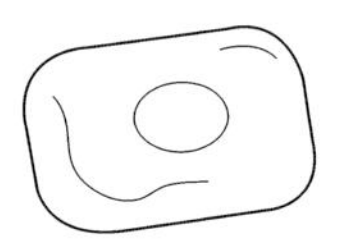

BAR SOAP

This is an inexpensive way to make markings on fabric. It's best to use white soap and shape it into a thin point, similar to a piece of chalk. Soap lines will disappear when the fabric is washed.

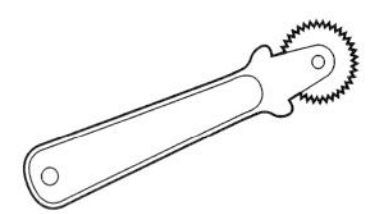

TRACING WHEELS

Tracing wheels are a wonderful way to transfer pattern markings when paired with dressmaker's carbon paper. It consists of a small handle with a metal wheel at the end. Some have serrated edges, which are useful for making perforations, while others are smooth around the edges, which works well for markings. Some tracing wheels come with two wheels - one marks the pattern piece while the other is adjustable and marks the seam allowance. To mark a pattern, lay the carbon paper down with the marked side up. Then lay fabric on top, pin the pattern piece to it and, using a tracing wheel, trace around the pattern, pressing down and transferring the markings on to the wrong side of the fabric.

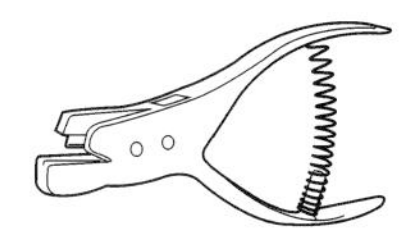

PATTERN NOTCHERS

These are similar to hole punches and make small notches in the fabric that serve as pattern markings.

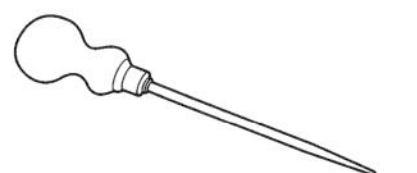

AWLS

Awls are simple tools with very sharp, pointy ends. They are sometimes used in pattern making to mark holes in a piece of fabric, but are generally used to punch holes in leather and other thick fabrics that need to be laced together.

PATTERN WEIGHTS

Pattern weights are used to weigh down a pattern on top of fabric when they can't be pinned. If you don't have weights, you could easily use a small tin of food or another household item to weigh down the pattern and fabric.

DRAPING TAPE

Draping tape is a thin, coloured tape used to create markings on a dress form. The tape offers an easy way to visualise your design on a three-dimensional form.

MEASURING TOOLS

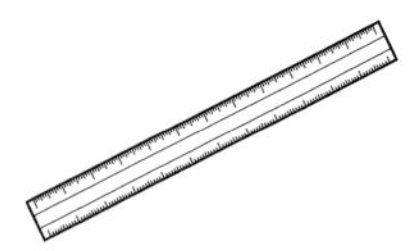

STANDARD RULERS

Standard rulers are used to draw straight lines. Measurements are labelled in inches on one side of the ruler and centimetres on the other.

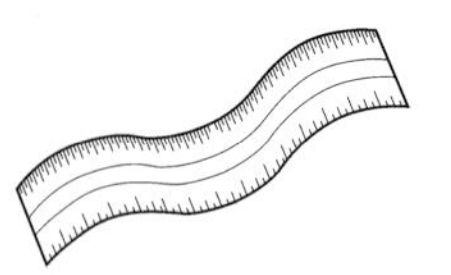

FLEXIBLE RULERS

Flexible rulers can bend around into a circle, making it easy to mark and measure sleeve caps and necklines.

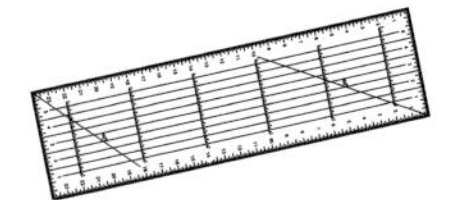

QUILTING RULERS

Quilting rulers are clear, transparent rulers with a grid of markings across the face. They come in a variety of sizes and shapes, including squares, rectangules, and triangles. When paired with a cutting mat and rotary cutter, it's easy to cut accurate, straight lines.

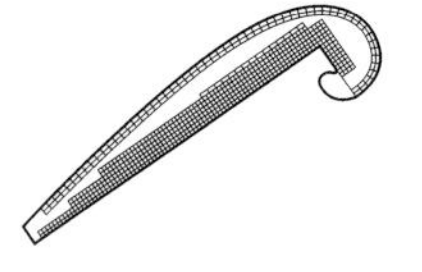

FRENCH CURVES

Often made of plastic or aluminium, French curves are used for drafting smooth curved lines. The French curve has many different curved shapes and widths to accommodate sleeves, necklines and any other curvy pattern pieces.

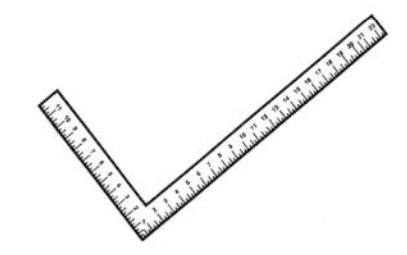

L-SQUARE RULERS

L-square rulers are used to line up fabrics with the grain and measure hem lines. They also help to make perfectly square corners.

MEASURING TAPES

Measuring tapes are flexible rulers made of cloth or plastic, and are a must-have for any sewer. Tapes are inexpensive and are very useful when taking body measurements. They are labelled in inches on one side and centimetres on the other.

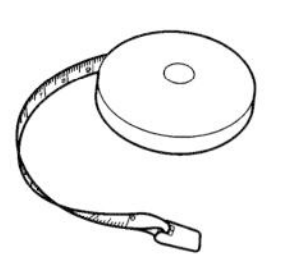

RETRACTABLE TAPES

These are similar to industrial tape measures used for DIY projects. The tape is usually plastic or aluminium, with inches on one side and centimetres on the other.

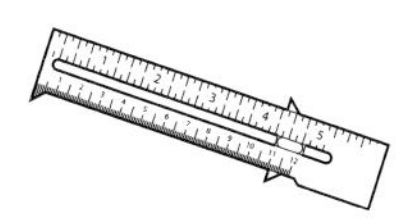

SEAM GAUGES

These are small rulers with an adjustable gauge in the middle that slides up and down. The gauge is used to mark and measure seam allowances and hem lines.

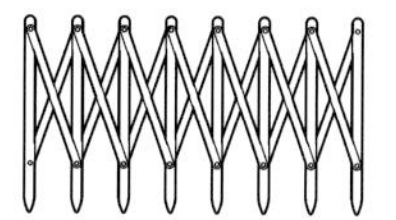

EXPANDING GAUGES

These gauges expand and contract, similar to an accordion, allowing you to mark buttons and pleats at equal distances from each other.

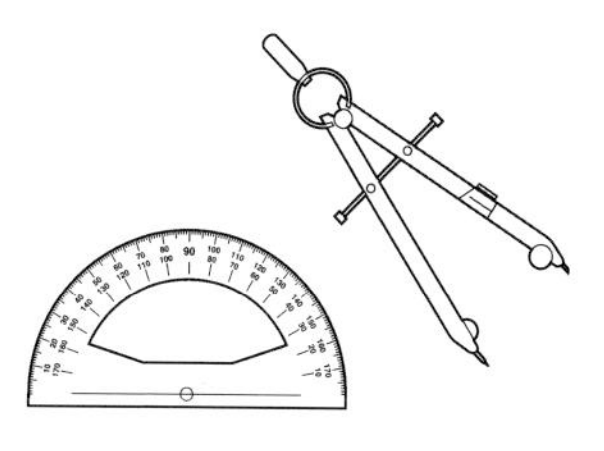

PROTRACTORS and COMPASSES

While often used for geometry, protractors and compasses can come in handy when mathematical measurements are needed for a pattern. Protractors help measure and draw exact angles by degrees, and compasses work well for drawing exact circles (you can easily make your own compass with a piece of string and a pencil attached to the end). Alternatively, a quick way to create a circle is to trace around a cup, plate or other round object.

CUTTING TOOLS

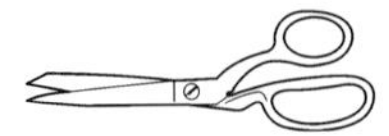

SHEARS

Sometimes referred to as dressmaking shears, these are the most common type of sewing scissors. While standard scissors have straight handles, shears have a bent handle, making it easier to cut fabric that is laid out on a table. They are usually 15–23cm/6–9in in length, giving you a longer blade for cutting. The finest shears are made from metal cutlery steel. Lower-end shears have metal blades and plastic handles. Quality shears are a wise investment.

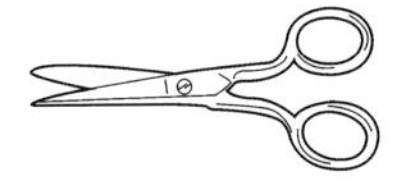

SCISSORS

Scissors have straight handles, are often less than 15cm/6in in length, and range in quality. Finer blades will cut through fabric and are also used in embroidery work, while general scissors work well for craft projects and paper cutting.

PINKING SHEARS

These shears are shaped like standard shears with a bent handle, but the blades have a unique zigzag finish. The zigzag cut minimises fraying edges, so it's ideal to use pinking shears for trimming seams and raw fabric edges.

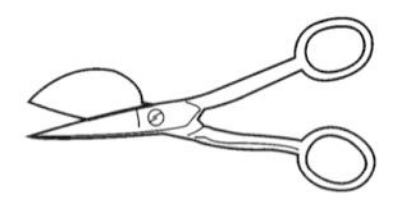

APPLIQUÉ SCISSORS

These scissors are used for fabric appliqué work. They have one standard blade and one rounded blade, which slips between and separates the bottom layer of fabric as the top layer is cut. This helps to make precision cuts very close to the stitching.

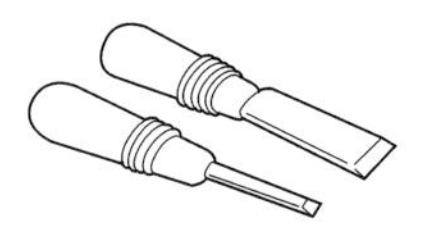

BUTTONHOLE CUTTERS

Buttonhole cutters are straight tools that have a sharp chiselled end, and are used to press and cut through buttonholes. They also help avoid cutting through the ends of buttonholes, which is common when using normal scissors.

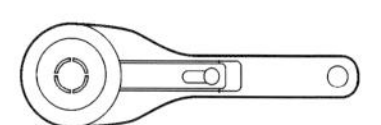

ROTARY CUTTERS

Rotary cutters are a must-have tool for sewers. They are single-handled tools with a round blade at the end that extends when cutting, but can be pulled back for safety purposes when not in use. The cutter can be used free-hand by guiding it along pattern lines to cut fabric. A rotary cutter is most often paired with a quilting ruler to cut very exact lines that are flush with the ruler's edge. A cutting mat surface is needed under the fabric; otherwise the blade will cut and scratch the surface below.

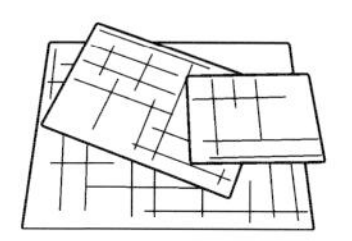

CUTTING MATS

Cutting mats protect your table from the scratches made by rotary cutters and cutting knives. They come in many different sizes, with grid marks covering the surface. Markings run vertically and horizontally and some are angled at 45 degrees for bias cutting. When paired with a transparent quilting ruler, it's easy to measure and cut exact lines and proportions of fabric. Some cutting mats are self-healing and will spring back from blade cuts.

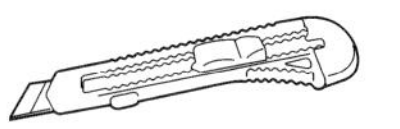

CUTTING KNIVES

These are one-handle tools with a small angled razor blade at the end. They are ideal for cutting appliqué templates, paper stencils and other craft projects.

HANDY TIP

It's good practice to have scissors and cutting tools professionally sharpened every other year, or more often as needed. Dull blades and knicks in the blade make it more difficult to cut through fabric and may cause snags. Some synthetic fabrics such as nylon, polyester, rayon and lamé will dull scissors and sewing needles faster than other fabrics. Sewing scissors should never be used to cut paper, as the paper will dull the blades. Always keep a pair of craft scissors in your sewing room for paper needs.

SEWING TOOLS

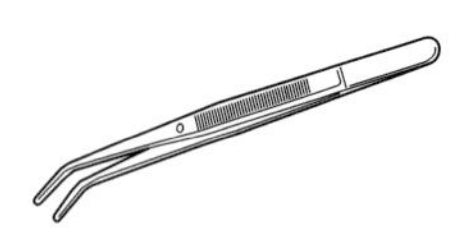

TWEEZERS

Commonly used for beauty and hygiene purposes, tweezers are also a valuable tool for threading overlockers. The two curved sides are pressed together to grasp a piece of thread and pull it through parts of the machine that are hard to reach with fingers.

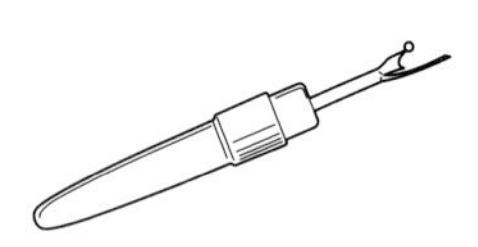

SEAM RIPPERS

Seam rippers are a must-have tool for any sewer. They have a short handle with a sharp hook and poker at the end that allows you to rip seams apart. Sizes and handle colours vary.

PINS

Pins are a sewing necessity and are used to pin fabrics together before sewing, to pin and tuck a garment, for basting and hemming, to create markings, for garment fittings and for many other tasks. Pins can be long, short, T-shaped, glass topped, flower topped (which are handy when ironing with pins in place because the head lays flat on the fabric) or shaped like a safety pin.

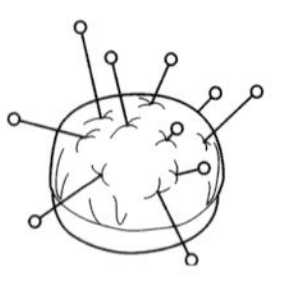

PINCUSHIONS

Pincushions are used to hold sewing pins, since a table scattered with sharp pins is less than efficient. They can be made from fabric (such as the classic tomato cushion) or can be magnetic (so that pins can lie on top).

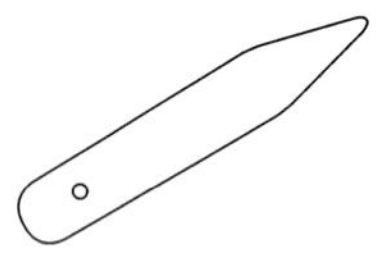

POINT TURNERS

Point turners are often made from plastic or wood and look like a large animal's tooth with a dull point at the end. They are used for poking out the corners of a bag or pillowcase and for pushing out curved seams.

ROULEAU LOOP TURNERS

Loop turners are long metal tools, similar to cooking skewers, used to turn small tubes of fabric the right side out. At one end is a metal circle that you hold to push the fabric through, and the other end has a hook that grasps the fabric. If you don't have this on hand, simply attach a large safety pin to one end of the fabric and pull it through to the other end.

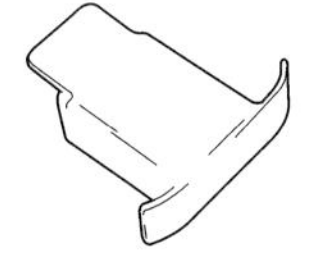

SEAM GUIDES

These are small rectangles of metal or plastic that attach to your presser foot and help guide your fabric to make exact seam widths. They are helpful when sewing lines with a very wide seam allowance, beyond the lines marked on your machine plate.

BODKINS

Bodkins have a blunt end and look like long needles. They are used for stringing elastic through a casing, such as a waistband or sleeve. A simple safety pin, however, can do the same job.

SEAM SEALANT

Seam sealant is a liquid used to seal the ends of fabric, overlocked threads or seams, and to keep them from fraying. Very little liquid is needed to create the seal. It's important to test on a fabric scrap first to make sure the sealant doesn't stain the fabric.

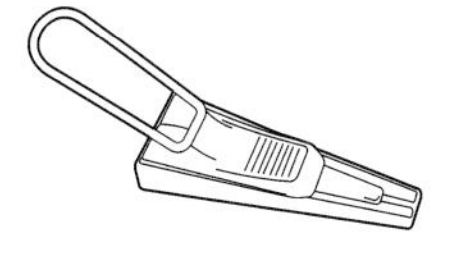

BIAS BINDING MAKERS

Bias binding makers are used for making bias binding. The simplest ones are small metal devices that are wide at one end and narrow at the other. Fabric is cut into long bias strips and fed through the back end of the bias binding maker. The binding comes out smaller and folded in towards the centre. As the fabric emerges, it is ironed down, and is then ready to be used. Electronic bias binding making machines are also available, which ensure more accurate results, but are only worth the investment if you plan to make a good deal of bias binding.

PRESSING TOOLS

IRONS

Irons are the standard tool used to press and flatten clothing by using heat and steam. An iron was traditionally a flat piece of metal that was warmed over a stove, but today irons are electronically charged and have all sorts of bells and whistles. The heat is adjustable and is typically labelled according to the type of fabric being used. Fabrics that tend to wrinkle easily, such as linen and cotton, often require a higher heat setting, while synthetic and some woollen fabrics should be pressed with a lower heat. Irons also have a compartment to hold water, which, if the iron is set for steam, is released as steam while pressing.

IRONING BOARDS

Used as a pressing surface, ironing boards are portable with collapsible, hinged legs, are adjustable in height and can be large enough to stand waist-high or small enough to sit on top of your table. Most ironing boards are made of a flat board wrapped in layers of heat-resistant fabric.

IRONING PADS

Ironing pads are also ironing surfaces made of heat-resistant fabric that can lay directly on a table or workspace. They are portable and ideal for use when travelling.

PRESSING MITT

A pressing mitt looks similar to an oven mitt and allows you to hold fabric in place around tight curves and other difficult areas while you iron, so your fingers and hands are protected from the heat.

TAILOR'S HAMS

These are ham-shaped ironing surfaces that are used for pressing curved areas and spots that are hard to reach when fabric is laid on a standard ironing board. The tailor's ham is stuffed with a dense heat-resistant filler and covered with wool fabric on one side and cotton on the other. The wool side is used for fabrics requiring low to medium heat, and the cotton side is used for fabrics with higher heat temperatures.

SEAM ROLLS

Seam rolls are similar to hams, but are long, narrow stuffed forms with wool fabric on one side and cotton on the other. The size and shape are ideal for pressing seams, especially on the arms and legs.

SLEEVE BOARD

A sleeve board is a smaller, narrower version of an ironing board, and is used for pressing sleeves.

WOODEN PRESSING BAR

This is a small wooden tool, angled on one side and used to press seams without the use of an electric iron. It's a great 'unplugged' method that's safe for children to use, and is useful for pressing hard-to-reach areas of a garment.

POINT PRESSERS and CLAPPERS

These are all-in-one wooden pressing tools with a flat side and a few points. The flat side enables you to make a sharp press on straight seams; it is also used to flatten bulky areas, such as interfaced collars and pleats, by using the flat side as a clapper to hit the areas to be flattened. The points are used for pressing hard-to-reach areas, such as the seams of shirt collars.

PRESSING CLOTHS

These are pieces of fabric that can withstand high temperatures, and are used to cover fabrics that don't do well under direct heat. Cloths can be shop-bought or simply pulled from your fabric stash. Thin cotton, silk and some woollen fabrics make excellent pressing cloths.

MACHINE PRESSER FEET

A presser foot is the small metal attachment that presses your fabric down on to the machine plate, holding fabric in place as you sew. Feed dogs come up from below the machine plate, guiding the fabric through. Every machine comes with a standard foot, sometimes called an all-purpose or zigzag foot. Some machines also come packaged with a zipper foot and a buttonhole foot. Additional specialty feet can be purchased separately online and in machine dealer shops. Although there is a wide range of feet available, this section focuses on the most common varieties. Please note that styles and names may vary from brand to brand, and that a standard foot can perform most of the tasks you'll need. My machine runs 98 per cent of the time with a standard, buttonhole or zipper foot.

When deciding what feet to buy for your machine, weigh out the cost versus how often you'll use the foot. Some generic brand feet will also work well with your machine and are a good way to practise before investing too much money.

STANDARD (also called zigzag)

This is an all-purpose foot that comes with every machine. It works well for most functions, such as straight lines, zigzags and forward-feed stitching. When in doubt over what foot to use, standard is often a great choice.

STRAIGHT STITCH

This type of foot is used for straight stitching only, as the opening on the foot is quite small and requires the needle to be in the middle position. It's an excellent choice for delicate fabrics because it presses more surface area on the fabric, giving you more sewing control.

ZIPPER

A zipper foot comes packaged with most machines, and is a must-have sewing item. The foot is narrow with openings on both sides, allowing you to sew down both sides of a zip or piping very close to the zip coils. The needle position is moved from right to left when sewing.

STANDARD BUTTONHOLE

A standard buttonhole foot comes packaged with most machines and is used when sewing buttonholes on a manual setting. The plate has a wider opening than a standard foot, making it easy to spot the end of the buttonhole stitches and stop you from overstitching on either end of the hole.

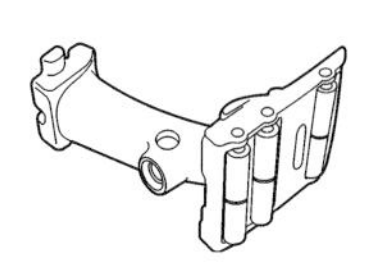

ROLLER

A roller foot has one or more small rollers that help guide fabric through the machine. It is ideal for vinyl, oilcloth, leather, velvet and other fabrics that tend to stick beneath the presser foot. A Teflon or non-stick foot is also suitable for these fabric types.

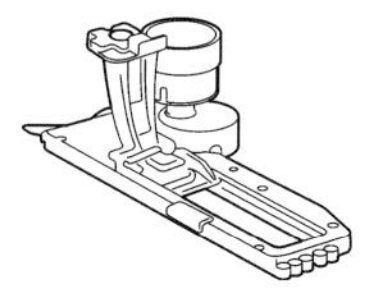

AUTOMATIC BUTTONHOLE

This type of foot is larger than a standard buttonhole foot, has a wider opening and works with automatic buttonhole settings to make precise buttonholes. Note that not all machines have these capabilities.

WALKING/EVEN FEED

This is a popular foot among quilters and is used when additional control is needed to feed the fabric. It works in a similar way to the feed dogs on the bottom of your machine, feeding and moving the fabric additionally from the top. A walking foot can overfeed fabrics, making it too powerful for some lightweight and delicate fabrics, but suitable for heavier fabrics.

FREE-HAND QUILTING/ DARNING

This type of foot is used for free motion sewing, mostly in quilting. The feed dogs are pulled down away from the machine plate and fabric is sewn freely in any direction to create interesting designs across the top of a quilt.

¼ IN SEAM

This type of foot is similar to a standard foot, but with a ¼in (6mm) edge to the foot and horizontal ¼ in markings across the top. This makes it easy to line up and sew ¼ in seams, squares and other lines when quilting.

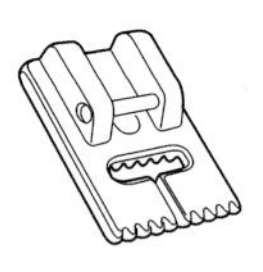

PINTUCK

A pintuck foot has small grooves on the base of the foot making it easy to sew pintuck-width seams on the outside of a garment or bag for a decorative look. Pintuck feet come with a range of grooves from three up to nine or more.

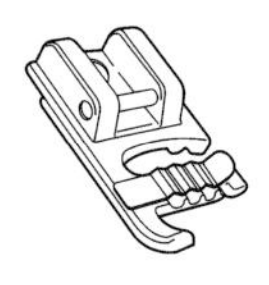

CORDING

A cording foot has open grooves on the bottom, similar to a pintuck foot, allowing cording and piping to pass through in a straight line as it is sewn into a cord casing.

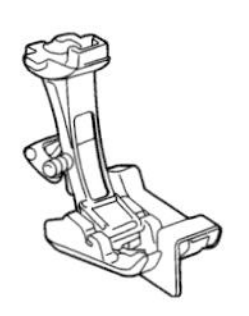

BLIND HEM

This foot is used for blind stitching hems on clothing or curtains. Similar to hand stitching a hem, blind stitching performs a pattern of three forward stitches (which do not show on the outside of the garment) and then one zigzag stitch (which catches the two fabrics and stitches them together). When the fabric is turned over, only the small zigzag stitch appears, but is barely noticeable. A blind stitch foot has a narrow blade in the middle to guide the folded fabric edge while sewing.

RUFFLER

This is an intimidating looking foot with a similar concept to the gathering foot - to gather and ruffle fabric. It has more precision and settings compared to the gathering foot, and actually creates small pleats in the fabric that look like ruffles.

GATHERING

This nifty foot gathers fabric as you sew. By adjusting the tension and stitch length on your machine, you can adjust how much fabric is gathering at once.

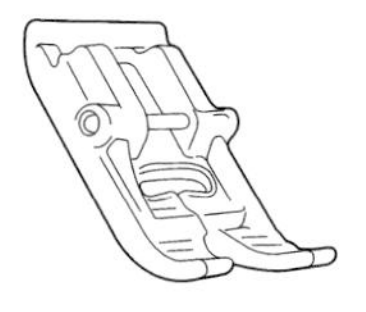

TEFLON and NON-STICK

Teflon and non-stick feet are designed to glide over vinyl, plastic, leather, oilcloth and other fabrics that tend to stick between a standard metal presser foot and the needle plate.

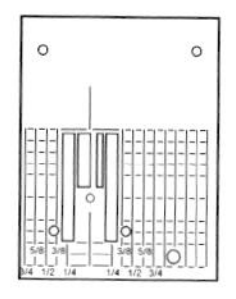

SINGLE-HOLE NEEDLE PLATE

This is used in conjunction with some presser feet to give additional control to sewing and to reduce puckering. Like a straight stitch foot, this has one small opening, providing greater surface area to press on the fabric. There is also less chance of fabric or thread being sucked down into the needle plate.

MACHINE NEEDLES

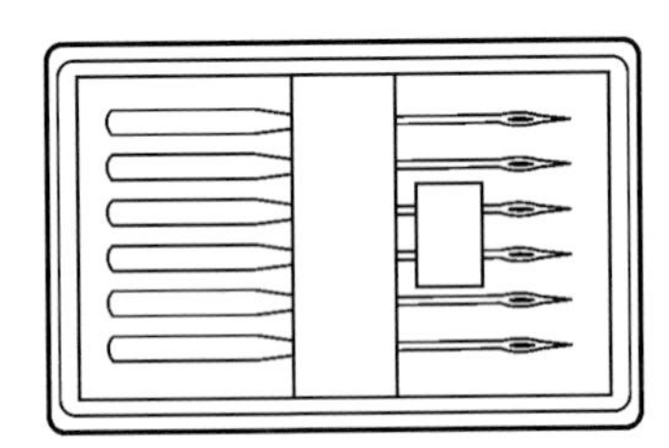

Just as sewing machines have advanced and multiplied, so too has the variety of machine needles available. To get the most out of your sewing, two things are important to remember when it comes to machine needles:

- Always start each sewing project with a fresh needle. Change needles whenever you notice skipped stitches or snags in the fabric. Keep in mind that synthetic fabrics tend to dull sewing needles faster than natural fibres and require more frequent changing.
- Select a suitable sewing needle for your project – some needles work better for certain fabric types and weights. For most sewing projects, a universal needle in varying sizes does the trick, but for specialty projects you may need a ballpoint, sharp or jeans/denim needle.

WHAT MAKES A NEEDLE?

Though needles are small, their function is tremendous. Needles puncture through fabric, connect the top thread to the bobbin thread, pull everything back up and create a stitch in a fraction of a second. Impressive indeed. To ensure the finest stitching possible and to avoid skipped stitches, sewing needles have been manicured into the best shape possible.
A needle is made up of six different parts:

SHANK: The large upper part of the needle with one round and one flat side. When the needle is inserted into the machine, a small screw is tightened against the flat side, holding the needle in place.
SHAFT (OR BLADE): The length of the needle below the shank, down to the point. Needle size refers to the thickness of the shaft – the thicker the needle shaft, the larger the needle size and vice versa.
GROOVE: A skinny canal on the back of the needle shaft that keeps the thread running smoothly down to the bobbin thread.
EYE: The small hole where the thread is inserted. Your thread should always feed through the eye smoothly and should fit into the back groove. If it doesn't, either your thread is too thick or your needle is too small.
POINT: The very tip of the needle. Point shapes vary for different types of fabric.

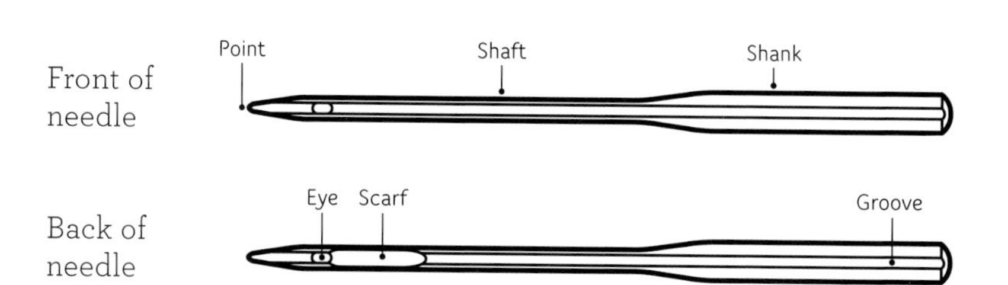

SCARF: A small notch on the back of the needle above the eye. This indentation allows the bobbin to get very close to the eye of the needle and catch the thread with precision, reducing the amount of skipped stitches.

PICKING THE PROPER NEEDLE

It would be easy to sew with the same needle all the time, but since fabrics are different, there are specific needle types and sizes that will give you better sewing results. Heavy fabrics such as denim and leather require a large, powerful needle to puncture through thick fabric (such as a Sharp HJ 100/16 needle), while dainty charmeuse sews nicely with a skinny Universal H 60/8 needle.

NEEDLE SIZES

Needles are categorised according to size first, followed by fabric type and point. Most home sewing machines around the world are from one of three needle systems: 130/705 H, the 15x1 H or the HAx1. Sound confusing? Well, it is and it isn't. The 'H' stands for *hohlkehle*, a German word meaning 'hollow shape', which refers to the needle having a scarf. The numbers next to the H are printed the same way on every pack of needles, and simply reference the system being used. For the most part, the three systems are interchangeable, so as long as your machine is part of that system it's not an important figure to remember (check the needles that come with your machine to be sure). What is important, however, is the printed numbers that refer to needle size or the thickness of the shaft, such as 80/12 or 70/10, etc. The larger numbers on the left (60 to 120) refer to European sizing and the smaller numbers on the right (8 to 19) refer to the North American system. The European numbers refer directly to the size of the shaft, with a size of 0.80mm being shortened to a measurement of 80 NM or 'number metric'. The North American numbers are a similar, yet arbitrary system that has been developed over the years. The table overleaf lists European and North American needle sizes. ▶

European needle size	North American needle size
Size 60	8
Size 65	9
Size 70	10
Size 75	11
Size 80	12
Size 90	14
Size 100	16
Size 110	18
Size 120	19

The numbers are always listed together on needle packages and charts, so don't worry too much about remembering them both. A European size 110 needle is always paired with an American size 18, and so on. You only need to remember this:

- A large needle size (90/14 or 100/16) means a larger needle, and is used for heavier fabrics.
- A small needle size (60/8) means a smaller needle, and is used for lightweight fabrics.
- Needles for medium-weight fabrics fall somewhere in between.

When choosing a needle, first start with the weight of your fabric and pair it with a suitable needle size. Each fabric entry in this book lists appropriate needle sizes and types for that fabric. Note that some needle packs come with a variety of needle sizes so that you can be prepared for sewing with different weights of the same type of fabric.

NEEDLE TYPES

Now that you've decided on a needle size, look at the type of fabric you're sewing with to decide which type of needle you need. Some fabrics, such as knits, work better with a duller ball point so that it doesn't snag the fabric, while other fabrics, such as microfibres, do well with a very sharp point. Most fabrics fall somewhere in between and require a universal needle. Some needles are also categorised according to the type of stitching that will be used, such as top stitching or embroidery. These names are printed on the needle pack, along with a letter category, such as HS, HJ or HM next to the needle system numbers. The H always means *hohlkehle*, S means stretch, J means jeans, M means sharp or microfibre, and so on. Some codes are not as obvious, but the most important thing to remember is the needle size and type. The two charts opposite list the most common needle types available and their abbreviations.

Type of needle	Description
Universal	An all-purpose needle used for many types of fabric. It has a sharp point for woven fabrics but a slight ball at the end to accommodate some knits. When in doubt, a universal needle is a safe and obvious choice.
Sharp/ Microtex	A skinny needle with a sharp point at the end that pierces through fabrics with a high thread count, such as microfibres, synthetics and some natural fibres. Sharp needles need to be changed more frequently than other needle types.
Ballpoint	The preferred needle for sewing with knit fabrics. The point is slightly dull, which reduces the risk of damaging or snagging knitted fibres when sewing.
Jeans/Denim	A very sharp, strong needle meant for sewing through dense fabrics such as denim and leather.
Stretch	Intended for extremely stretchy knits such as elastane. The needle has a deeper scarf and a medium ballpoint to prevent skipped stitches.
Leather	A very sharp needle with a cutting point at the end. Used only for leather, suede, faux leather and other vinyl types of fabric.

Needle type	Abbreviation
Sharp/Microfibre	HM
Jeans	HJ
Stretch	HS
Ballpoint	H-SUK
Top-stitching	N
Metallic	MET
Embroidery	HE
Quilting	HQ
Twin Needle	ZWI
Chrome Finish	CF
Leather	NTW

READING SEWING PATTERNS

Have you ever read a mathematical problem five times in a row and still felt confused? Reading a sewing pattern can feel much the same way until you understand the language and symbols involved. Once you understand how to use a pattern, you'll feel confident starting new projects.

When selecting a pattern, consider your skill level and how much you want to spend, and don't be afraid to push yourself beyond your comfort zone! Sewing is not rocket science. With a few skills under your belt, you'll be surprised how you can jump up to a more advanced pattern. To help you along, this section covers sewing pattern basics.

PATTERN TYPES

STANDARD PRINTED PATTERNS:
Patterns that are printed on tissue paper with corresponding instructions on separate pages. They are packaged in envelopes and sold online and in most fabric shops. Big name brands such as McCall's, Butterick, Simplicity, Vogue and Burda have large catalogue books filled with photographs that are available for you to thumb through in-store.

INDIE PRINTED PATTERNS: Patterns developed by independent designers have been creeping into the marketplace over the past few years. Independent pattern makers such as Oliver + S, Sew Liberated, Portabellopixie, Amy Butler and Anna Maria Horner offer patterns that may cost a little more compared to the large retailers, but are often more detailed, well-written and easy to follow.

E-PATTERNS: Typically sold in small online shops by indie makers, these patterns are provided as PDF documents that can be downloaded and printed from your home computer. Each page needs to be pieced together with tape to make one large pattern piece. E-patterns typically cost less than indie printed patterns, but more than standard patterns.

READING STANDARD PATTERNS

The front of a standard printed pattern is labelled with:

- The pattern name.
- Photos and illustrations of the finished look, plus other views/versions.
- The pattern reference number – also found in pattern catalogues and pattern drawers or racks.
- Skill references such as 'easy-to-sew' or 'intermediate'.
- The pattern size. Most patterns have different versions, with a range of six different sizes in each, so make sure you get the appropriate size. Using your bust, waist and hip measurements, refer to the sizing information provided on the back of the envelope to decipher your size. Don't fret if your pattern size is different to your shop-bought garment size – just go with the pattern size that fits you best and think of how fabulous you'll look in the finished product!

The back of a pattern envelope is labelled with:

- Suggested fabrics that work best with the pattern type and style (there are often a few options listed).
- Fabric and interfacing amounts, labelled in yards or metres and broken down according to a 115cm- or 150cm-wide (45 or 60in) fabric. The yardage has been figured according to the layout of pattern pieces. Note that there's often an A, B or C view included in the pattern. Make sure you're reading information for the appropriate view to select fabrics and trim yardage.
- Notions that are needed, such as trims, zips, threads, etc.
- Sizing measurements to help you decipher your garment size. Measure your bust, waist, hips, etc. to get an exact pattern size.

INSTRUCTION PAGES

Before starting a project, read through the instructions to familiarise yourself with the steps. Tape the page up on the wall above your sewing machine for easy reference or keep it close by. Note that labels, illustrations and symbols will vary from brand to brand, but some basics are the same:

PATTERN PIECES: Each pattern uses a key of illustrations to represent the right and wrong sides of the fabric, interfacing, etc. It's important to note the right and wrong side markings to ensure that pattern pieces are cut and sewn properly.

CUTTING OUT THE PATTERN: Cut out the tissue pattern pieces first and then follow the illustration for laying them out on to the fabric. The illustration included in the instructions shows the best possible way for laying pieces out. A with-nap layout means that all the pattern pieces should be placed in the same direction, so that the nap of the fabric will be consistently positioned on the garment. For a without-nap layout, the pattern pieces are placed in opposing directions. It's important to take note of whether the fabric is folded, how it is folded (with right or wrong sides together) or if pieces are cut as a single layer, on the fold, etc.

SEWING: The instructions walk you step-by-step through the sewing process. The placement of some steps might not make sense at the time, but remember that there's an order to the project. Pattern makers have found the most efficient sewing route that will give you the best results. Have confidence and press on!

THE PATTERN ITSELF

Whether printed on tissue paper or standard paper, most commercial pattern pieces are the same, and are labelled with markings for various sizes and symbols that guide you. The more often you sew with patterns, the more familiar the language and symbols will become. Here are some basics to get you started:

SIZING DASHES: Each size is labelled with various dashed lines. Find the dashes that correspond to your size and always cut on the same dash for each pattern piece.

GRAIN LINE AND BIAS: It's important to cut your pieces with the grain line in mind so that your sewn garment drapes properly or so printed fabrics run in the proper direction. The grain line is marked on the pattern piece by a large arrow and runs parallel to the selvedge of the fabric. This is the finished edge of the fabric, usually marked with the designer's name or dotted printing codes. When laying out the pattern pieces, make sure the marked run parallel to the selvedge, unless indicated to cut on the bias. A bias cut makes a 45-degree angle with the selvedge (picture an invisible diagonal line in the fabric). Cutting something on the bias provides more give and stretch to

the pattern piece (which is good for sleeves, trims and pieces with curves).

NOTCHES: These skinny triangles help you to match pattern pieces together. A single notch is used for front pattern pieces and a double notch for back pieces. Cut along the dotted line and when you get to a notch, cut a small triangle pointing out from the fabric and then continue cutting along the dotted line again. When pinning and sewing, line up the notches together on the appropriate pieces.

CIRCLES OR RECTANGLES: Typically, a set of circles or rectangles indicates the beginning and end of a function, such as gathering, pleating, etc., but refer to the key of symbols used on your pattern for clarification.

DARTS: Not to be confused with notches, darts are large triangles that indicate where the fabric should be joined together to create a dart, which makes a dress or skirt more fitted. Use a fabric marker or pins to mark where darts should go on your fabric.

BUTTONHOLE: Patterns will use small lines to indicate where a buttonhole should be sewn. Transfer these markings to your fabric using a fabric marker or pins.

CUT ON THE FOLD: A large rectangular box with the words 'cut on the fold' indicates where a pattern piece should be laid on the fold of the fabric. This is used for pattern pieces that are symmetrical, such as T-shirts, skirts and dresses.

SEAM ALLOWANCE: It's important to sew with the seam allowance indicated on the pattern to ensure that your garment fits properly. Seam allowance means the distance you are sewing from the edge of the fabric. Your sewing machine needle plate has lines marking these various allowances. If markings have worn off, use a ruler to measure and make a simple mark on your machine to guide you. Typically, the edge of a presser foot is 6mm (¼in).

GLOSSARY

ABUTTED SEAMS
Often used for thick fabrics where sewing would result in bulky seams. Two fabric edges are typically left raw and 'butted' up right next to each other, then sewn with a flatlock or zigzag stitch to hold them together.

BLENDED FABRIC
A mix of various fibres combined together to create a stronger, more versatile fabric.

CALENDARING
A process that creates a surface finish on a fabric, such as sateen.

CELLULOSE
The structural component in plants and trees that is obtained from wood pulp and cotton. It is used to make some synthetic and sustainable fabrics.

DENIER
Measurement used for the mass density of fibres, such as microfibre fabric. Denier is also used as a unit of measure for nylon tights.

DISCHARGE DYEING
A dyeing process that uses bleach to remove colour in a recurring pattern.

DIRECT TO GARMENT (DTG) PRINTING
An at-home printing method that uses inkjet printers and fabric sheets to digitally print on to fabric.

FLAT-FELLED SEAMS
An alternate method for sewing seams. Both sides are finished and the seam is sewn flat to help reduce bulk. Used for thick fabrics such as denim.

INTERFACING
A type of fabric that's attached to specific pattern pieces to provide extra support and shape to clothing, such as shirt collars or pockets. Interfacings are somewhat stiff yet soft and are either sewn-in or fused to other fabric with an iron. The term should not be confused with facings, which refers to some pattern pieces that interfacing is attached to - those pieces that face inwards on clothing, giving the edges of your design a finished look (like the inner edge of a jacket).

KNITS
Fabrics that are knitted and linked together by connecting loops using needles (rather than being woven). Knit fabrics often have stretch and are comfortable to wear.

LENO WEAVE
Warp yarns that are twisted around each other in a figure of eight pattern.

LINING
Used to line clothing when fabrics are scratchy or see-through, to hide interior seams and finish off looks, for comfort or for a luxurious feel. Linings are typically sewn separate from the outer garment and are attached in one or two pivotal spots, such as the waistband, hem or around arm holes.

MAN-MADE FABRICS
Fabrics such as acetate and rayon that are manipulated from plant and wood cellulose as substitutes for natural fibre fabrics.

MANUFACTURED FABRICS
A category that includes synthetic and man-made fabrics.

NATURAL FIBRE
Fibres that come from nature such as plants, wood and animal fleece.

NAP
A raised pile on the top of a fabric. Nap can be very small, as with flannel, or quite tall, like terry towelling.

NEEDLE BOARD
An ironing surface covered with metal pins that is useful when ironing velvet. The pins help raise the velvet pile up and keep it from crushing under the iron.

PILE
A type of weave that creates a nap, or pile of plush threads on top of the fabric surface. Pile can be very small, as with flannel, or quite tall, like terry towelling.

PLAIN WEAVE
The most common weave. It is made of warp threads that run vertically and weft threads that run side to side.

PRESS CLOTH
A cloth used to cover and protect a fabric while ironing.

SELVEDGE
The finished edge of a fabric. It is usually marked with the designer's name or dotted printing codes.

OVERLOCKER (SERGER)
A three-to-four thread spooled machine used to sew finishing seams on garments and hems. Machines have a cutting tool that cuts the fabric edge as you sew.

SLACK-TENSION WEAVE
A type of weave where groups of yarn are bunched together in certain parts of the fabric to form a puckered look.

STABLE KNIT
Knit fabrics with little to no stretch.

STAY TAPE
Sheer, straight tape used when stability and support are needed in the seams without adding bulk.

SUSTAINABLE FABRICS
Fabrics that support environmentally friendly products and processes over those that pollute and hurt the environment. Fabrics include hemp, bamboo, organic wool and organic cotton.

SYNTHETIC FABRICS
Fabrics made from man-made, synthetic fibres meant to mimic the properties of natural fibres. Fabrics include polyester, acrylic and nylon.

THREAD COUNT
The number of threads in a one-inch square. When referring to cotton fabric, the higher the thread count, the more luxurious and soft the fabric.

UNSTABLE KNIT
Stretchy knit fabrics. They can be either two-way or four-way stretch depending on how many directions the fabric can stretch in.

WALE
The vertical plush lines on corduroy fabric.

WAX-RESIST DYEING
A method of dyeing where wax is used to resist, or hold back, the dye in certain areas of the textile in order to create a pattern.

WOVENS
A large classification of fabrics that are woven with threads in a variety of methods such as plain weave, twill, ribbed, satin, brocade, damask, etc. Fabrics typically have no stretch.

INDEX

Acknowledgements

Last year the words 'dream big' bounced around in my head. And writing a book was the perfect 'big' I had hoped for.

To the creative people at RotoVision publishing, a huge thank you for taking a chance on me and helping me feel like a student again. I loved the writing process more than I could have imagined. Thank you also to my fabulous editor Jane and clever book designer Emily for being patient and walking me through the ins and outs of book publishing. Thank you to my local library for the free WiFi and comfy tables to camp out on for hours. Thank you to the MADE blog readers who keep me motivated to share new ideas, explore and improve my skills. To my Granner and mum who taught me to sew when I was 10, thank you for sharing your talents with me. Our talents are only as good as what we do with them and you both spread creative goodness wherever you go.

Finally, the phrase is a cliché, but the biggest thank you goes to my family. I honestly couldn't have done it without a willing husband, who was on-board from the beginning and stepped in to be Mr Mum for weekends in a row. Many thanks my dear. And to my Lucy and Owen who asked, 'You're going to the library again??', thank you for spending those Saturdays hanging out alone with Dad. It's nice to be back to our Saturday morning doughnut routine.